EAST-SOUTH TRADE
Economics and Political Economics

Edited with an Introduction by

Marvin R. Jackson

Routledge
Taylor & Francis Group
LONDON AND NEW YORK

First published 1985 by M.E. Sharpe

Published 2015 by Routledge

2 Park Square, Milton Park, Abingdon, Oxon OX14 4RN
711 Third Avenue, New York, NY 10017, USA

Routledge is an imprint of the Taylor & Francis Group, an informa business

ISBN 13: 9780873323642 (pbk)

Soviet and Eastern European Foreign Trade

SPRING–SUMMER–FALL 1985/VOL. XXI, NO. 1–2–3

East–South Trade Economics and Political Economics

Edited with an Introduction by:
MARVIN R. JACKSON

Marvin R. Jackson

The Economics and the Political Economics of East-South Relations in the 1980s: An Overview and Review of the Literature

The international emergence of the Soviet Union and its recently consolidated entourage of satellites in the 1950s appeared to many to pose a formidable threat to the economic interests of the developed capitalist countries in the less developed countries. The Soviet-type economies offered stable and rapidly growing markets in return for capital equipment that incorporated a rugged, intermediate-level technology more suitable to factor proportions of the LDCs and easy to maintain. In the bargain, the Soviet Union and its allies not only appeared ready to grant generous credits in the form of projects that could be repaid in future goods flows, but they also were more than willing to send cadres of technicians to set up plants and to train relatively large numbers of persons from the LDCs, both on the project sites and in their own educational facilities. That training was mixed with not a little political indoctrination and that mutual economic advantages were supplemented with more than a little anti-imperialist, anticolonialist feeling among the LDCs all seemed to add up to very significant capabilities for the Soviet bloc to wage economic warfare against the capitalist states in the rest of the world.[1]

As matters turned out in this, as well as other threats perceived during the Sputnik era, the seeming advantages of the Soviet-type system were not or could not be realized. Already in 1966 one book written on what we now call East-South trade concluded:

> (1) it is small, (2) it has grown rapidly but at a slower rate since 1960, (3) it is heavily concentrated on relatively few countries and commodities, (4) it has yielded [mostly] economic advantages to both sides, (5) it is quite closely linked to the Communist aid program, and (6) it has been beset by a number of difficulties such as instability, re-exports by Communist countries, and the accumulation by some developing countries of large credit balances in their clearing accounts with communist countries.[2]

According to the author of that book, while East-South trade had been growing at an impressive rate of 13% per year, in 1964 it only amounted to little more than 1% of world trade. It was about 5% of total South trade and less than 10% of total East trade. As we shall see below, matters hardly are different today. In fact, most of the six points listed above would still apply to the qualitative aspects of East-South economic relations.

In spite of this record there remains considerable interest today in East-South economic relations. Recent publications on the subject pose two contradictory views.

One view represents strategic concerns evident in both the Carter and Reagan administrations over the seeming expansion of Soviet influence in the South during the 1970s, not through direct economic means but when economics followed successful political takeovers by Marxist or anticapitalist revolutionaries. So, whereas Soviet commitments to military and economic aid just balanced, each at about $8,500 million, from 1954 to 1972, from 1972 to 1979 military aid commitments were four times economic aid. Here a changed political strategy may well have been based on the economic rationality of comparative advantage in industry.[3] So to China, North Korea, and Cuba, committed communist governments, were added Vietnam, Laos and now, we assume, finally Kampuchea. Governments committed to some form of Marxist revolutionary cause took over in Afghanistan and South Yemen, and then in Africa in Ethiopia, Angola, Mozambique, the Congo, Benin, and even elsewhere. In Latin America influence was extended into Nicaragua, temporarily in Grenada, and other places. And conflict with third parties pushed many countries[4] closer to the East, as in the cases of India, Syria, Iran, Libya, and Iraq. Of course, from the Eastern point of view not all was movement forward, as in the cases of Egypt, Sudan, Somalia, and Indonesia. So, if the economic attractions of trade with centrally planned economies proved insufficient to expand the influence of the East in the South, then perhaps trade could be made to follow the sword. Fears were particularly aroused over the growing maritime power of the East and for the critical supplies of oil in the Middle East.[5]

Other opinion sees an expansion of East-South economic relations as a promise rather than a threat. Here one finds the influence of those who believe that the dependence of the South on the West is responsible for the former's lack of development. Some samples of this view are found in the published papers of a 1980 conference on East-West-South economic relations held by the Vienna Institute for Comparative Economic Studies. For example:

> Since the industrial West has hitherto played the major role in economic and political relations with the South . . . it is natural that Western governments and enterprises should bear the brunt of the vigorous criticism of the ways in which these relations have been conducted.

It is suggested that the TNCs (transnational corporations) are unlikely to implant their production capacities in accordance with the long-term needs of the host countries. Shorter-term interests—the earning of profits from cheap labor—are thought likely to dominate the TNCs' investment pattern.[6]

The proponents of this view, not all of whom are found in the East or the South, see a need to replace conventional means for conducting international economic relations with some kind of new international economic order, one, they seem to assume, that will bear more than a faint resemblance to the way countries of the East have conducted their affairs within the confines of the Council for Mutual Economic Assistance (CMEA). Unfortunately, some who express this view may be poorly informed either about how CMEA has worked or about how CMEA countries, especially since 1976, have conducted their discussions with the South.[7] They are also guilty of having assumed both too much compatibility of East and South country interests and too much similarity of CMEA institutions with those proposed for the NIEOs. In the only research we have found especially dedicated to the subject, Collin Lawson concludes

> In rejecting the LDC demands [for some NIEO], the CPEs have not only asserted that they intend to retain their present trading practices vis-à-vis LDCs, but also have claimed that those practices meet the NIEO demands. The evidence suggests that this claim is not self-evidently true, and in some respects is wholly false. . . . CPE support for LDC proposals to reform the institutional framework of the international economy has been less than enthusiastic. . . . In this particular debate CPEs have narrowed their attention to issues of direct, and mainly economic interest to themselves.[8]

Neither the view that the East is a great threat nor the one that sees its system as a solution to trade-induced problems of development answers an important question about the facts of East-South trade that may undermine both.

If the Soviet sword is an efficient substitute for the attractions of an economic system in swinging trade of the South from the West to the East, then why has so little of it swung? And if the interests of the South have been so badly damaged by trading with the West according to the conventional rules of international commerce, then why have East-South economic relations not prospered more?

Could it be that the main barrier to expanded East-South economic relations and, at the same time, the main explanation for the dominance of West-South trade lies in the ineffectiveness of the economic institutions of the East for conducting international business? Are these institutions so weak that they even have a hard time attracting trade flows when the East has a decided political advantage in some given country of the South? Is part of the difficulty evidenced in negotiating some sort of "new international economic order" revealed by the problems exhibited already in negotiations to expand and improve the role of the institutions of CMEA? And is a growing awareness of the considerable weaknesses of institutions in

CMEA among countries of the South part of the reason why relatively little substantial effort is being committed to constructing a "new international economic order"?

This triple issue of *Soviet and Eastern European Foreign Trade* has been assembled to seek some answers to these questions. Most of the papers are written by specialists from the Soviet Union and Eastern Europe. They are presented as current examples of writing in the East on the subject and, as has been the case in other issues under our editorship, are viewed as being interesting as much for what they do not say as for what they may say about the topic.

On the subject of East-South economic relations there is so much unsaid in papers by specialists from the East about important aspects of the question that we have decided to include papers by some Western specialists, especially some that might not otherwise be available to the reader. In this case we wish to thank the Centrally Planned Economies Service of Wharton Econometric Forecasting Associates and Dr. Jan Vaňous, formerly the chief economist of the Service and now director and chief economist of PlanEcon, Inc., for permission to reproduce several invaluable papers first published as Current Analyses for customers of the Service. They are to be commended for recognizing the educational value of republishing the papers in this journal.

The papers fall into three or possibly four categories. First, we present those covering the South group as a whole, beginning with István Dobozi's useful survey and including papers on arms trade, a subject usually avoided by any economist from the East. The second group of papers focuses on the Middle East, where location and radical Arab socialism motivated close ties with the CMEA countries even before the OPEC oil-price revolution. A third group of papers covers three countries—Cuba, Mongolia, and Vietnam—that may be properly seen as in the South considering their levels of development, but which are now members of CMEA. The next paper on South Yemen, or officially the People's Democratic Republic of Yemen, represents a possibly distinct group of countries in the South, those which are currently controlled by what the Soviet Union considers as "vanguard" revolutionary parties.[9] Had suitable papers been available on Ethiopia, Angola, Mozambique, or

Table 1

Share of CMEA Country Foreign Trade with the Less Developed Countries

	Exports					
	CMEA			UN		
	1975	1980	1982	1975	1980	1982
Bulgaria	10.7	13.4	17.2	13.1	15.2	19.0
Czechoslovakia	8.6	8.7	8.4	9.1	9.7	12.0
GDR	4.4	7.2	8.0	5.3	7.4	8.7
Hungary	6.4	11.0	13.3	7.0	14.8	19.4
Poland	8.6	9.7	13.8	8.7	10.7	15.0
Romania	22.5	—	—	19.9	20.8	29.9
USSR	13.7	13.8	16.1	18.5	18.6	13.6
Total				13.3	15.4	14.6

	Imports					
	CMEA			UN		
	1975	1980	1982	1975	1980	1982
Bulgaria	4.1	3.9	6.1	5.9	5.4	7.7
Czechoslovakia	5.6	5.5	4.4	6.3	6.1	6.5
GDR	4.4	6.2	4.6	5.1	6.7	4.4
Hungary	6.8	9.5	10.3	7.6	10.1	9.5
Poland	4.9	9.4	5.8	5.0	10.7	7.5
Romania	14.6	—	—	13.9	31.4	32.2
USSR	11.2	11.4	11.4	16.7	15.9	16.7
Total				10.9	13.5	13.3

Sources: *Statisticheskii ezhegodnik stran-chlenov soveta ekonomicheskoi vzaimopomoshchi*; United Nations, *1984 Yearbook of International Trade Statistics*, vol. 1, special table G.

even Nicaragua, we would have included them here. The volume is concluded by papers on India and Argentina, and then by a paper by István Dobozi in which he tries to capture factors that will affect all CMEA countries in a forecast of Hungary's future relations with the South.

Our choice of Dobozi's papers to begin and end this volume not only recognizes his numerous contributions on the subject but also is intended to give the first and last words to someone in the one

Eastern country whose economists write factually and analytically about the foreign trade of the East. Hungary's advocacy of more market forces within CMEA would be consistent with advocating a greater role for such institutions between the East and the South. Before commenting on the substance of the general papers by Dobozi and the Soviet economist Khaldin, we owe the reader some statistical overview.

Statistical sources and problems

Three international agencies provide the commonly cited statistics on East-South trade: (1) the CMEA, (2) the United Nations, and (3) the International Monetary Fund. As Table 1 indicates, the data sets do not usually agree. This is because of differences in exchange rates used, different categorization of countries, and different sources of the original information (from country sources or from data "mirrored" in the records of trading partners). In some notable cases such as Cuba, only incomplete data are available from any of the sources. Beyond this the "direction-of-trade" statistics of the CMEA countries distort the true direction by the application of official rather than realistic exchange rates for the ruble and the dollar. For example, a recent study by Jan Vanous shows that in 1980, 8.6% of Czech exports measured in actual foreign trade prices went to LDCs. The share would have increased to 11.9% had comparable world market prices been used.[10]

Table 1 shows the trade shares of individual member countries of CMEA with the LDCs according to two views, the CMEA and the UN. The patterns are similar. Recently, Hungary, Romania, and Bulgaria have all shown significant increases in their shares of exports to LDCs. But only Romania has increased its import shares in any important way, and this is largely because it is the only one of the group that takes most of its imported crude oil from LDCs. Hence its increased share is mostly due to increased prices of oil on world markets. Recently all the CMEA countries except the Soviet Union and, in 1982, Romania have had larger export shares than import shares, and they tend to have important export surpluses with the LDCs.

Table 2

Shares of the Foreign Trade of the LDCs with the West and the East

	1965	1970	1975	1980	1981
Shares of LDC imports	100.0	100.0	100.0	100.0	100.0
Developed market economies	75.0	78.4	70.1	66.6	66.6
European CPEs and USSR	4.1	3.2	3.5	3.5	3.6
All CPEs	4.6	3.5	4.0	4.2	4.4
Shares of LDC exports	100.0	100.0	100.0	100.0	100.0
Developed market economies	69.0	72.4	70.2	70.3	67.0
European CPEs and USSR	5.3	5.1	4.3	2.8	3.3
All CPEs	6.9	6.3	4.8	3.6	4.0

Source: United Nations, *1982 Yearbook of Foreign Trade*.

Table 2 looks at the information from the point of view of the LDCs as a group (more details on categories of LDCs are presented in Table 3). Here the CMEA export shares of about 15% are reflected in the relatively small import shares of about 3.5% for the LDCs. The increases in OPEC oil prices had the effect of reducing even further the share of exports from LDCs taken by CMEA countries. Here again the CMEA countries appear to be more dependent on the LDCs than the latter are on the CMEA countries.

Dobozi's introductory paper adds some important points of detail to these statistical patterns which saw the other members of CMEA turn a large deficit of 1980 into a $3.0 billion surplus by 1982, a year in which the Soviet Union registered a $1.1 billion deficit. He suggests that the Soviet position is motivated by a broader set of considerations than applied by the smaller CMEA countries when they sharply cut imports from the LDCs in 1981 and 1982. The surplus with LDCs in those two years would have largely offset deficits with the West had they been in convertible currencies. Dobozi does not address this difficult question and instead asks why the East exports mostly machinery to the South while importing mostly raw materials. His suggested answer is that the East has failed to sufficiently promote trade with the newly industrializing countries. Going a step further, he predicts that in order to modernize its own antiquated industrial structure, the East will have to turn to imports from those countries in the South that have succeeded, the so-called "newly industrialized countries" (NICs). At the same time, he sees that the small East European countries will become increasingly dependent on imports of raw materials from sources other than the Soviet Union. Dobozi sees a future of challenges to the East as it becomes economically more dependent on the South.

Soviet Professor Khaldin presents a contrasting, orthodox view of West intentions and the superiority of the East's motives and devices. He blames any impediments in the way of greater East-South economic relations on the inability of some South countries to develop a planned system as a complement to that of the Soviet Union. He advocates greater use of Soviet specialists on a for-pay basis in LDCs, greater involvement of Soviet contracting organizations in foreign projects, and greater use of tripartite cooperation involving a Soviet-South pair on projects in a second South country.

Economic aid and the arms trade

Neither Dobozi nor Khaldin raises the sensitive issues of aid and arms exports covered by the Cooper-Fogarty paper and those from Wharton. According to Cooper and Fogarty, in the past ten years Soviet military aid has outrun economic aid by 2.5 times. The former has usually put the Soviet Union second only to the United States as arms supplier to the world (together they supply well over half of world arms sales). By contrast, Soviet economic aid has been small compared to that of the United States, and like that of the United States, declining. Something like 50–55% has been concentrated on countries along Soviet borders and on North African states, with most of the rest going to Cuba, Vietnam, Angola, and Ethiopia. There are enough Soviet failures to suggest no certain economic position will follow the political acts of granting military and economic assistance.

According to Wharton, in 1983 Soviet arms exports were nearly one-fifth the value of exports to nonsocialist countries; except for small sales to Finland and Austria, they went mostly to the LDCs and made up over 50% of total Soviet exports to this group. Wharton also estimates that 70–80% of sales were for hard currencies and nearly three-fourths on credit. Arms sales, then, would be a major source of Soviet hard currency earnings, with something like $4–6 billion per year recently generated from sales to the South. This is a higher figure for both the absolute value and the share of arms sales in total hard currency earnings than given by some other estimates.

Bulgaria's share of arms exports in total exports is smaller than in the Soviet case, but probably they generate an even larger share of Bulgarian hard-currency earnings. This is clearly so in the case of such earnings from the LDCs.

As noted, the Wharton estimates of earnings in hard currencies from Soviet arms sales to the South are higher than other recent estimates. Rajan Menon, for example, cites figures showing only $1.6 billion or 8.4% of total hard currency was earned this way in 1978.[11] Part of the difference is over what part of arms sales is for hard currency. Other problems are encountered in determining the value to place on physical quantities of arms shipments. At least one recent study suggests that the basis of evaluation used by the CIA and the U.S. Arms Control and Disarmaments Agency seriously understates the values.[12] Since the much-cited estimates of Cooper and Fogarty have these purported biases, they must be used with some caution.

East and Middle East

The Middle East has been an area of special interest to the Soviet Union and the East European countries because of proximity, support of anti-Western revolutionary and anti-Israeli movements, and potential economic profits in the oil-for-arms trade.

As Table 3 suggests, successful development of trade following these interests has not been easy.[13] The Soviet Union and Eastern Europe took larger shares of exports from the Middle East than from the non-OPEC developing countries as late as 1977. Following that year the position of the East in the exports of the Middle East slipped seriously. The relative strength of the East in the imports of the Middle East was already weaker in 1977 and became still worse in following years. Behind these movements were the changing orientations of some Middle Eastern regimes, further effects of the second round of OPEC price increases, balance-of-payments adjust-

Table 3

Shares of Exports and Imports of Various Country Groups to and from the USSR and Eastern Europe

	1977	1978	1979	1980	1981	1982	1983
In exports of:							
Oil-exporting countries	0.3	0.3	0.2	0.2	0.3	0.3	0.3
Non-oil developing countries	7.7	7.7	6.7	6.8	7.1	6.7	6.8
African countries	1.9	1.8	1.5	1.5	1.8	1.6	1.6
Asian countries	2.8	3.6	3.5	3.3	2.7	2.6	2.6
Middle Eastern countries	9.3	6.1	3.4	2.5	2.4	3.1	3.4
In imports of:							
Oil-exporting countries	2.3	2.4	1.8	2.6	2.2	1.5	1.6
Non-oil developing countries	5.7	5.8	5.4	4.8	4.4	4.6	4.5
African countries	1.6	1.4	1.5	1.4	1.4	1.7	1.7
Asian countries	1.7	2.5	2.7	2.3	1.8	2.0	1.9
Middle Eastern countries	3.9	3.5	2.5	2.0	2.9	2.9	2.3

Source: International Monetary Fund, *Direction of Trade Statistics Yearbook 1984*, pp. 18, 24, 30, 36, 48.

ments in some East European countries (Poland, Romania, Hungary), and the relative competitiveness of the East against the West and the new challengers from the South.

Given these complications, we are fortunate to have available the paper by Jan Vaňous, which both compiles and explains the complicated record of recent statistical information. He concentrates on (1) the volume of oil purchases by the East and the motives behind it, (2) the character of exports from the East to the Middle East, and (3) the role of Middle Eastern relations in financing acquisitions of hard currency by the East. Out of the innumerable important details he records, Vanous discovers an extremely interesting triangle of mutual East-South-West benefits:

> Middle East purchases of East bloc goods are paid for partly by deliveries of oil and partly by surplus cash earned from oil sales in the developed West; East bloc re-exports of Middle Eastern oil to the developed West augment the cash surplus and the entire trade surplus of the East bloc in the Middle East is used to offset the East bloc payments deficit in the developed West; the surplus the

> developed West earns in its payments transactions with the East bloc is then used to offset its own trade deficit in the Middle East.

One of Vaňous's findings is that in 1982, Bulgaria stood number one in the CMEA in the share of its export earnings from nonsocialist markets that were earned in the Middle East (actually the six Middle Eastern countries studied in detail by Vaňous). This trade has had the important benefit to Bulgaria of providing a flow of oil that, directly or as products, was sold for hard currency and used to pay off Bulgaria's debts to the West.

A Bulgarian view of that trade reflects nothing about that country's now secret data on oil imports and exports or on its balance of payments. Sasha Grozdanova does record that over 50% of Bulgaria's exports to Arab countries are machinery[14] (of course, leaving out the detail of their important arms component noted above) and that, in return, Bulgaria's imports are 80% industrial materials (again, the share of oil is not revealed). Grozdanova echoes Dobozi's theme of the need to meet increased competition for Arab markets by better marketing, higher quality goods, and developing better service backup and involvement in turnkey operations. Still, her emphasis ends on those more conventional approaches of the East to bilateral negotiations by governmental delegations and even more complicated ones within a multicountry CMEA framework. This reflects conservative views in Bulgaria that will probably keep that country from making the reforms of foreign trade necessary for effective international competition.[15]

Syria provides an interesting country focus of CMEA relations with an Arab country in the article by Kozolaev. This is more because of politics than economics. The volumes of trade flows, as registered above by Vanous, are no greater in Syria's case than Egypt's, while those with Iraq, Libya, and non-Arab Iran are much larger. Since the Soviet-Syrian Treaty of Friendship in 1980, Syria has received massive arms supplies and economic aid from CMEA countries to sustain its leading role against Israel. Also, since Iraq's shift West, Syria is Moscow's leading window in the area and supports the region's most durable example of Arab socialism.[16] Judging by Kozolaev's paper, most of the CMEA's economic assistance has been directed to some 250 major projects, of which only

Table 4

Exports to and Imports from the Soviet Union and Eastern Europe of Selected Communist and Client LDCs (million U.S. $)

		1970	1975	1979	1980	1981	1982
China	X	183	530	1,078	1,204	889	885
	M	205	546	1,221	1,035	932	1,013
Mongolia	X	80	207	310	370	387	486
	M	230	532	963	1,103	1,144	1,328
North Korea	X	188	277	489	526	401	545
	M	271	330	456	514	452	479
Vietnam	X	33	85	277	299	295	353
	M	287	313	857	932	1,178	1,197
Cuba	X	681	2,321	3,592	3,413	3,338	4,124
	M	780	1,827	3,587	4,016	4,437	4,851
South Yemen	X	0	0	4	8	8	8
	M	5	24	122	110	148	113
Afghanistan	X	35	91	221	407	439	384
	M	41	99	311	425	480	577
Angola	X	0	0	38	72	12	5
	M	0	0	122	187	192	105
Ethiopia	X	1	6	37	57	42	20
	M	7	11	110	235	210	274

Source: United Nations, *1984 International Trade Yearbook*, vol. 1, special table G.

38 seem to have been supported by the Soviet Union. Perhaps most interesting is the explanation of the development of Syria's oil resources, leading to its elimination of import dependence and, instead, to a net export position which generates about 70% of the country's total export earnings.

Vaňous's data also suggest a focus on Iran, as that country has recently exported more oil to the East than its rival Iraq. The view of Soviet-Iranian economic relations given by V. Ivanenko also concentrates on joint projects, a conventional emphasis that might be expected, given his position as secretary of the joint Soviet-Iranian commission. He describes a number of major projects built in Iran with Soviet assistance, including the largest Iranian steelmill at Isfalan, the multipurpose hydroelectric project on the Araks River, and the linking of Iran's rail system with Europe through the Soviet Union. The USSR also laid two gas pipelines, one of which supplies gas to the Soviet Union in compensation for Soviet gas supplied to Western Europe.[17] According to Ivanenko, the Iranians have had to pay no hard currencies. Instead, from 1970 to 1980 they sent 73 billion cubic meters of natural gas to the Soviet Union and, more recently, petroleum. Some of the latter, noted by Jan Vaňous, was part of a swap of Soviet petroleum to Romania which brought in return food and other products that would have cost the Soviets hard currencies. Of course, any Iranian deliveries of gas or oil to the Soviet Union tend to increase that country's net available exports of hard goods.

Relations between Iran and the CMEA countries have recently been conditioned very much by the war between Iran and Iraq. In fact, shortly after the war there appeared to be a shift of Soviet support from Iraq, which had been very close to the CMEA since breaking diplomatic relations with the United States in 1967. Vital military supplies were suspended to Iraq, only to be quietly restored as the war's tide swung toward Iran. In the meantime, Iraq turned to a willing France in 1981 and since 1983, through the good offices of Saudi Arabia, to the United States for economic assistance and other help. Future relations between Iraq and the CMEA are now uncertain.[18]

The South as Members of the CMEA

Table 4 shows the foreign trade of the Soviet Union and Eastern Europe with a special group of countries in the South, those in which communist parties are now solidly in power (not included are Kampuchea and Laos) and three in which communist or Marxist groups dominate but face serious counterrevolutionary threats (Afghanistan, Angola, and Ethiopia). The data in the table do not show Soviet deliveries of military aid.

The pattern of Soviet and East European trade with these countries differs from trade with the other LDCs, generally having larger imports per capita and, at the same time, relatively large imports compared to exports. At some point such differences deserve to be explored in analytical research.

From the point of view of the Soviet Union and the East Europeans, especially the former, political (and military) success seems to have an economic cost of a liability for long-term economic support. One wonders if such economic cost makes Soviet leaders hesitant to support revolutions. In any case, it is not their only potential problem.

The cases of China and Yugoslavia, if not also of Cuba, suggest that independent revolutions and coups far from Soviet borders create a major risk of deviations from the brand of socialism preferred by the Soviet Union. Moreover, the newly successful revolutionary leaders may have ambitions on neighboring territory, even if it is in the hands of another revolutionary power.

Still, new allies in the South offer a number of potential economic benefits. Cuba and Vietnam now supply tropical fruit; the latter sends natural rubber. Besides some useful industrial raw materials (nickel and cobalt from Cuba, potential offshore petroleum from Vietnam), these countries also have rapidly growing populations. Perhaps the future will see a special socialist form of the *gastarbeiter* coming to the aid of the CMEA members whose populations no longer grow.

Two solidly socialist countries in Table 3, China and North Korea, are not members of the CMEA. Their trade with the Soviet Union and Eastern Europe is also marked by a conspicuous lack of the large import deficits that evidence the economic assistance and credits flowing to the other countries.

Only three countries in the South have joined the CMEA so far. Mongolia, whose socialist government has been in office far longer than any in Eastern Europe, did not join until 1960. Cuba did not come in until 1972. Then Vietnam joined in 1978. The three are covered by two papers in this issue, a background paper by Lawrence Theriot and JeNelle Matheson of the U.S. Department of Commerce and one by the Bulgarian economist, Georgi Marinov.

Theriot and Matheson point out that Mongolia has benefited from a rising flow of Soviet assistance since the Sino-Soviet split. The trade deficit alone was about $2 billion from 1970 to 1977; as shown in Table 3, it has increased rapidly since then on an annual basis. In addition, other aid came in the form of below market prices on Soviet exports of petroleum products to Mongolia. A third benefit came when Mongolia was able to rid itself of a threatened permanent inundation of Chinese workers and specialists.[19] The specialists were replaced by less threatening persons from the Soviet Union.[20]

The future of Vietnam could also be influenced by a renewal of close ties between Beijing and Moscow. But clearly there is no sign of that in the paper by P. Navrozov and E. Plotnikov on Soviet-Vietnamese relations. They speak of "the aggressor of the North sanctioned by the American administration" and do not even mention China by name until well into their paper. But other disagreements among the socialist countries over Vietnam's policies are hinted by the fact that Navrozov and Plotnikov only mention the GDR, Czechoslovakia, Bulgaria, and Cuba as having agreements of friendship and cooperation with Hanoi. Does this mean that Romania, Poland, and Hungary did not, and was it because of their unhappiness over the situation in Kampuchea?

Worthy of attention is the Navrozov and Plotnikov note of the Soviet-Vietnamese joint enterprise, Vetsovpetro, operating out of Vungtan in southern Vietnam and undertaking exploration and possible development of the country's offshore oil and gas reserves. Such a development must attract the East European countries even more. This tone is clear in Marinov's paper on Bulgaria's relations with the three less developed members of CMEA. In fact, what is most interesting about this paper is its open recognition of the need to develop and promote "traditional" exports from these countries in return for the industrial capital goods and technology of the Euopean members of the CMEA. Now that Vietnam may have "resolved" the Kampuchean issue in its favor and opened the door to possibly better relations with the West, including the United States, it will be interesting to see how close it aligns its trade with the CMEA. Evidently it is not happy with the results of Soviet cooperation in offshore oil development.[21] But as late as 1983 that had not affected the share of Vietnam's imports supplied by the Soviet Union and Eastern Europe. That share, roughly estimated, rose from about 48% in 1979 to 64% in 1983.[22]

If Vietnam were able to develop export supplies of hard goods, it well might follow the path of Romania, one that was less consistently used by Cuba when it could, according to Theriot and Matheson. In 1975 about 46% of the total of Cuban exports and imports was with noncommunist countries. That share fell to 25% by 1977, while the Soviet share of total Cuban trade moved up from 52% in 1970 to 62% in 1977. As Table 3 shows, Cuban imports from Soviet and East European sources rose dramatically after 1975. The noncommunist share of those imports in 1983 was only about 21%.[23]

Cuba's exports to the industrial West also have fallen dramatically, from $766 million in 1980 to $463 million in 1983 according to the IMF's Directions of International Trade. This, in turn, required Cuba to enter into a rescheduling of its debts in convertible currencies which amounted to some $3.2 billion at the end of 1983. Cuba's position has required increasing levels of Soviet economic aid, which recently reached about $4.5 billion annually, including subsidies in above-market sugar prices. Military aid adds another $950 million per year to the figure. According to some reports, the Soviet Union is now asking the East European countries to carry increasing shares of the burden of supporting Cuba.[24]

Socialist client governments in the South

One may wonder how Cuba's foreign trade is influenced by its military role in Africa. The two countries with an important Cuban presence, Ethiopia and Angola, have been granted observer status in the CMEA. Along with Mozambique they are recognized by the Soviet Union as "socialist oriented," a designation which recognizes their lack of development and significant political and economic instability but even more suggests the unwillingness of the more developed countries in the CMEA to have them withdraw from the world-capitalist orbit.[25] As can be seen by the cases of Angola and Ethiopia in Table 4, this group of countries is already a significant economic burden. That we did not find recent papers on them in the foreign trade literature surveyed for this journal may indicate a nervousness that must have grown even greater with the intensity of famine in Ethiopia and the possibility of American and South African engineered realignments in Angola and Mozambique, which saw them both sign agreements with South Africa. Ethiopia, with all of its problems, seems to be the most secure Soviet client in Africa and recently has taken the formal step of forming the first ruling Marxist-Leninist party on the continent.[26]

Table 5

Exports to and Imports from the Soviet Union and Eastern Europe of Selected Third World Countries (million U.S. dollars)

		1970	1975	1979	1980	1981	1982
Argentina	X	81	464	651	1,970	3,458	1,839
	M	18	94	118	119	128	69
Brazil	X	109	734	1,177	1,479	1,935	1,286
	M	75	316	276	282	330	526
India	X	421	862	1,060	1,664	2,131	2,440
	M	295	742	1,087	1,733	1,926	1,796
Pakistan	X	83	69	69	141	151	144
	M	93	108	298	300	236	193
Bangladesh	X	0	36	81	64	60	68
	M	0	59	83	106	75	64

Source: United Nations, *1984 International Trade Yearbook*, vol. 1, special table G.

Just opposite Ethiopia and the Horn of Africa in Asia is another Soviet client, South Yemen, or more properly the People's Democratic Republic of Yemen. It is the single case of a thriving communist party in an Arab country and the only one having an avowed Marxist government.[27] Unlike Ethiopia, South Yemen has had no contingent of Cuban troops, even though it assisted Ethiopia in its war against Somalia in 1977–78 and then launched its own war against the neighboring Yemen Arab Republic. That war was settled by the Arab League. The League's influence would seem another contradiction, but it arose out of South Yemen's resumption of diplomatic ties with Saudi Arabia and the other conservative Arab countries in 1976. As a consequence, imports from OPEC countries, and recently the United Arab Emirates in particular, have been significantly higher than those noted in Table 3 from the Soviet Union and Eastern Europe. In fact, the CMEA countries seem to have provided only about 10% of imports recorded for the country in 1983.[28]

This is hardly the impression given by the paper of D. Al Khadat, a Yemeni graduate student in Bulgaria. He provides a long list of projects supported by CMEA members, including the important development of a fishing fleet by the Soviet Union that possibly could have other uses. This assistance is said to have covered 61% of total capital investment in the first five-year plan and the early years of the second of the country. With domestic sources covering 22%, it appears that noncommunist sources were about 17%. A list of countries providing those sources is also given in this relatively rare source on the country's development problems.

Two special cases

Two papers in our collection deal with countries that cannot be called "clients" of the CMEA, but that for various reasons have special trade relations with it. Table 5 provides the contrast between India and Argentina and their neighbors in these terms. If we discount Cuba, then in 1981 India and Argentina ranked first and second as Southern trading partners with the Soviet Union and Eastern Europe.

One can not help but ponder the complexities of international life that draws Asia's largest communist country close to the world's biggest capitalist power, while Asia's largest democracy seems always pushed from the United States and pulled toward the USSR. India's high volume of trade with the Soviet Union and Eastern Europe, reaching over 25% of total exports and over 10% of total imports, dwarfs the volumes of trade in the same direction for Pakistan and Bangladesh. The paper by N. Bogatyi and A. Ol'shanyi points with pride to the fact that the Soviet Union is now India's most important trade partner. Exports of the CMEA countries to India are dominated by machinery and equipment, but the authors fail to tell us the reason Soviet exports have an even greater component of machinery and equipment is that the Soviet Union is India's main supplier of arms. Arms exports include the advanced MiG 29 and 30 and the T-80 tank. Now India even has a license to manufacture the MiGs.[29]

Following a now familiar pattern, Bogatyi and Ol'shanyi provide an exhausting list of specific projects that involved participation by CMEA partners, including an impressive 38% of India's steel output from Soviet partnership, as well as 40% of its petroleum refining and 10% of electric power generation from the same sources. They claim that Soviet-provided facilities for ferrous metallurgy outperform those built by West Germans and Britains. This suggests that India would be an excellent case study of the comparative benefits of East and West project technologies since there are so many examples from both sides in the country.

The authors try to defend the benefits of the CMEA's bilateral clearing arrangements for India and also praise more recent examples of Indian-CMEA partner cooperation in third markets.[30] But here the CMEA countries must cope with India's increasing industrial know-how, one which now accounts for a rapidly growing share of Indian exports to the bloc, including a dominating position in some categories of Soviet imports. India is now shopping for more competitive Western technologies for its imports of capital goods and faces growing trade surpluses with the CMEA. While it probably would be willing to take for soft goods or against clearing accounts even more crude oil and petroleum products than the 14% and 39% shares already in its imports from the CMEA, the latter hardly wishes to lose much needed hard-currency earnings. Does this mean that the CMEA must become even more reliant on its ability to supply arms to India?

Argentina may have been a case where the Soviet Union wanted to balance its trade with arms exports but failed because of circumstances beyond its control. The fact that Soviet-Argentine trade is so completely dominated by the latter's exports of food products, mostly grain following the American embargo of 1980, causes V. Kornyshev to write with care in his paper. He resorts to presenting figures only for the total volume of trade and nicely ignores the significant decline in trade since 1981. Clearly the Soviet Union would like to buy Argentine grain with something besides dollars. Kornyshev admits that Argentina's "considerable positive balance" does stand in the way of a further development of trade with the Soviet Union. But his suggestions about how Soviet exports might be increased include nothing but conventional devices which have not proved successful. Oddly, he does not discuss Argentina's debt problems. Perhaps they, as much as anything, lie behind the several commitments to buy Soviet machinery that are listed in the paper.

The future of East-South economic relations

The final paper in this volume is István Dobozi's effort to project Hungary's trade with the South through the end of the century. He begins with a review of major factors influencing Hungarian-South economic relations up to now, most of which he emphasized in his first essay. Our concern now is to identify the factors he emphasizes as dominating the future. They are the following:

1) Increasing relative shortages of raw materials available from the Soviet Union;

2) Continued difficulties in resolving effective specialization of machinery production in the CMEA;

3) A lack of dynamics in East-West trade, compared to the 1970s;

4) Rapid growth and product diversificaiton in the exports of manufactures from the developing to the developed capitalist countries;

5) Rapid growth of South-South trade;

6) More rapid economic growth in the South than either the East or the West.

From this list he concludes that Hungary's own economic future is going to be determined by the success it has in exporting to the South, a success he understands as depending on the continued rationalization of Hungary's system of market socialism. It might be too much to have asked Dobozi to forecast the critical variables in that rationalization. Perhaps it is enough to see that significant change is underway in Hungary and that it is imperative that change be continued.

By implication, the future for the rest of Eastern Europe and the Soviet Union is considerably more gloomy than for Hungary. Poland has proposed significant changes but lacks the political cohesion to make them. The new Soviet leader may be inclined to search for reforms; but after so many failures in that country, we all know that inclinations will not be enough. Nothing in the other countries suggests any real commitment to decentralization and market discipline, not even in Bulgaria. But perhaps the new Soviet leadership will catalyze change.

We will end with what may be a ray of hope for the East. In all the literature searched for this introduction and certainly in the papers included here, we found nothing approaching a rigorous econometric analysis of the determinants of East-South trade. Perhaps that exercise would show more future for the kinds of policies and institutions that have made understanding this segment of the international division of labor so hard.

Notes

1. See, for example, Robert Loring Allen, *Soviet Economic Warfare* (Washington, D.C.: Public Affairs Press, 1960).
2. Carole A. Sawyer, *Communist Trade with Developing Countries: 1955–65* (New York: Praeger, 1966), p. 83.
3. This point is made by Daniel Pineye, "The Bases of Soviet Power in the Third World," *World Development*, 11:12 (December 1983), pp. 1083–95.
4. Case studies of most are found in *The New Communist Third World*, edited by Peter Wiles (New York: St. Martin's Press, 1982).
5. For some of the details, see the collection of essays in *Soviet Policy in Developing Countries*, edited by W. Raymond Duncan (Huntington, N.Y.: Krieger, 1981), and monographs by Stephen T. Hosmer and Thomas W. Wolfe, *Soviet Policy and Practice toward Third World Conflicts* (Lexington, Mass.: Lexington Books, 1983), and Elizabeth Kridl Valkenier, *The Soviet Union and the Third World: An Economic Bind* (New York: Praeger, 1983).
6. See the editor's introduction to *East-West-South: Economic Interactions between Three Worlds*, edited by Christopher T. Saunders (New York: St. Martin's Press, 1981), pp. 2, 4.
7. A glaring example of scholasticism of the left is Albert Szymanski, "The Soviet Union's Economic Relations with the Less Developed Countries: A Response to Clawson," *Review of Radical Political Economy*, 14:3 (Fall 1983), pp. 63–70. The views attacked are more "radical" but somewhat better documented and accurate—see Patrick Clawson, "The Character of Soviet Economic Relations with Third World Countries," *Review of Radical Political Economy*, 13:1 (Spring 1981), pp. 76–84.
8. C. W. Lawson, "Socialist Relations with The Third World: A Case Study of the New International Economic Order," *Economics of Planning*, 16:3 (1980), p. 159.
9. A useful view of these political distinctions is found in Wallace Spaulding, "Checklist of the 'National Liberation Movement,'" in *Problems of Communism*, March-April 1982, pp. 77–82.
10. Jan Vaňous "The Real Facts about Czechoslovak Foreign Trade," *The ACES Bulletin* (now *Comparative Economic Studies*), 24:1 (Spring 1982), p. 15.
11. "The Soviet Union, the Arms Trade and the Third World," *Soviet Studies*, 34:3 (July 1982), p. 387.
12. See Moshie Efrat, "The Economics of Soviet Arms Transfers to the Third

World—A Case Study: Egypt,'' *Soviet Studies*, 35:4 (October 1983), pp. 437–56. Efrat reviews the methods used by (1) the CIA–USACDA, (2) the Stockholm International Peace Research Institute, (3) the trade residuals method (used by Wharton), and (4) his own method based on recipient country data. He concludes, ''American official estimates of the value of Soviet military aid to the Third World are grossly mistaken; its value is at least two, and more probably, three times as high as their assessments'' (p. 454).

13. Neither have the political relations according to a useful review of them by Karen Dawisha, ''The USSR and the Middle East: Superpower in Eclipse?'' *Foreign Affairs* (Winter 1982/83), pp. 438–52.

14. As might be expected given Bulgaria's lower development level, the machinery share in exports is somewhat lower than the average for the other European members of CMEA, but significantly higher than that for neighboring Yugoslavia (see the data provided by Vanous).

15. A more complete view of Bulgaria's situation is found in Marvin R. Jackson, ''Recent Economic Performance and Policy in Bulgaria,'' in *East European Country Studies 1983. A compendium of Papers Presented to the Joint Economic Committee, Congress of the United States* (Washington, DC: US GPO, 1985), forthcoming.

16. Useful background on Syria is found in Robert G. Neumann, ''Assad and the Future of the Middle East,'' *Foreign Affairs* (Winter 1983/84), pp. 237–56.

17. Gu guan-Fu, ''Soviet Aid to the Third World, an Analysis of its Strategy,'' *Soviet Studies*, 35:1 (January 1983), pp. 80–82.

18. See *Radio Liberty Research*, August 4, 1983, and *The Economist*, November 24, 1984. The many ups and downs of recent Soviet-Iranian relations are reviewed in Shahram Chubin, ''The Soviet Union and Iran,'' *Foreign Affairs* (Spring 1983), pp. 921–49. Chubin contends that the country has not become dependent of Soviet and other CMEA sources of military supplies in spite of the renewable three-year military agreement signed in July 1981, which has brought as many as 1,500–2,000 Soviet advisers to Iran.

19. See Tania A. Jacques, ''Mongolia and Socialism'' *Problems of Communism*, March-April 1981, pp. 76–79, which reviews two recent books, Robert Rupen, *How Mongolia Is Really Ruled: A Political History of the Mongolian People's Republic, 1900–1978* (Stanford, Cal.: Hoover Institution Press, 1979), and Sechin Jagchid and Paul Hyer, *Mongolia's Culture and Society* (Boulder, Colo.: Westview Press, 1979).

20. *Far Eastern Economic Review*, March 29, 1984, and January 10, 1985.

21. See the *Far Eastern Economic Review*, January 31, 1985. Additional background can be found in Douglas Pike, ''Writing on Vietnam,'' *Problems of Communism*, November-December 1981, which reviews several recently published books on Vietnamese communism.

22. Calculations are based on figures for noncommunist trade published in the International Monetary Fund, *Directions of International Trade 1984*, p. 395, and figures for the Soviet Union and Eastern Europe published in the United Nations, *International Trade Yearbook*, given in Table 3.

23. The 1983 trade shares are estimated by the author on the basis of noncommunist trade in the IMF, *Directions of International Trade*, and the figures found in Table 3. For a detailed presentation of Cuba's economic and foreign trade

situation, see *Soviet and Eastern European Foreign Trade*, 20:3 (Fall 1984) which is dedicated to a long paper by Ricardo Acciaris, "Cuba's Economic Relations with Latin America and the Caribbean."

24. See *Radio Liberty Research*, January 18, 1984.

25. See Valkenier, pp. 97–103. In Africa the Soviet Union signed treaties of friendship and cooperation with Egypt in 1971, which was abrogated by Egypt in 1976, Somalia in 1974, which was abrogated by Somalia in 1977, Angola in 1976, Mozambique in 1977, Ethiopia in 1978, and the Congo in 1981. The treaties are normally for 20 years. For some detailed analysis of them, see Zafar Imam, "Soviet Treaties with Third World Countries," *Soviet Studies*, 35:1 (January 1983), pp. 53–70. For another view of the issues of ideological status, see the introduction by Wiles and Smith in Wiles, pp. 13–20.

26. See the report in *Radio Liberty Research*, September 7, 1984. On Cubans, East Germans, and Soviets in Ethiopia, see *The Economist*, February 11, 1984, and *Radio Liberty Research*, March 29, 1984. Two recent and informative sources on Ethiopia are Paul B. Henze, "Communism and Ethiopia," *Problems of Communism*, May-June 1981, pp. 55–74, and Alan Abouchar, "The Firm in Abyssinia: Capitalism, Socialism, and Economic Development in Ethiopia," *The ACES Bulletin* [now *Comparative Economics Review*], 26:4 (Winter 1984), pp. 25–42.

On Angola and Mozambique, see Gerald Bender, "Angola: Left, Right and Wrong," *Foreign Policy*, no. 43 (Summer 1981), pp. 63–71; N. MacQueen, "Mozambique's Widening Foreign Policy," *World Today*, January 1984, pp. 22–28; *The Economist*, December 24, 1983, January 14, 1984, and January 5, 1985; *Radio Liberty Research*, January 18, 1984, and March 29, 1984.

A useful political survey is Sam C. Nolutshungu, "African Interests and Soviet Power: The Local Context of Soviet Policy," *Soviet Studies*, 34:3 (July 1982), pp. 397–417. The essays in Wiles, ed., *The New Communist Third World* are also especially useful.

27. See Arnold Hottinger, "Arab Communism at Low Ebb," *Problems of Communism*, July-August 1981, p. 17.

28. Again, the estimate is a rough one combining Table 3 with information on noncommunist countries from the IMF, *Directions of International Trade 1984*, pp. 400–01.

29. See *Radio Liberty Research*, March 6, 1984.

30. For example, in 1977 India and the Soviet Union signed contracts to supply Indian equipment to steel projects built with Soviet assistance in Egypt, Turkey, Bulgaria, and Cuba. Possibilities also existed for such projects in Algeria, Libya, and Nigeria. See Gu Guan-Fu, p. 80.

István Dobozi (Hungary)

Prospects for East-South Economic Interaction in the Changing International Environment

I would like to raise a few major issues that are very relevant when dealing with East-South relations. I think that over the past few years East-West relations in the framework of the world trade system have received tremendous attention, and the East-West issue has overwhelmed the whole financial and economic system as a result of the debt problems affecting Eastern Europe and the increasing politicization of East-West economic relations.

To a large extent these major processes in the East-West segment of world trade shifted attention from the economic operations of the East European socialist countries in the Third World. This is a regrettable fact because there have been several interesting changes in this area. I would like to highlight those changes that took place in the seventies and early eighties.

First a few words about the magnitude of the trade flows I am talking about. East-South trade represents about 2% of the world trade, i.e., it constitutes a marginal flow. In absolute terms the socialist countries' exports to the South in 1982 amounted to $22 billion, their imports from developing countries to $20.5 billion. More than half of East-South trade is accounted for by the Soviet

---

The author is Head of Department, Institute for World Economics, Hungarian Academy of Sciences. This is a slightly revised version of a lecture before the North-South Academy of the Vienna Institute for Development (Vienna, October 13, 1983). Vienna Institute, *Occasional Paper*, 83/4.

Union. The share of the Soviet Union in East European countries' imports from the South was 63%, whereas in exports it amounted to 53%. The interesting aspect of the flows between East and South is that relatively speaking, they are significantly more important for the East European countries than for the developing countries. Whereas the share of East-South trade in the overall exports and imports of the socialist countries in 1982 was 13.8% and 13.2%, respectively, the share of the socialist countries of Eastern Europe, the Soviet Union included, in the overall trade of the Third World countries was significantly lower. In 1981, for example, in the total imports of developing countries, the share of the socialist countries was 5.3%, and in exports it was only 2.5%. This is a striking contrast. In the seventies the share of the developing countries in the overall trade of the East European socialist countries steadily increased. In some countries the increase was almost revolutionary. For example, in the case of Romania's exports, the share of the developing countries went up from 9.6% in 1970 to 28.1% in 1981. In the case of Hungary there was a significant increase, although it was not as revolutionary as in the case of Romania. The overall increase was significant for the East European countries, especially until 1981, when the share of the developing countries in overall East European exports was 17.4%, as opposed to 13.2% in 1970. The share of the developing countries with respect to imports increased from 9.7% in 1970 to 13.2% in 1982.

Interestingly enough, this did not happen with respect to the Third World countries. The share of the socialist countries in the total trade of the developing countries decreased. This divergency is due to the fact that East-South trade has been developing at a significantly lower rate of growth than the Third World countries' exports and imports vis-à-vis the West and the South. Whereas between 1970 and 1981 the exports of the developing countries to the West increased 9.5 times, their exports to the East European countries grew only fivefold.

As far as the *balance of trade* is concerned, a few interesting things can be observed. The socialist countries have been able to accumulate significant balance-of-trade surpluses in their trade with developing countries. In 1982 the surplus of the socialist countries other than the Soviet Union, the CMEA Six (CMEA: Council for Mutual Economic Assistance), was $3 billion, whereas the Soviet Union registered a $1.1 billion negative trade balance with the developing countries. Nineteen eighty-two was an exceptional year for the Soviet Union since it had consistently experienced positive balances with the Third World. This has not been the case with respect to Eastern Europe because, as a result of the first oil shock and partly as a result of the second one, the CMEA Six had registered a negative trade balance with the South for a few years. This has changed, and since 1980 the CMEA Six has accumulated consistent and increasing surpluses with developing countries. One understands the significance of the surplus in the socialist countries' trade with developing countries if it is put into a broader framework of trade relations, more specifically, East-West economic relations, where the socialist countries consistently have large balance-of-trade deficits. The interesting problem here is whether the socialist countries will be able to use their balance-of-trade surpluses with the South to offset their balance-of-trade deficits with respect to the West. This is not just a hypothetical question; it has practical relevance. The balance-of-trade surplus registered by the socialist countries is to a significant extent in hard currency, which can be used to finance partially the trade deficit vis-à-vis the West. In 1982 the surplus of the CMEA Six vis-à-vis the South amounted to 72% of these countries' deficit vis-à-vis the West, which provided the socialist countries a chance to finance part (smaller or bigger depending on individual cases) of their hard currency deficit vis-à-vis the West.

Nineteen eighty-two may seem an exceptional year. But it was not. In 1981 the surplus of the CMEA Six with respect to the South was bigger than that group's trade deficit with respect to the West. This then suggests that if their surplus vis-à-vis the South had been in hard currency, the socialist countries would have gained a net hard currency benefit from their trade with the nonsocialist world and would have been able to use their surplus vis-à-vis the South not only to counterbalance the deficit with respect to the Western countries but even to accumulate a marginal surplus. This is of course a tricky and underresearched subject, and no firm conclusion can be drawn concerning the precise magnitudes. The picture is very diverse. Some of the socialist countries use clearing arrangements to a larger extent than other CMEA countries in their Third World-related transactions. Those countries which conduct most of their trade with developing countries in hard currency are able to use the surplus very flexibly to offset deficit in East-West trade. Those countries which have accumulated surpluses mainly in clearing accounts are not as flexible. Hungary, for example, conducts nearly two-thirds of its trade with developing countries in hard currency. This is approximately the case with respect to Poland and some other countries. The Soviet Union seems to be an exception, relying heavily on clearing settlements.

I do not want to go into details because not all of us are financial experts; and when it comes to clearing and settlements, one needs to be an expert to discover the real implications of the problem. But what I have said is in a broad way indicative of the fact that some of the socialist countries, especially over the last few years, have used their trade with developing countries for balance-of-trade adjustments vis-à-vis the West.

One of the reasons why the socialist countries, especially the non-Soviet member countries of the CMEA, decided to cut back imports from the developing countries significantly in 1981 and 1982 was probably a reflection of the very serious situation they encountered in their trade with the West. Just to give a few specific figures: in 1981 the CMEA Six cut back imports from developing countries by 12% and in 1982 by 11%. This drop was much bigger than the drop in the socialist countries' imports from other relations. Even the Soviet Union was forced to cut back imports from developing countries in 1982. It is important to distinguish between the Soviet Union and the other CMEA member countries because, for a number of reasons, they behave differently. The structure of trade is different; the trade policy of the Soviet Union is definitely motivated by a broader set of considerations, whereas the small CMEA countries' policy in the East-South context stems predominantly from economic considerations.

Interestingly enough, it was the South toward which the socialist countries could rapidly expand their exports, and they did so rather successfully over the past few years. But in 1982 the earlier rapid dynamism of the CMEA countries' exports to the South stopped, and a decline of 19% was registered mainly as a result of balance-of-payments constraints, which particularly hit those developing countries with which the socialist countries had built up strong economic relations. This applies mainly to the oil-exporting countries of the Middle East and North Africa, with which the East European countries had rather successfully expanded their exports. As an indication of the success of this policy, I cite a few figures indicating how significantly the share of the OPEC countries went up in the socialist countries' total exports to developing countries. Whereas in 1970 only 16% of the total Third World-related exports of the socialist countries went to OPEC, in 1982 it was 32%. If we take the CMEA Six, the change is even more dramatic: the share of OPEC in the CMEA Six's Third World exports went up from 10% in 1970 to 42% in 1981, which then went down to 38% in 1982, reflecting the liquidity problems some of the major oil exporting countries faced and which, of course, also influenced East-South economic relations.

This is broadly the overall quantitative picture of East-South economic relations. It is important now to look at the *structure* of those relations. I am probably overwhelming you with figures, but I think it is important to know these figures before dealing with policy issues.

The interesting aspect of the trade structure between socialist countries and developing countries is that it reflects the character of the socialist countries, their status in the world economy as *intermediate economies*.

When one compares East-West trade with East-South trade, this intermediate nature of the socialist countries is very clearly identifiable. While the socialist countries' trade with the South exhibits very traditional features of an international division of labor between a Northern country and a Southern one, this picture, to a considerable extent, repeats itself in the East-West context, where the East European countries play almost the same role as the South plays in the East-South context, with some degree of modification, of course. If one looks at the specifics, there are differences in degree rather than in kind. Just a few figures: the socialist countries' South-related import picture is dominated by primary commodities. In 1980 the share of primary commodities in the CMEA Six imports from the South was 90%, which had increased from 81% in 1970. As far as manufactured goods are concerned, the share is correspondingly low, and moreover it declined from 18% in 1972 to 9% in 1980. The export picture is almost the opposite. The share of manufactured goods was 79% in 1980, and the share of primary products was 20%. Interestingly enough, the share of manufactured goods did not increase during the seventies; on the contrary, there was a slight decline from 84% in 1970 to 79%. By these figures I wanted to indicate that the structural picture of East-South trade is far from being healthy; it reflects some major underlying forces, some of them internal to the socialist countries, some of them external to them. But broadly speaking, I feel that the overall composition reflects neither the capabilities of the socialist countries nor the potentials that are inherent in East-South economic interaction in general.

A very interesting question comes up: Why are the socialist countries' imports of manufactured goods from the South so insignificant? Why did the share of manufactures even drop in the seventies? One of the major reasons is that the socialist countries were not able to integrate themselves into a dynamically unfolding division of labor in the area of manufactured goods between some developing countries and the industrially developed countries. I am referring, of course, to the NICs (newly industrializing countries), which have been the prime movers on the part of the South to push manufactures exports to the developed countries. The socialist countries did not establish an organic, strong economic contact with the NICs, with the partial exception of Brazil. This shows that the major changes in manufacturing industrialization that unfolded in the seventies and before in some parts of the South went almost unnoticed by the socialist countries. Surprisingly enough, therefore, the share of the socialist countries in NICs' exports declined, although it had been very insignificant even before. Let me just cite the case of my country. In the case of Hungary's Third World-related imports, the share of the ten well-established NICs (Brazil, Argentina, Mexico,

Hong Kong, Singapore, South Korea, Taiwan, the Philippines, Malaysia, and Thailand) went down from 39.2% in 1977 to 26.2% in 1982. This picture is totally distorted by the dominance of Brazil. All the socialist countries import basically a few important agricultural products from Brazil. So the relatively high share of the NICs in Hungary's overall Third World-related imports does not reflect Hungary's real involvement in the NIC process. As far as the export side is concerned, whereas in 1973 the share of the ten NICs in Hungary's exports to the Third World was 10.7%, it went down to less than 3% in 1982.

I did a statistical analysis to find out the share of East European countries in the foreign trade of several NICs. The picture shows the socialist countries' combined share being absolutely insignificant and in some cases even less significant than that of Austria. Although in 1981 Austria imported $141 million worth of commodities from South Korea, the value of the socialist countries' imports was less than $20 million. As far as exports are concerned, whereas Austria exported $50 million worth of commodities to South Korea, the value of socialist countries' exports to that country was only $7 million. One can cite more figures for Hong Kong, Brazil, Singapore, Argentina, Mexico, Malaysia, the Philippines, and Thailand, but the situation is no better. Although Austria does not stand very high with respect to some of these countries, the Netherlands, as a comparative example, alone outperforms Eastern Europe as a whole in most cases.

What causes this lag? One often cited reason is that some of the NICs are overly conservative in their internal policy and conduct a foreign policy which is antagonistic toward the East European countries. I think that this aspect has been blown out of proportion. My hunch is that the foreign trade strategy of the CMEA countries was not imaginative enough, not aggressive enough. The East European countries have also been slow to grasp the real importance of integrating themselves into the NIC process. All this goes a long way toward explaining the insignificant share of manufactured goods in the socialist countries' imports from developing countries. But it does not explain why the share of manufactured commodities in the socialist countries' overall exports to the South tended to decline.

This is partly related to the overall NIC problem. The NICs have been the most dynamic manufactures market in the South, actually in the world. If you are not able to establish an organic, strong link with the most rapidly developing markets in the area of manufactured goods, then you have probably set yourself on a course of declining importance in world manufactures trade. And this has happened. Moreover, not only in the case of NICs but also with several major OPEC countries, the socialist countries have tended to lose ground in the area of manufactured goods to alternate suppliers. So there is a problem with the overall competitiveness of the East European countries' manufactured goods exports to the South.

This is an overall picture which, I am stressing again, is not very healthy, neither from the point of view of the East European countries nor from that of the developing countries.

I would like to turn now to discuss a few major forces that will shape the *future of East-South economic relations*.

There are a few major forces one can identify which will govern East-South economic relations over the next 10 to 20 years. There is an underlying trend in the East European countries for the *labor force to become increasingly scarce and increasingly expensive*, especially if one takes into account sluggish productivity growth. From this fact one can draw certain conclusions about prospects for East-South economic relations. The socialist countries will be increasingly forced to import manufactured goods from the South in order to upgrade and modernize their industrial structure. The structural policy of the CMEA countries at the moment can be termed inadequate with respect to needs and requirements. This policy tends to result in new development amounting to putting one more layer on the existing structure. As a result industrial structures get very complex and overly diverse. Such development cannot be very successful since the lack of resources for development hinders the emergence and growth of new branches and new lines of production. This is to a large extent because the socialist countries bear the burden of those factories and industries that have been created in the past and somehow managed to stay alive and whose guaranteed survival is at the expense of the new sectors. The South potentially can clearly play a role in the adjustment policy of Eastern Europe by freeing resources in those sectors where the socialist countries have clearly lost their comparative advantage. Through conscious structural policy the socialist countries may make themselves room for adjustment by redeploying certain industries to the South and by accelerating manufactured goods imports from developing countries. As you know, this has been the case with respect to Western Europe and North America, and you also know that the structural accommodation of the increased manufactured goods imports from the South was a painful process, especially for Western Europe; but it should happen. Otherwise the East European countries will find it very difficult to compete on the world markets because of the inferior quality of their products, which results from an overly complex economic and industrial structure. The socialist countries have the potential advantage over the market-economy countries of anticipating such changes and implementing this adjustment in a planned way. This advantage, however, is not automatically captured. Earlier I talked about a recognition lag on the part of Eastern Europe concerning the importance of certain processes in the Third World. There should be a push toward recognizing the need and importance of a structural shift toward less labor-intensive lines of production in Eastern Europe.

There is a set of "environmental factors" that shapes the prospective evolution of East-South economic interaction. It is related to the changes in the major trading areas of the individual socialist countries. With respect to the CMEA, the important variable will be the rapidity of the integration process. One of the major "environmental factors" in the CMEA related to prospective East-South relations is natural resources. As you all know, CMEA integration has to a large extent been an extractive industry integration. The extractive sector has been the prime mover of integration. One can see a deceleration in the integration process as a result of the problems which the socialist countries have encountered in the area of extractive industry. Several Soviet economists point out that the Soviet extractive industry has entered into a new stage in its evolution which cannot be termed dynamic. In some sectors of the Soviet extractive industry there has been a significant deceleration of growth, and in the case of oil production there has been a levelling-off tendency, as opposed to a very dynamic output increase over the past decades. This, of course, will also reflect on the Soviet Union's ability to export natural resources to Eastern Europe.

Over the past few years there have been significant shifts in Soviet resource exports to Eastern Europe. Natural resources tend to become increasingly hard commodities in Eastern Europe, almost being the equivalent of hard currency, and they are very difficult to obtain.

This is the current situation. On the basis of the underlying forces in the CMEA, I do not foresee any major improvement over the next 10 years in this area. Actually the situation could get even worse, which then might result in serious policy implications for the CMEA Six. Our projections indicate that a rise in imports of several major fuels and minerals from nonsocialist countries (mainly developing countries) to meet the needs of East European countries seems inevitable. The projected 1990 import needs from Third World sources was published in my "World Raw Material Markets until the Year 2000—Implications for Eastern Europe" (*Raw Materials Report*, 1983, no. 2). The forecast was prepared for two scenarios: the first assumes that the efforts for demand management (improved conservation performance) will not produce the desired results; the second assumes that the efforts to moderate demand will prove successful, that the growth rate of raw materials and energy consumption will slow down considerably, and that there will be a marked improvement in specific input use. The second scenario indicates that even if problems get bigger and bigger in the CMEA in the area of natural resources supply, there is a policy option for the East European countries to decelerate their rate of growth of energy and raw materials consumption, which historically has been excessively rapid as a result of these economies' tendency to overconsume. There is a large reserve to decrease the margin of overconsumption; but of course it is related to a set of factors among which I consider the most important to be the institutional setup of the East European economies. I do not foresee a major deceleration in the growth rate of energy and raw materials consumption in general without a genuine institutional incentive impulse at home.

Even if a conservation policy proves to be successful, the import needs of these countries vis-à-vis the Third World will still become staggering in terms of requirements for finance. For scenario II the combined imports for six commodities (oil, natural gas, copper, bauxite, iron ore, phosphate rock)—at current prices—will amount to about $40 billion in 1990.

Thus there is going to be competing demand among the socialist countries for Southern manufactures and raw materials. Previously I talked about the necessity to accelerate manufactured goods imports from the South—my very firm belief is that this should take place. On the other hand, the acute problems in the area of natural resource supply will make this evolution toward accelerated manufactured goods imports very difficult, if not impossible, depending on the volume of import needs of the socialist countries with respect to major minerals and fuel. So this is a major question mark, a policy dilemma for the East European countries as to how to proceed in this contradictory situation.

Another complicated issue is the manufactured goods cooperation problem in the CMEA. Unfortunately, the problems the socialist countries face in the area of manufacturing integration are not much smaller than those they face with respect to extractive industry integration. The qualitative problems of CMEA integration are reflected very strongly in the area of manufacturing integration. This is a process that cannot be directed solely from the center. Manufacturing integration needs independent enterprise actors, and even the best planning center is not able to direct a microintegration for very obvious reasons. Manufacturing integration within the CMEA has become very strongly tied to the national economic reforms within the CMEA. I do not foresee any major progress in the area of manufacturing integration without the necessary institutional changes in the national economies. Before this happens, manufacturing integration will not be able to offset the lost dynamism in the area of CMEA extractive industry integration. If this is the case, manufacturing integration will not be as adequate for the individual member countries as the objective situation of the countries would require. It would act as a push factor again, nudging these countries toward those trading areas with which they are able to engineer genuine cooperative links in manufacturing.

One can now turn to the East-West segment of the socialist countries' foreign economic relations as it relates to East-South relations. In the seventies East-West economic relations had their ups and downs. Broadly speaking, East-West economic relations have developed rather dynamically, and the general dynamics of East-West trade was determined by the import needs of the socialist countries. The eighties will see a different situation where instead the export capabilities of the socialist countries will determine the dynamics of East-West trade. If we look at the East European countries' export capabilities objectively and the receiving policy environment in Western Europe, then one cannot be very optimistic about the potential for growth in East-West trade. There is going to be sluggish growth in East-West trade even if the West should recover from the recession. The debt situation of the East European countries is obviously a constraining factor. Furthermore, the tendency toward increased politicization of East-West trade will act as a factor deterring the East European countries from East-West relations to some extent, and the degree of this deterrence will vary in the individual socialist countries. The politicization attempts on the part of the United States, which have some implications for Western Europe as well, and the resulting policy uncertainty in the context of East-West economic relations will not go unnoticed by some of the East European countries and potentially may result in a redirection of efforts to trade with alternative actors. If this is the case, then again the South appears as a potential alternative trading partner.

An important environmental factor is related to what is happening in the Third World itself. I cannot be very specific on this because of lack of time, but I think that it is probably correct to say that over the next ten years, the Third World as a whole will develop at a significantly higher rate of growth than the rest of the world, even if the present short-term situation does not warrant such a forecast because the South is in a deeper recession than the West or some segments of the East. I think that as the West recovers from the present economic malaise, so will the South. Objective conditions existing in the South will warrant a significantly higher rate of growth for these countries and, by implication, a significantly higher rate of growth of import demand. So, as in the past decade, in the eighties the developing countries will be the most dynamically expanding import markets. There is going to be a continuing shift of economic dynamism toward extra-European territories, and the East European countries will try to capture the opportunities for rapidly growing import demands, although the rapidity of the import increase among the developing countries will not be as strong as it was in the seventies.

This is broadly the situation. There are certain push and pull factors, which as a net result will push the socialist countries toward the South and may result in a significantly increased share of developing countries in the overall foreign trade of the East European countries.

As far as my country is concerned, with an imaginative trade policy the Hungarian economy would be able to increase the share of developing countries in its overall exports to 20—25% by 1990 and to about 30% by 2000 which, of course, would be a revolutionary increase as compared to the present situation.

There is nothing inherently good in increasing the share of the developing countries in the overall trade of the socialist countries. Neither these countries nor any other country in the world is run by attaching inherent goodness or badness to certain groups of countries or relations. I think that as a result of the above-mentioned factors, partly internal and partly external to the socialist countries, the economic importance of the Third World for the East European countries will significantly increase and vice versa.

I left totally untouched the organizational and institutional infrastructure of an accelerated East-South economic scenario. One can very firmly say that the present institutional machinery of East-South interaction will not be able to back an accelerated development over the next ten to twenty years. I believe that there is a correlation between the East European countries loosing ground in the Third World and the institutional machinery of East-South trade. Modernization of the existing organizational background of East-South economic relations will be necessary.

M. KHALDIN (USSR)

Contemporary Forms of Commercial and Economic Cooperation between the USSR and the Developing Countries

Economic interchange between the USSR and the developing countries in the present stage is a complex system of intergovernmental economic relations including, in addition to traditional foreign trade operations, credit-financial and scientific-technological relations and assistance in the construction of projects in the leading sectors of production and in the infrastructure of the liberated countries.

The growth of the economic potential of the USSR and the developing countries, the heightened level of international specialization in their economies, the accumulated positive experience in mutual cooperation, and a growing mutual political trust have placed on the agenda of the day the question of the formation and deepening of a stable and mutually advantageous division of labor between partners in the interests of increasing the effectiveness of the economy of the USSR and strengthening the economic independence of the liberated governments of Asia, Africa, and Latin America.

The comprehensive development of foreign trade and economic and scientific-technological relations between the Soviet Union and the liberated countries, which embraces not only commerce but also

---

 "Sovremennye formy torgovo-ekonomicheskogo sotrudnichestva SSSR s razvivaiushchimisia stranami," *Vneshniaia torgovlia*, 1984, no. 3, pp. 24–29. Translated by Michel Vale.

The author is a professor of economics and holds a doctorate in economics.

the sphere of material production and services, has created favorable preconditions for diversifying the forms of commercial and economic cooperation and has strengthened the organizational and legal basis of that cooperation.

Soviet foreign trade organizations are carrying out systematic work to discover, approve, and implement new forms of economic interchange between the USSR and the developing countries, taking into account useful foreign experience and the practice of international economic relations.

A transition to large-scale and multileveled economic relations requires the continuous refinement of the mechanism of administration and of the organizational forms of economic cooperation. Practice has taught us that it is necessary to create new organizational institutions with broader possibilities for applying day-to-day measures and for making coordinated decisions in the interests of the further growth of commercial and economic cooperation between the USSR and the developing countries.

Intergovernmental mixed commissions on economic and scientific and technological cooperation have proven to be an organizational form which fits the increased scale of commercial and economic cooperation between the USSR and many developing countries.

These commissions and their national sections include leading officials in the planning, financial, production, and foreign trade ministries and agencies, as well as those from scientific organizations which have the necessary competence for the development, application, and execution of contracted measures for the further development of bilateral commercial and economic relations. Subcommittees and working groups consisting of specialists from the different countries are set up in the principal areas of cooperation to work on current and long-term problems.

The functions of these mixed committees include evaluating the results achieved in the main areas of cooperation, examining problems that arise and determining methods for dealing with them, working out national and joint measures for developing mutual economic relations, the preparation of drafts for joint documents on external economic questions, and finally, the discovery of new areas of cooperation and planning them over the long term.

The participation of representatives from the concerned production ministries and agencies in the work of the committees ensures that the obligations of foreign economic relations are duly coordinated with the needs and means of the national economies of the respective parties to cooperative ventures, and measures to ensure the coordinated growth of economic exchange are promptly implemented. The intergovernmental nature of the decisions and documents adopted introduces elements of planning into commercial and economic relations and increases the responsibility of the respective partners for meeting their mutual obligations.

The first intergovernmental mixed committees between the USSR and the developing countries were created in the '60s, and by the middle of 1983 there were about twenty such committees operating in the area of economic and scientific and technological cooperation. These committees actively assist the development of commercial and economic cooperation between the USSR and such countries as Algeria, Angola, Argentina, Afghanistan, India, Iraq, Libya, Madagascar, Morocco, Mexico, Mozambique, the Peoples' Republic of Yemen, Peru, Syria, Uruguay, Ethiopia, and certain others.

The activity of the mixed committees is a logical complement to cooperation in planning. As one of the forms of scientific and technological exchange, it has a deep impact on commercial and economic cooperation and accordingly has very promising long-term prospects from the standpoint of a stable and planned development of bilateral relations, which in the final analysis will stabilize the development of the various sectors of the economies of the liberated countries that are partners of the USSR.

Of course, this form of cooperation is especially effective in relations with those developing countries which have introduced the principles of planning into their economic practice across a broad front and have a large state sector in their economies as well as established national planning bodies. Developing countries with a socialist orientation, which consider planning an important factor in their social and economic policies, have shown the most interest in this form of cooperation.

Given the instability of the world markets, *long-term commercial contracts* have begun to play a growing role. They help to increase the effectiveness of planning in production and financing, make possible prompter transfer of technology in the processing of raw materials, economize on labor, material, and financial resources, and reduce transport costs in foreign trade operations. Used widely, long-term commercial contracts stabilize and expand the scale of foreign trade turnover and broaden the use of new forms of commercial and economic cooperation with the liberated countries.

Soviet foreign trade organizations have been carrying out commercial operations with the developing countries on long-term contracts for a rather long time. In contrast to ordinary commercial contracts on the purchase and sale of raw materials, long-term contracts are concluded as part of intergovernmental agreements on economic and scientific and technological cooperation, which provide for the granting of credits for long-term projects, the delivery of machinery and equipment, the proffering of technical assistance in construction and engineering, etc. In other words, long-term commercial contracts in Soviet foreign economic practice are usually tied in with economic and scientific and technological assistance to the developing countries and sometimes reap the results of this cooperation.

The deepening of the international division of labor is furthered by *cooperation in processing donor raw material* in the form of swap transactions or transactions on a donor basis. In this case one party saves on the construction of additional productive capacities, and the already existing production capacities of the other party are more fully utilized, and ultimately trade grows. In the early '70s Soviet foreign trade organizations made some test swap transactions that provided for the delivery of Soviet raw materials for processing in enterprises in the developing countries, after which the final products were repurchased by the Soviet Union on the basis of a single ongoing contract.

The area in which this form of cooperation between the USSR and the developing countries might potentially be used is rather broad, but it can yield a special effect in relations with neighboring developing countries that have large production capacities in the processing of some types of Soviet raw materials bearing a high cost per unit weight.

The appearance of several new forms of cooperation is closely related to the growth in economic and technical assistance of the USSR to the developing countries. This type of cooperation has been going on since the mid-'50s in the form of deliveries of complete equipment and materials, the carrying out of various planning and surveying projects, geological prospecting, maintenance, construction, commissioning plants, adjustment work, and in the training of skilled personnel. In the '70s, in the interests of mobilizing the domestic resources of the developing countries and speeding up technology transfer to them in the construction and operation of cooperative projects, Soviet organizations began to assume the responsibility of carrying through all the work involved in completing covenanted projects and delivering turn-key factories, ready for operation. The least developed liberated countries, which do not have the necessary skilled personnel, production capacities, and financial resources, as well as the oil-exporting developing countries, have shown a special interest in developing this kind of cooperation in order to save time in constructing projects in key sectors of their economies.

Considering these interests on the part of many developing countries, the Soviet Union has since the '70s begun to practice another form of economic and technological assistance, namely, *cooperation under conditions of a general contract*. In constructing on contract the Soviet Union assumes the responsibility to carry out all the tasks in constructing a project, which guarantees the client in the developing country that the project will be handed over on time in full conformity with the planned specifications, thereby eliminating the waste of the foreign currency and of the technological and labor resources of the client. The proportion of construction under general contract in the total volume of Soviet assistance to the developing countries increased from 15% in 1975 to 46% in 1982. In connection with the increase in the volume of work carried out on the basis of contractual agreements, an administration for construction on contract abroad and an all-union office, "Stroipodriadeksport," were set up under the auspices of the USSR State Committee on Foreign Economic Relations; these agencies deal with questions of constructing foreign projects on a general contractual basis, including in the developing countries.

A new modification of contractual relations is *construction accompanied by marketing of the finished product*, in which the contractor not only does all the construction and assembly work in projects but also organizes the production and sale of the final product in the initial stages of operation of the new enterprises. Many developing countries encounter difficulties employing the latest technology because of the low level of professional training of local cadres and believe a solution to the problem of extending the obligations of the foreign contractor constructing a factory include the operation of the new production capacities.

At the present stage the developing countries have shown an interest in employing the efforts of Soviet foreign trade organizations not only to construct but also to operate agreed upon ventures with a view toward ensuring their profitable functioning at the very outset, as soon as the enterprise has begun operations.

In light of this trend the *long-term leasing* of enterprises constructed in the developing countries with the assistance of the USSR is both logical and possible, with these enterprises then being operated with the participation of Soviet specialists. Settlement in these operations could take place with the final product of the leased enterprise being shared proportionally to the expenditures of the respective partners. Another form that helps solve some of the problems in commercial and economic cooperation between the USSR and the developing countries does not require the handing over of the property rights of a plant or factory built in the developing countries with Soviet assistance; it ensures that the partners each receive the necessary quantities of output for a specified period.

With the beginning of operations of many plants and factories constructed with Soviet assistance in the developing countries, operations *involving repurchase of the output of these facilities* were begun.

The relevance of these operations is due to the interest that the partners from the developing countries have in utilizing the production capacities of new enterprises, organizing a reliable outlet for their products on foreign markets, and in the final analysis ensuring the profitability of these enterprises. But the Soviet Union is also interested in importing certain types of products. As an example we can mention deliveries of cast iron, rolled ferrous metals, and metallurgical and crane equipment from plants built with Soviet and Indian cooperation. In the first half of the '70s Egypt supplied a considerable quantity of cold rolled sheet steel; large orders of Soviet foreign trade organizations for stampings of tractor parts and ocean-going vessels were filled by the forging factories and shipyards of this country, built with Soviet assistance.

At the end of the '70s oil, natural gas, bauxite, silica, ferrous and nonferrous metals, yarn, canned goods, chemical fertilizers, and even some types of machinery and equipment were exported to the Soviet Union from plants and factories built on a cooperative basis in the developing countries.

In 1976–80 the proportion of products from enterprises constructed with Soviet cooperation reached 20–25% of the total volume of Soviet imports from the developing countries.

One of the promising forms of foreign economic relations of the Soviet Union is *cooperation on a compensation basis*. In the practice of commercial and economic cooperation between the USSR and the developing countries, this form works as follows: the Soviet Union provides earmarked credits and material resources, new production capacities are built in the developing country with the assistance of Soviet organizations, and the debt of the developing country to the Soviet Union is paid off (compensated) by deliveries of the output of the plant or factory built on a compensation basis (less frequently, by delivery of the output from other enterprises).

Compensation ventures are built mainly in key sectors of the economy of the developing countries (fuels and raw materials, the processing industries, etc.). A compensation agreement is usually tied to export-import and commercial operations and embraces the productive, financial, and commercial interests of the partners, thereby ensuring that both sides share in the responsibility for the effective construction and operation of the ventures over the rather long periods the agreements are in effect.

Compensation cooperation helps expand the export resources of the developing countries and guarantees them a reliable outlet over a long period of time; it increases their solvency, gives them a source of credits on a noncurrency basis, alleviates the problem of paying off their foreign indebtedness, and stabilizes economic interchange between the cooperating countries.

At the present time the Soviet Union has about thirty compensation agreements with the developing countries, the most important of which are agreements with Afghanistan (1963) and Iran (1966) for natural gas, with Guinea for bauxites (1969), with Syria and Iraq for oil (1969 and 1975), with Morocco for phosphates (1978), and with the Congo (1981) for polymetallic ores.

Trilateral cooperation, which grew in the '70s under conditions of international detente, involves joint participation of organizations of socialist, developed capitalist, and the developing countries in the construction of large-scale projects on the territories of the developing countries. This form of cooperation helps economize on the material resources of all partners by reducing the costs of construction and operation of the projects, increasing the competitiveness of the proposed transactions in commercial and technical respects, and accelerating the beginning of operations of a project, especially if it is a large factory or plant.

For the developing countries, trilateral cooperation broadens their access to advanced technology, multiplies their production capacities on more favorable financial conditions, and promotes the growth of their national exports on the markets of socialist and developed capitalist countries.

Trilateral cooperation attracts the Western partners by virtue of the possibilities it offers for expanding exports on the markets of the developing and socialist countries, increasing the utilization of their production capacities, and reducing the size of credits necessary to pay construction costs.

As practice has shown, trilateral cooperation grew through the construction of enterprises in the mining industry in the African countries, enterprises in the processing industry, infrastructure projects in Latin American and Asian countries, and the construction of large-scale industrial and infrastructural projects under general contractual conditions in the petroleum-exporting developing countries.

By 1982 Soviet foreign trade organizations had arranged trilateral cooperation with more than 200 firms in the developed capitalist countries, including Finland, the FRG, France, Italy, Austria, Japan, and Switzerland. The projects in trilateral cooperation with USSR participation have been enterprises in nuclear power plants and heating plants, ferrous metallurgy, the chemical and petrochemical industries, construction materials, the mining industry (including prospecting for minerals), and the development of transport networks in the developing countries.

By 1978 the Soviet Union had participated in the construction of many projects on a trilateral basis in 46 developing countries.

This form of cooperation is employed in various versions: Western firms act as subcontractors for equipment, materials, and services in the construction of projects built by Soviet organizations; Soviet organizations provide equipment, materials, and services on contract for projects constructed by Western firms, and finally there is joint participation of Soviet organizations and capitalist firms at all stages of construction of projects in the developing countries. As economists have observed, "In this form of cooperation all its participants gain: the country in which the project is being built obtains an enterprise that is highly competitive economically and technically, suppliers of equipment acquire the possibility of expanding their exports and exchanging both technical and commercial experience, and finally, this form of joint participation promotes the further deepening of the international division of labor and cooperation, which is in consonance with the ideas of strengthening peace and detente."[1] Trilateral cooperation, which flourished during the years of detente, encountered obstacles due to the exacerbation of international tension, to every possible type of economic sanction from Western countries against the socialist and some of the developing countries, and to the attempts of the American administration to transform foreign economic relations into a tool for exerting the grossest political pressure.

In this situation prospects are broader for *cooperation by the USSR with the developing countries on the markets of third countries*, which may be seen as a modification of trilateral cooperation, but without the participation of developed capitalist country firms, which have embarked on a path of undermining international economic cooperation. This form of relations expands the export possibilities of the partners on the basis of the principles of a just division of labor, increases the competitiveness of their products on the markets of the developing countries, and thereby enables the partners in general to obtain advantageous contracts and make use of the business connections of the participating parties in the interests of developing their commercial and economic relations. Understandably, this form of cooperation is utilized by the USSR primarily with those developing countries that have sufficient economic potential and many years of experience in bilateral cooperation.

Hence it is natural that the pioneer in joint entry with the USSR on the markets of third world countries has been the friendly Republic of India. The long-term trade agreement signed between the USSR and the Republic of India on December 26, 1970, includes Article 12, which says: "Both governments will assist the development of cooperation between industrial commercial enterprises in both countries for the purpose of pooling their resources and know-how in order to satisfy their desire jointly to expand markets in third countries and to meet the needs flowing from programs for industrial development in third countries." The mutual desire to develop cooperation on the markets of third countries (especially the developing countries) has also been specified in subsequent intergovernmental documents regulating Soviet-Indian commercial and economic cooperation.

In the context of the documents, cooperation on the markets of third countries between the USSR and India is promising in two areas. First, it can bring mutual benefits in the joint construction of projects in third developing countries within the framework of economic and technological assistance, especially in the case of construction of projects on a general contractual basis. In this case each party can serve both as the general contractor and the subcontractor, with both responsible for performing stipulated portions of the work in constructing the project.

Second, cooperation on the markets of developing countries is possible in ordinary commercial operations if the merchandise-supply systems of the partners on the markets of the third countries differ in density and effectiveness.

The first experience in Soviet-Indian cooperation on the markets of the developing countries showed it to have fruitful prospects for building large-scale industrial projects. Thus, when ferrous and nonferrous metallurgy enterprises were built with the USSR in Algeria, Iran, Turkey, and Nigeria, Indian firms and organizations were the subcontractors to Soviet general contractors, built some public projects and roads, and supplied metal constructions and certain types of equipment produced by Indian industry. According to the Indian evaluation, India's participation and cooperation with the USSR on markets of third countries increased the utilization of their production capacities and strengthened India's position on world markets.[2]

Brazil has demonstrated an interest in cooperation with the USSR on markets of third countries. A number of Brazilian companies are now studying possibilities for such cooperation on the markets of Latin America and Africa. One of the possible cooperation projects between the USSR, Brazil, and Peru concerns the construction of a tunnel for channeling water resources into desert and arid regions on the Western shore of Peru to irrigate farms and run hydroelectric power stations.[3]

Considerable attention has recently been devoted by many developing countries, and even some international economic corporations, to a form of cooperation involving the creation of mixed companies on the territory of the developing countries, with organizations from socialist countries having participating shares. The view is that the activity of mixed companies as a new form of economic exchange among the developing countries fits the socioeconomic conditions in these countries; it meets both the needs of the organization of postsale service of equipment purchased in socialist countries and demands with regard to strengthening and expanding the organizational network for servicing mutual foreign economic operations. In some developing countries mixed companies with foreign participation are considered almost the only possible form of economic cooperation with foreign countries.

However, certain ideas of an ideological and social character seriously limit the possibilities of socialist countries having participating shares in mixed companies on the territory of developing countries. Soviet foreign trade organizations refrain from such participation in mixed companies in the realm of material production in developing countries.

But since no surplus value is created in international trade and services, and the profit of mixed companies derives exclusively from the advantages and benefits flowing from the participation of the cooperating parties in the international division of labor and has nothing to do with the exploitation of one party by the other, socialist countries can have shares in mixed companies on the territory of developing countries in the domain of trade and services. Soviet foreign trade organizations have a working share in a number of mixed companies involved in transport and financial servicing of foreign trade organizations of the USSR and its partners in the developing countries, as well as in inspecting and technically servicing Soviet export products in some developing countries, although the number of such companies remains very limited.

The effective utilization of many of the approved forms of commercial and economic interchange in connection with the further growth in Soviet production of items for export to the developing countries creates the necessary conditions for the formation and deepening of a stable, mutually advantageous international division of labor between the USSR and the developing countries and for reaping the advantages and benefits deriving from it.

The key targets in the formation and deepening of stable and mutually advantageous international division of labor between the USSR and the developing countries require a further increase in the volume of goods put into circulation by commercial and economic cooperation, and the Soviet Union is taking the necessary measures in this direction. But the tremendous potential of the USSR in the domain of "invisible trade" with the developing countries, first and foremost, in the realm of services, is still not sufficiently realized. The Soviet Union has a tremendous scientific and technological potential, while the developing countries are experiencing an acute shortage of specialists in many key areas of production, technology, and science. Soviet specialists are today working across quite a broad front in the developing countries, although as a rule only within the framework set down by Soviet commitments to providing economic and scientific and technological assistance to these countries. The development of new forms of cooperation involving sending Soviet specialists to provide paid services to the developing countries over and above the existing commitments of the USSR to provide economic and scientific and technological aid is a timely, viable, and mutually advantageous goal for the USSR and the developing countries.

It is not difficult to see that new forms of commercial and economic cooperation of the USSR with the developing countries will intensify the interplay of foreign trade, economic assistance, and scientific and technological relations, as well as credit and financial and transport operations among the partners in the interests of forming and deepening a stable and mutually advantageous division of labor between the USSR and the developing countries.

The participation of the USSR in the construction of projects in the developing countries logically becomes cooperation on general contractual conditions and on a compensation basis, and this expands the volume of mutual trade both through the return delivery of the products manufactured by cooperatively built projects to the USSR and through the additional export of Soviet machinery, equipment, and materials to the developing countries. The positive experience of bilateral cooperation makes the transition to trilateral cooperation on the markets of the developing countries a possibility, and this means a further growth in economic interchange among the partners. The forms of cooperation mentioned above have been substantially enriched by a growing exchange in science and technology and have received more and more financial and transportation support. Cooperation in planning makes it possible confidently to determine the scale, structure, and pace of development of foreign economic ties and at the same time to carry out the necessary economic measures in the interests of developing mutual economic exchange. The organizational underpinnings of these complex foreign economic relations are effectively provided by intergovernmental mixed commissions. The system of traditional and new forms of economic exchange between the USSR and the developing countries persuasively debunks all the various bourgeois "theories" according to which commercial and economic relations between states with different social systems are inhibited by "the specific characteristics'' of the organizational and legal foundations of conducting the foreign economic relations of the USSR. In reality the state monopoly over foreign trade and other forms of foreign economic relations which we have in the USSR is able to respond promptly and flexibly to newly arising needs of international economic exchange and to actively assist the development, testing, and practical introduction of new forms of such exchange.

The international division of labor between the USSR and the developing countries has concrete historical forms. Hence Soviet foreign trade organizations intend to continue to improve the system of forms of economic interchange with the liberated countries, thereby expanding the channels of economic contact with them in the interests of consolidating peace and mutual cooperation.

Notes

1. For more details see *Postroeno pri ekonomicheskom i tekhicheskom sodeistvii sovetsgogo soiuza*, Moscow, ''Mezhdunarodnye otnosheniia,'' 1982, p. 251.
2. *Indo-Soviet Cooperation and Indian Economic Development*, R. K. Sharma, ed., New Delhi, 1982, p. 105.
3. UNCTAD, *Trade relations among countries having different economic and social systems*, Report by the UNCTAD Secretariat. TD/B/912, July 23, 1982, Geneva, p. 30.

Orah Cooper and Carol Fogarty
(United States)

Soviet Economic and Military Aid to the Less Developed Countries, 1954–78

Introduction

The USSR launched its aid program in the mid-1950s to promote Moscow's foreign policy interests in the Third World. In the 24 years since then the USSR has responded to aid opportunities in target areas throughout the world with nearly $47 billion of economic and military pledges to 73 countries. It has trained 50,000 students from 98 developing countries in academic disciplines and nearly 75,000 LDC nationals in military and technical skills. The record for Soviet personnel serving in LDCs in a single year (1978) was nearly 28,000 economic technicians and 11,000 military technical personnel (not including troops stationed in Egypt in the early 1970s).

Moscow's basic political objectives have remained constant—to erode Western influence and substitute its own, to counteract the Chinese challenge to its "leadership" of national liberation movements, and eventually to persuade Third World countries that Soviet Communism offers the only viable solution to their economic problems. To accomplish these objectives Moscow has provided less developed countries with alternative sources of arms, capital, and technical services on attractive terms. Initially the Soviets gave

Soviet Economy in a Time of Change, vol. 2, October 10, 1979 (Washington, D.C.: GPO, 1979).

The authors are research analysts with the Office of Economic Research, Central Intelligence Agency.

preference to emerging states that followed a "noncapitalist path of development" and were on the road toward becoming "national democratic states." Ideology was overtaken by pragmatism in the mid-1960s, when aid was offered with less concern for the political orientation of potential clients.

Anxious to assert a big power image in the Third World, the Soviets tried to fill the vacuum left by the withdrawal of colonial powers, while securing a foothold in areas of strategic importance. Moscow found arms its most direct and fastest route to influence in these countries, which often were able to obtain economic assistance from noncommunist sources, but not military aid.[1] The Soviets also provided military personnel and advanced weapons systems to states and nationalist groups ripe for conflict, most recently to the Arab belligerents in the Middle East and for nationalist movements in southern Africa.

Nearly two-thirds of Moscow's $47 billion commitment and three-fourths of its $32 billion of deliveries since 1954 have been military related. In the first years of the program, when some developing countries were reluctant to accept large amounts of military assistance from Moscow, economic commitments roughly equaled the military. In the past 10 years military aid has outrun the economic 2.5 to 1, and for most of those years the Soviets have held second rank, after the United States, as an LDC arms supplier.

Moscow has never been able to compete on a broad scale with the West, either in the size or kind of economic aid programs it has offered. Nonetheless the heavy regional concentration and high visibility of its program often have given Soviet aid an impact beyond its size. Military aid has been competitive and has given Moscow prestige as a major international arms supplier. While major Western powers would not or could not provide the modern weaponry developing countries craved, Moscow responded rapidly, often with favorable payment conditions. Because many new states felt that their political futures and even their survival hung on military stature and assured arms supplies, the Soviets were able to entangle many military clients in a web that deepened and prolonged their dependence on the USSR.

Moscow can respond quickly to crises with air- and sea-lifts of large numbers of men and matériel to trouble spots. Its most spectacular operation was in the 1973 Middle East war, when the Soviets poured $4 billion worth of arms into Arab belligerents' inventories within 15 months. The 1975 venture into Angola was another bold display of Soviet supply capability. This was followed in 1977–78 by massive support to Ethiopia—on a scale unprecedented in the Soviet arms supply record for a single country.

Economic assistance is viewed by Moscow as a low-cost expedient for forging links with the developing world. On few occasions has this aid—or the trade which has emanated from it—been cut off as a result of political changes in LDCs, strained relations between LDCs and the USSR, or changes in Soviet military supply policy toward a particular LDC. In Egypt, for example, Moscow's aid and trade programs continue in spite of Cairo's abrogation of major military and friendship treaties in 1976. While economic aid provides the materials, personnel, and ideas to encourage the growth of socialist institutions in aid-receiving countries, it also has established relationships which sometimes help assure the USSR certain strategic raw materials and goods and services from the LDC.

Operations of the program

Moscow's first important use of aid was in Egypt. Using Czechoslovakia as a front, the Soviets answered Nasser's call in 1955 for arms with a $250 million military aid package. The accord opened the door for a large Soviet military and economic presence in the Middle East. Egypt's acceptance of Soviet arms was followed by Western refusal to construct the Aswan Dam and a Soviet economic aid commitment to Egypt that reached nearly $1.5 billion. The $4 billion arms supply relationship that evolved required some 17,000 Soviet military personnel (including troops) in 1971 to maintain it and created a relationship that crippled Egyptian military readiness after the cutoff of Soviet supplies.

Economic and military assistance programs usually have worked in tandem. Generally, major military aid recipients accepted arms aid first, often during periods of perceived threats. These have frequently come with liberal terms, such as: (a) discounts from list prices, which averaged 40% but were as high as 75%; (b) repayments stretched over 8 to 10 years at 2% interest; and (c) payments in LDC commodities rather than hard currency. Terms are no longer as concessional, and most sales, even to long-established recipients, are at higher prices than in the past and often for hard currency or oil. Discounts are no longer typical, and in some cases prices may even be above those charged other customers.

Moscow's economic and military aid has been limited by historic ties and political affinities of LDCs. Thus, despite apparent Soviet willingness to sell to almost any less developed country, arms sales have been heavily concentrated in the same areas where Soviet economic aid has been extended. The largest share of the military and economic assistance has gone to nations on the Soviet borders, as well as to radical North African-Middle Eastern states. Together these countries have received more than 55% of Soviet economic aid commitments and nearly 50% of the military.

Military

By 1974–78 Soviet military sales accounted for about 20% of the nearly $125 billion world sales to LDCs, while deliveries represented more than 25%.[2] Through these sales less developed countries were able to obtain a wide array of modern military equipment, including their first jet fighters, supersonic jets, guided missile systems, and missile attack boats. Soviet sales in 1974–78 averaged $3.3 billion annually (in actual prices charged; $4 billion in U.S. production costs) and accounted for 55% of the nearly $30 billion of LDC arms orders placed with the Soviet Union in 1955–78.

The Soviet $17 billion economic aid program has had a very different history. Deliveries have been slow, LDCs could get the aid elsewhere, and they could often obtain newer technology from noncommunist sources. Project aid, the backbone of the program and always difficult to administer, has sometimes brought more grief than blessings. The program, initiated in 1954 by the flamboyant Khrushchev, pledged large amounts of development assistance which Moscow later found it could not always deliver as rapidly as expected by LDCs. After the first decade of aid, when only 40% of the $3 billion commitment was delivered, commitments were made after more careful studies to assure project viability. Gradually fewer open lines of credit for development were offered. These were first replaced by commitments to specific projects and more recently by more general framework agreements. These newer agreements in principle, which specify broad outlines for cooperation, are intended to allow flexibility in project negotiations and implementation.

The basic operation of the economic aid program has not changed much over the more than two decades of its history:

a) Economic aid is still targeted at a few recipients that receive large credits often for highly visible, heavy industrial projects in the public sector.

b) Almost all Soviet aid is tied to equipment purchases in the USSR. Rarely are commodities or hard currency extended.

c) Moscow provides extensive technical assistance to help overcome the lack of local skills in implementing and operating aid projects. The USSR dispatched nearly 28,000 Soviet technicians to LDCs in 1977 and 1978, of which 65% acted as advisers and training officers on Soviet aid-assisted projects. These technicians have conducted geological surveys, drawn up plant designs, and supervised and performed technical tasks in the construction and operation of some 1,100 projects which the USSR has built or is building in LDCs. Large numbers of Third World personnel are still going to the USSR for training in addition to some 550,000 that have been trained locally.

d) At least 95% of Soviet economic aid must be repaid—traditionally over 12 years at 2.5 to 3% interest. Occasionally the terms are more lenient, such as those usually given Afghanistan (which allow up to 50 years for repayment) and recent credits to India (20 years plus a three-year grace). Especially since the mid-1960s, however, credits have sometimes carried commercial-like terms that include down payments, allow only 5 to 10 years for amortization, and carry high rates of interest. Most Soviet credits are repaid in commodities, often in the output of plants built with Russian aid. Soviet terms compare with average U.S. terms for official development assistance of more than 35 years and less than 3% interest; also, grant aid has comprised more than half of U.S. aid in recent years.

e) Increasingly the USSR has extended economic assistance that will yield mutual benefits, such as border dams in Iran, pipelines to carry natural gas from Iran and Afghanistan to the USSR, oil exploration in Iraq in return for oil, and geological surveys and exploration for minerals which the USSR has conducted in at least 30 countries of the developing world. The most recent example is the 1978 accord with Morocco to exploit phosphates with which Morocco will repay its debt to the USSR.

The shifting aid picture

Military

Soviet arms sales more than doubled in 1974–78, compared to 1969–73 (in a world market that had quadrupled), based largely on the massive resupply and buildup in the Middle East since the October 1973 war and huge amounts of aid to Ethiopia in the past two years. In addition, the Russians moved more heavily into commercial sales, as opposed to concessional aid, because of the availability of large OPEC funding for arms.

Before 1974 Moscow's military customers had included: Egypt, its only $4 billion customer; Syria, a $2.3 billion client; India and Iraq, each in the $1.5 to $2 billion class; Indonesia, an $875 million client before 1965; Iran, Afghanistan, and Algeria, whose orders ranged from $350 to $600 million; and some two dozen LDCs that received small, often negligible amounts of arms.

The larger sales following the 1973 war were accompanied by both accelerated training programs for LDC personnel in the Soviet Union and additional Soviet and Cuban support cadre in less developed countries that had purchased new modern equipment. The numbers of Soviet advisers and maintenance personnel in the LDCs rose to some 6,700 in 1974 and to 11,000 in 1978, with the largest numbers stationed in the Arab radical states and in Ethiopia (1978).

Kuwait and Iran bought military equipment in the USSR (a $50 million Kuwaiti order for missiles in 1977 and Iran's $800 million worth of ground equipment after 1973). Other oil producers (Algeria, Iraq, and Libya) placed over $7 billion of orders for Soviet equipment after 1973, which accounted for more than 40% of Moscow's $6.5 billion of arms sales in 1974–78. At least another 15% of Soviet sales were placed by LDC customers whose purchases were financed by rich Arab states.

The loss of Moscow's most important customer, Egypt, was the most notable change in Soviet arms client patterns after 1973. The loss was accompanied by: (a) the emergence of Libya as Moscow's largest arms buyer (after 1973); (b) the marked expansion of Soviet sales to Iraq, Syria, Algeria, and India; and (c) the dramatic $2 billion supply relationship established with Ethiopia in 1977–78—unprecedented in sub-Saharan arms procurement history. Moscow also added half a billion dollars of orders to its 1973 initial arms sales to Peru—its only Latin American customer (apparently a temporary one).

While these initiatives clearly reflect Soviet geopolitical interests, reemphasizing Moscow's determination to maintain a presence in the Middle East and Indian Ocean areas, the Russians clearly have profited from these sales, which now cover a large deficit in Soviet trade with LDCs and supplement Soviet hard currency earnings.

Economic

Fewer changes have occurred in Soviet economic assistance. The most notable has been a shift to the use of broad "framework" agreements and an increase in the number of large commercial accords. The framework accords are agreements in principle which usually agree to explore possibilities for cooperation in designated areas, without allocating definite amounts of aid until project-by-project studies are completed. Accords are then drawn for each project, either with supplier-type credits, commercial arrangements, concessionary aid terms, or a combination of these arrangements for different parts of the package. At the same time that Moscow introduced framework agreements, it tried to synchronize its own requirements and production plans with those of LDCs through joint Soviet-LDC committees. Moscow also has tried to expand its economic relationships through joint ventures (still limited to shipping and fishing), which Moscow is using in the case of fisheries to circumvent some of the limitations imposed on its own fishing fleet by the 200-mile territorial waters limits.

Despite possibly harder terms in the overall, Moscow has continued to extend its largest credits to a selective few. In general, the size of credits has increased. Partly because of higher project costs and also because of the kinds of project support provided, commitments in the past five years rose 1.5 times over those in the previous five years. Extensions in 1974–78 thus have accounted for almost half of the total amount of aid provided over the entire program period. Deliveries went up 25% in 1974–78 but without marked improvement in the rate of drawdown.

The program 1977–78

Despite a definite upward annual bias in Soviet military and economic commitments to LDCs in the latter part of the 1970s, annual pledges have fluctuated widely because of: (a) changing political exigencies and, for the military, emergency and resupply operations; (b) long periods required for implementing economic aid and for absorbing military receipts into LDC inventories; (c) prolonged negotiations required for finalizing economic and military agreements and the lack of an annual rhythm in signing accords; (d) economic or political constraints within the USSR, which affect aid determinations; and (e) the apparent lack of LDC interest, in some cases, in accepting Soviet offers or initiating requests.

The most dramatic swings in Soviet aid history occurred for both the economic and military programs in 1977–78. Military pledges jumped to an all-time record ($5.2 billion) in 1977 and then plummeted in 1978 to their lowest level since 1973 ($1.8 billion). On the other hand, more than $3.7 billion of new economic assistance in 1978 followed the 1977 seven-year program low and broke all former Soviet economic aid extension records. These transactions demonstrated Moscow's continuing interest in expanding and reinforcing its Third World connections. On the other hand, the kinds of agreements signed in 1977–78 made it apparent again that Russian aid had become as pragmatic as it is political. Moscow's military support to Ethiopia had a strong geopolitical basis; the assistance for mining phosphates in Morocco was motivated by economic factors.

The increasingly commercial cast of Soviet assistance has been noted in: (a) the harder repayment terms and higher prices for most military sales; and (b) the $1.5 billion of hard currency earnings Moscow has gleaned annually over the past several years from military sales (possibly as much as $2 billion in 1978). It also is reflected in an interest in exploiting aid possibilities which eventually will provide goods to help support Soviet domestic industrial operations. The most noteworthy recent example of Soviet interest in LDCs' material supply potential is the widely publicized $2 billion Moroccan phosphate deal, signed in 1978. In this latest Soviet initiative to cultivate external long-term supply sources for raw materials, the USSR is hedging against possible domestic shortages, either as a result of resource depletion or prohibitive extraction or processing costs. Under the Soviet-Moroccan accord the Russians have contracted for their first phosphate imports, with a 30-year supply line of 10 million tons a year.

Military

Moscow has been pushing its more lucrative, more easily effected military sales program. Sales for the two-year period (1977–78) were high despite the 1978 decline and despite Indian, Iraqi, and Syrian purchases of large amounts of Western equipment in their first important moves to diversify arms supply sources. India broke a 17-year tradition by placing a $2 billion order for Anglo-French Jaguars, which it selected in preference to the MIG-23 and SU-20 aircraft offered by the Russians. Iraq also bought $2 billion of arms (largely Mirage aircraft) from the West in the past two years, more than double its total previous purchases. The $240 million Syrian purchase of the Franco-German Hot and Milan antitank missile systems was Damascus's largest order ever placed in the West.

In addition to continuing a heavy supply program to its already important arms customers, Moscow's most decisive supply action was in the Horn of Africa. Following political decisions made late in 1976, the USSR shifted its alliance from Somalia to Ethiopia in an arms buildup unprecedented in size or character in the sub-Sahara.

The $2 billion of modern weaponry to Ethiopia provided a class of sophistication new to the region and far beyond the capabilities of the Ethiopian military establishment to operate or maintain. Thus in 1977 Addis Ababa sent a contingent of about 300 military trainees to the USSR, following this in 1978 with almost a thousand. At the same time, about 1,300 to 1,500 Russian technicians in Ethiopia (in 1978) performed training and maintenance functions.

Arms for Ethiopia accounted for about 30% of total Soviet arms sales in 1977–78. Four of Moscow's traditionally large arms customers—Libya, Algeria, Syria, and India—accounted for another 55% of total Soviet sales with their nearly $4 billion of orders for a wide range of weapons. Among the remaining 22 less developed countries that purchased arms from the USSR in 1977–78, countries with Soviet supplied arsenals such as Afghanistan, South Yemen, and Iraq bought more than $600 million of weaponry; Tanzania bought air and ground equipment, and Peru contracted for aircraft.

Deliveries under these accords scored new records in 1977 and 1978, rising to almost $4 billion in the latter year. These deliveries enabled military hardware to maintain its top rank as Moscow's most important export to the Third World. By the end of 1978 the Soviets had delivered about 85% of their total arms commitment to Third World clients. The 1977–78 deliveries included an impressive array of first-time Soviet exports of advanced weaponry to the Third World, such as:

MIG-25 jet fighters to Algeria and Libya;
IL–76 transports to Iraq; and
SU-22 jet fighter-bombers to Peru.

Among other important deliveries were: the first MIG-23 jet fighters to sub-Sahara (Ethiopia) and the late model MIG-21 bis to Syria and Ethiopia. Syria also received continuing supplies of surface-to-air missiles, OSA-II guided missile patrol boats, T-62 tanks, and a wide assortment of ground armaments.

The heavy flow of advanced weaponry which the USSR is pouring into LDC inventories has created an added burden on Soviet services for training local personnel in maintenance and use of the equipment. About 1,900 LDC nationals were in the Soviet Union at the end of 1978 for training. At the same time, almost 11,000

Soviets (double the number in 1973) were in less developed countries in advisory-training roles to assemble and maintain equipment and instruct local units in combat techniques and the use and maintenance of new weapons.

Syria, which claimed the largest number of Russian technical personnel in 1973, continued as the top claimant in 1978, by which time it had received $2 billion of additional Soviet weapons. The next largest Soviet technical contingents were in Ethiopia, Libya, and Angola; each of these countries had received large arms shipments after 1973. At the same time, the 1,500 Soviets stationed in Somalia early in 1977 all had departed by year-end.

Economic

Soviet economic aid, still a program of opportunity, depends not only on Moscow's assessment of cost-benefits but also on LDC response to aid overtures and the kind of assistance offered. Soviet commitments rebounded to an all-time high in 1978 from their eight-year 1977 low. The $3.7 billion of credits extended in 1978 was more than double the previous record year, 1975, and represents more than a fifth of all Soviet economic assistance committed to the Third World over the 24 years of the Soviet aid program. The 1978 peak followed $400 million of extensions in 1977.

Even the 1978 data tend to understate the full extent of Russian economic aid initiative because many new accords carry no price tag. These general "framework" agreements depend on project consideration, which draw actual allocations out over long periods. In 1977–78 framework agreements were signed with Afghanistan, Costa Rica, Guyana, Morocco, Mozambique, Syria, and Ethiopia. Only in the case of Morocco and Syria have definite commitments already been made for specific projects. These amount to $2.3 billion.

Eighty-five percent of the aid extended in 1977 went to India—Moscow's first new aid to that country in more than a decade. Because a large part of the credit will be for an alumina plant in which the Russians have a special interest, and because of Soviet eagerness to cement ties with this important Chinese neighbor, the terms of the credit were more concessionary than in earlier aid to India. The only other important agreement in 1977 was a $30 million credit to Jamaica—Moscow's first to that country—for geological prospecting, a cement plant, and training schools. During 1977 the Soviets also entered into large contracts, probably mostly on commercial terms, for: (a) a second gas pipeline from Iran to the Soviet border; (b) a dam in Iraq to irrigate 1.6 million hectares of land and to provide 500 MW of power; and (c) a 240 MW powerplant in Iraq.

The large pledges in 1978 stemmed almost entirely from the $2 billion Soviet-Moroccan accord—the USSR's largest commitment to a single project in the Third World—and $1.2 billion of industrial development credits to Turkey. The aid to Turkey increases the amount of credits made available under a 1975 framework agreement for financing (a) expansion of the Soviet-built steel and aluminum plants, (b) powerplants, and (c) a new oil refinery. Looking to the future, Soviet and Turkish authorities also are viewing other possibilities for cooperation, which could involve billions of dollars of additional Soviet assistance.

Pakistan was the only other important aid recipient in 1978. A $220 million credit for financing increased costs at the Karachi steel mill brings Soviet aid to the project up to $650 million, three-quarters of Moscow's total aid to Pakistan. Smaller amounts of aid also went to South and North Yemen, a token amount was extended to Latin America for power projects, and virtually nothing to sub-Saharan Africa despite big expectations in Angola and Ethiopia.

Soviet nonmilitary technical personnel in the Third World rose on the average by a third between 1975–76 and 1977–78. While large increases in the number present were noted in Africa, the Middle East, and South Asia, the African share of the more than 25,000 technicians present each year (in 1977–78) gained 5 percentage points over 1975–76. A large percentage of the Soviets stationed in Africa continued to work outside the aid program; Soviet aid projects in Africa probably employed only half the Soviet technicians present on the continent. The rest of the Russians worked as administrators, teachers, and doctors on commercial construction jobs (as in Algeria, Libya, and Nigeria). Soviet technical personnel assigned to other areas of the Third World worked more often on aid projects, except in a few countries such as Iraq and Iran, where the Soviets had captured large commercial contracts. Altogether the Soviets earned an estimated $50 to $75 million of hard currency a year from the nonproject, nonaid technical services they provided in 1977–78.

Effectiveness of the program

Reduced Western influence in Third World countries has not necessarily led to a corresponding rise in Soviet influence. New governments often have translated anticolonialist positions into strong nationalist policies jealous of any foreign influence. Despite the commitment of some LDC governments to a "socialist" system, they usually have wanted their own brand of socialism and have not been attracted to Soviet communist ideology, either by economic or military aid. Nonetheless the Russians take a long-term view of the effectiveness of their program. While they continue to forge closer ties with a group of strategically situated LDCs, the Soviets enjoy economic returns from both military and economic aid.

Military assistance has been less problem-ridden than economic aid despite occasional setbacks—notably in Indonesia (in the mid-sixties) and more recently in Egypt and Somalia. For the most part they have had only a temporary effect on Moscow's expanding Third World arms sales. Thus Soviet sales of military hardware more than doubled in the five years after the cutoff of supplies to Egypt, compared with the five years before.

Economic aid is often more able to endure strains created by new political alignments and changes in government. This holds true despite the disenchantment which often sets in during and after the economic aid implementation period. Time-consuming surveys and feasibility studies required before construction work, as well as institutional, human, and economic obstacles in many LDCs have hampered Soviet (as well as other) programs. The USSR has compounded the difficulties of administering its aid program by furnishing only materials, equipment, and technical guidance for projects.

Advantages to both donor and recipient have gone beyond the mere size of the exchanges as each party gains from the relationship. Many of Moscow's arms clients have had their aspirations for international power and prestige satisfied, while Moscow has built an LDC presence. In recent years Moscow also has garnered a windfall in hard currency and has kept its trade with LDCs out of the red with arms sales. The ranking position of the USSR as an LDC arms supplier, the sophistication of the weapons it provides, and the dependent relationship it has created, all have contributed to a big power image for Moscow. Soviet military technical assistance also has exposed LDCs to Soviet military institutions and techniques and undoubtedly has established important personal relationships with LDC military leaders. Through its aid program Moscow has obtained base rights in several countries, including the use of port facilities in Iraq and Syria (and previously in Egypt); during its venture into Angola, Mali and Guinea made their airports available; Moscow has used facilities in India (and previously in Somalia) for naval and air intelligence operations.

The Soviets also must view economic assistance as productive and inexpensive. Foreign aid has imposed a negligible drain on Soviet domestic resources, despite burdens sometimes created by aid requirements levied against an already taut planning cycle. In return for aid the USSR has received bauxite from Guinea, oil from Iraq, natural gas from Iran and Afghanistan, and alumina from Turkey and India. The closer economic relations expanded Soviet-LDC trade to $12 billion in 1977 (20 times above the 1955 level), representing 17% of total Soviet trade. Moscow's largest aid clients have become its major LDC trading partners. Egypt, India, Iran, and Iraq together accounted for nearly half of Soviet 1974–77 nonmilitary trade with the Third World. Countries in the Middle East and South Asia were largely responsible for the almost 100% increase in Soviet-LDC trade between 1973 and 1977.

The USSR also must consider its recent Moroccan deal a coup. This latest effort to expand long-term procurement possibilities for strategic materials is part of Moscow's continuing effort to supplement its own supplies. Since the early 1960s Russian geologists have inventoried the metals and minerals reserves of at least 12 countries in Africa, five in the Middle East, two in South Asia, and one in Latin America. Gas and petroleum exploration and exploitation assistance was provided 14 less developed countries. Until now the return flow has been limited to gas and oil, bauxite, and iron ore. By

1978 the USSR was receiving: (a) 13 billion cubic meters of natural gas a year from Iran and Afghanistan through Soviet-built pipelines, as repayment for economic and military aid; (b) 6 to 7 million tons of crude oil annually from Iraq and Syria from fields the Russians had helped to develop; and (c) 2.5 million tons of bauxite from Soviet developed mines in Guinea.

Economic aid also made positive contributions to the development of some LDCs. For example, Soviet plants in India account for: 80% of India's output of metallurgical equipment; 60% of heavy electrical equipment; more than half of India's oil production; and a third of its steel output and a fifth of the electric energy generated.

In several instances when the USSR jumped in with aid offers for major installations turned down by other donors, Moscow gained extra prestige. The Bokaro steel mill in India and the Isfahan mill in Iran are classic examples. Moscow scored in some countries by its help for developing public sector industrial complexes, though in some cases the administrative woes and underutilized capacity have dampened the recipients' original fervor. In Egypt Soviet aid provided: 70% of Egypt's power equipment; all of Egypt's aluminum production; three-fourths of the capacity at Egypt's only steel mill at Helwan; and refineries that fill half of Egypt's domestic needs.

Prospects in the early 1980s

While Moscow shifts its program tactics from time to time to accommodate to new political or economic currents, no reduction in the scale or content of the aid program nor in Moscow's strategy for leadership in the Third World has become apparent. Instead of backing off in the face of new massive OPEC funding for Moscow's most important aid clients, the USSR continued its small economic program even in oil-rich states, profiting from their wealth through larger arms sales and big commercial deals.

Military

On the military front there are no signs of a letup in the Soviet sales effort. A slowdown might come from a market that is saturated momentarily and is winding down its orders. The heavy sales of the past few years will in themselves dampen chances for large new orders because of the time it takes for LDCs to absorb the large stocks of modern weaponry pouring into their inventories. The recent quest for alternative arms sources by some of Russia's largest customers (that is, Iraq and India) could also lead to a gradual reduction in the scale of orders by some major Soviet buyers.

If the world arms market settles into a more even annual procurement pattern, Soviet sales probably also will follow suit, with annual sales falling into the $2 to $3 billion range. At a minimum the USSR will supply complementary equipment and large quantities of spare parts and technical support to countries that have been large Soviet arms buyers in the past. With the possibilities for increasing levels of instability in the Middle East, South Asia, and southern Africa, the USSR stands ready to offer rapid delivery of large quantities of equipment and services which would push Soviet sales even higher than before.

Economic

Economic assistance, while not expected to equal the 1978 record again in the next several years, should follow a more even pattern as definite commitments are negotiated under existing and new general framework agreements. Moscow is expected to maintain its aid tempo in traditional client areas—more often under framework agreements; at other times through specific accords for project assistance, as provided India in 1977. The Soviets also are expected to expand patterns of joint participation (in planning as well as in certain enterprises). They will continue to try to expand the commercial aspects of their program. Commercially oriented aid overtures to Latin America especially should gain momentum, as Moscow exerts pressures on Mexico for sales of all types of machinery and equipment. Moscow will undoubtedly pursue negotiations with Jamaica and Guyana to exploit their bauxite deposits as part of its search for additional supplies to satisfy the USSR's own needs.

Note on sources

The detailed information on Soviet foreign aid contained in this study is drawn from numerous official and nonofficial publications available to the public. A primary source for data concerning the Soviet program in the LDCs—aid extensions, drawings on credits, and technical assistance—is the annual reviews of the communist aid programs published by the Central Intelligence Agency. The most recent of the series, *Communist Aid to Less Developed Countries of the Free World, 1977*, was published in November 1978.

Official publications, journals, and newspapers from LDCs and the USSR also have been invaluable sources, particularly the USSR Ministry of Foreign Trade's foreign trade yearbook series and monthly foreign trade magazines. Other useful sources include publications of the United Nations and the Organization for Economic Cooperation and Development.

Appendix

Table 1

Soviet Economic Assistance to LDCs (in millions of U.S. $)

	1956–78	1956–73	1974	1975	1976	1977	1978
Agreements[1]	17,090	9,255	815	1,935	980	400	3,705
Africa	3,990	1,360	55	100	435	30	2,010
East Asia	260	160	100				
Latin America	965	410	215	255	40	30	15
Middle East	6,920	3,770	200	1,050	500		1,400
South Asia	4,955	3,555	245	530	5	340	280
Deliveries[1]	7,595	4,965	705	500	460	540	430
Africa	1,025	675	85	70	65	70	60
East Asia	145	[2]	[2]				
Latin America	195	85	15	15	35	25	20
Middle East	3,340	2,105	245	320	225	280	165
South Asia	2,890	1,955	355	95	135	165	185

[1]Components may not add to totals shown because of rounding.
[2]Negligible.

Table 2

Soviet Economic Credits and Grants to Selected LDCs (in millions of U.S. $)

	Total 1954–78	1977	1978
Total	17,090	400	3,705
Africa	3,990	30	2,010
North Africa	2,920		2,000
Algeria	715		
Morocco	2,100		2,000
Other	105		
Sub-Saharan Africa	1,070	30	10
Angola	15	5	10
Ethiopia	105		Negligible
Ghana	95		
Guinea	210		
Somalia	165		
Sudan	65		
Tanzania	40	18	
Other	375	7	9
East Asia	260		
Indonesia	215		
Other	45		
Latin America	965	30	15
Argentina	225		
Brazil	90		
Chile	240		
Colombia	210		
Jamaica	30	30	
Other	170		15
Middle East	6,920		1,400
Egypt	1,440		
Iran	1,165		
Iraq	705		
North Yemen	145		40
South Yemen	200		90
Syria	765		
Turkey	2,380		1,200
Other	120		70
South Asia	4,955	340	280
Afghanistan	1,265		
India	2,280	340	
Pakistan	920		220
Other	490		60

Table 3

Soviet Economic Technicians in LDCs[1]
(number of persons)

	1977	1978
Total	22,390	27,620
Africa	7,520	11,575
North Africa	3,120	6,680
Algeria	2,650	6,000
Libya	100	200
Morocco	150	250
Other	220	230
Sub-Saharan Africa	4,400	4,895
Angola	200	400
Ethiopia	150	600
Guinea	500	450
Mali	350	450
Other	3,200	2,995
East Asia	65	35
Latin America	490	350
Argentina	5	35
Bolivia	150	100
Brazil	25	25
Other	310	190
Middle East	11,195	11,885
Egypt	1,000	750
Iran	3,400	4,000
Iraq	3,800	3,950
Syria	1,200	1,100
Turkey	1,000	1,250
Other	795	835
South Asia	3,120	3,775
Afghanistan	1,300	2,000
India	1,100	1,000
Pakistan	500	575
Other	220	200

[1]Minimum estimates of number present for a period of a month or more. Numbers are rounded to the nearest 5.

Table 4

Soviet Military Relations with LDCs (in millions of U.S. $)

	Total 1956–78	1956–73	1974	1975	1976	1977	1978
Agreements[1]	29,655	13,035	4,225	2,035	3,375	5,215	1,765
North Africa	4,965	485	1,825	535		1,800	315
Middle East	14,960	8,860	2,025	640	2,100	1,235	100
Other	9,730	3,690	375	860	1,275	2,180	1,350
Deliveries[1]	25,310	11,240	2,310	1,845	2,575	3,515	3,825
North Africa[1]	3,875	435	150	380	810	925	1,175
Middle East	13,800	7,755	1,780	975	1,065	1,125	1,095
Other	7,635	3,050	380	490	700	1,465	1,555

[1]Components may not add to totals shown because of rounding.

Table 5

Soviet Military Technicians in LDCs (number of persons)

	1977	1978
Total	10,200	10,800
Algeria	600	1,000
Egypt		
Ethiopia	1,000	1,300
India	145	150
Iraq	1,050	1,100
Libya	990	1,300
Syria	2,170	2,400
Other	4,245	3,550

[1]Minimum estimates of number present for a period of a month or more. Numbers are rounded to the nearest 5.

Developments in Soviet Arms Exports and Imports, 1980–83

The recent release of the official *1983 Soviet Foreign Trade Yearbook* has made it possible for Western researchers to obtain an insight into the most recent developments in the commodity composition of Soviet trade in general and exports in particular. As has been true for a number of years now, the most important group of commodities in exports were fuels. In 1983 fuels accounted for 53.7% of total exports, 50.1% of exports to socialist countries, and 59.2% of exports to nonsocialist countries. Naturally, exports of crude oil and refined oil products were dominant exports in the fuel category, accounting for 41.6% of total exports, 35.6% of exports to socialist countries, and 49.0% of exports to nonsocialist countries. The second most important export item in 1983 was arms, which represented a 13.4% share in total exports to all countries, 8.4% of exports to socialist countries, and 19.6% of exports to nonsocialist countries. (Actually, at least in the case of socialist countries, the share of gas exports in total exports amounted to 10.3%, a somewhat higher figure than the share of arms exports.)

Although the Soviet Union does not publish any data on its arms trade, it is relatively easy to estimate its arms exports and imports, at least in comparison to other East European countries. Information on overall exports of arms and exports of arms to socialist and nonsocialist countries as well as data on imports of arms from socialist countries (five East European countries) can be readily extracted from official Soviet statistics using the so-called "residual analysis" described below. In addition, Western understanding of Soviet arms trade benefited from occasional access by Western analysts to internal *CMEA Foreign Trade Yearbooks* (published by the CMEA Secretariat for official use only), statistics excerpted from these yearbooks and published in other sources, and occasional

Centrally Planned Economies Current Analysis, Wharton Econometric Forecasting Associates, vol. 4, no. 62 (August 15, 1984), Jan Vaňous, ed.

Ranking of Soviet Commodity Exports According to their Value in 1983

	World		Socialist countries		Nonsocialist countries	
	In mil. rubles	In percent	In mil. rubles	In percent	In mil. dollars	In percent
Total	67,891	100.0	37,714	100.0	40,657	100.0
1 Oil and oil products	28,216	41.6	13,438	35.6	19,910	49.0
2 Arms	9,080	13.4	3,150	8.4	7,990	19.6
3 Natural gas	6,303	9.3	3,865	10.3	3,285	9.1
4 Rolled ferrous metal products	1,672	2.5	1,593	4.2	106	0.3
5 Coal and coke	1,301	1.9	1,053	2.8	334	0.8
6 Power-generating equipment	1,118	1.6	836	2.2	380	0.9
7 Trucks and garage equipment	891	1.3	541	1.4	472	1.2
8 Cotton	885	1.3	672	1.8	287	0.7
9 Passenger cars and motorcycles	715	1.1	466	1.2	335	0.8
10 Board lumber	694	1.0	333	0.9	486	1.2
11 Airplanes (civilian)	678	1.0	225	0.6	610	1.5
12 Fertilizers	670	1.0	433	1.1	319	0.8
13 Metallurgical equipment	668	1.0	189	0.5	645	1.6
14 Electric energy	619	0.9	516	1.4	139	0.3
All other items	14,381	21.1	10,404	27.6	5,359	13.2

Source: Arms—Wharton CPE Service estimate based on analysis of unspecified residual commodity exports to socialist countries and unspecified residual regional exports to developing countries in official *1983 Soviet Foreign Trade Yearbook* [Vneshniaia torgovlia SSSR v 1983 godu]; Other commodities—Wharton calculation based on data published in *1983 Soviet Foreign Trade Yearbook*.

slips by Soviet/CMEA statistical authorities. For example, the Soviets delete all arms transactions from trade statistics supplied to the CMEA Secretariat. Therefore a comparison of official statistics published in *Soviet Foreign Trade Yearbooks* with data on Soviet trade published in internal *CMEA Foreign Trade Yearbooks* reveals exactly the value of arms exports and imports. Another case in which the Soviets revealed their arms trade occurred in 1981 when two versions of the *CMEA Statistical Yearbook* (recently accessible to anybody) were published. In the earlier "anniversary version," the honestly reporting individual forgot to include arms in 1980 data in the broad CTN category V—chemicals, fertilizers, rubber, construction materials, and *other* goods. (CTN stands for CMEA Trade Nomenclature.) In the regular version of the yearbook, arms were dutifully lumped with unrelated commodities. The discrepancy in export and import data in the two versions of the *CMEA Statistical Yearbooks* exactly revealed the size of arms trade flows.

In analyzing the developments in Soviet arms trade with socialist countries, the task of the Western analyst is made easier by the fact that the Soviets include all arms trade in bilateral statistics and allocate it to the so-called "unspecified commodity residual," i.e., trade flows specified by country but not by commodity. In addition, the fact that the methodology of recording arms transactions is not uniform within CMEA—East European countries lump arms with machinery trade—makes it easier to calculate Soviet arms trade with Eastern Europe by comparing Soviet machinery trade statistics (which exclude arms) with mirror East European statistics (which include arms). The results of this comparison are presented in the table below.

According to our estimates, between 1980 and 1983, nominal ruble value of Soviet arms exports to six East European countries increased 39%, from 1,866 million rubles in 1980 to 2,600 million in 1983. In quantity terms Soviet arms shipments to Eastern Europe increased between 10 and 18%. Soviet arms imports from Eastern Europe grew considerably more rapidly during the above period—between 1980 and 1983 they increased 82% in current ruble terms, from 1,119 million rubles to 2,041 million rubles. The growth in these imports in real terms amounted to 44–55%. The faster growth in Soviet imports of arms than exports during 1981–83 probably reflects two developments. First, the Soviet Union was willing to accept more East European arms to offset the rapidly growing East European energy import bill from the Soviet Union. It may well be that the Soviets find East European arms and military components more attractive than imports of civilian (investment) machinery from Eastern Europe. Second, it is quite likely that the Soviets reexported at least some of the arms imported from Eastern Europe to the Third World, notably to Iraq, Syria, and possibly to Iran.

During 1980–83 the largest portion of Soviet arms delivered to Eastern Europe was sold to East Germany (23%), followed by Czechoslovakia (22%), Bulgaria (19%), Poland (18%), Romania (10%), and Hungary (8%). Soviet purchases of arms were concentrated in Czechoslovakia and Poland (27% each), Bulgaria (24%), East Germany (17%), and Hungary (5%). The Soviets appear to have purchased no arms from Romania during the above period.

With the exception of small sales of arms to Finland and even smaller sales to Austria, Soviet arms sales to nonsocialist countries are destined for the Third World. In recent years the largest Soviet buyers of Soviet arms (in order of their relative importance, based on our guess) were Iraq and Syria, Libya, India, Iran, Angola, Ethiopia, Algeria, etc. (Unfortunately, the bulk of Soviet arms exports to the Third World is included in the so-called "unspecified LDC export residual," i.e., trade identified by the Soviets as exports to developing countries in general, but not identified by country of destination. Therefore the country distribution of Soviet arms exports to this region can only be reconstructed on the basis of intelligence reports from the country of origin, i.e., the Soviet Union, or countries of destination, i.e., individual Third World countries.) We estimate that these exports increased from $5,570 million in 1980 to $6,440 million in 1981, $8,100 million in 1982, before declining slightly to $7,890 million in 1983. (It should be noted that these are arms *sales*, not arms deliveries, which would include gifts of arms and other types of arms aid.) According to our estimates, in recent years the share of arms sold for hard currency was somewhere between 70 and 80%. However, a large portion of these arms—probably around three-fifths—was sold on credit (for more detail, see *Current Analysis*, nos. 18 of March 19, 1984, and 22–23 of April 9, 1984).

Growth of Soviet Arms Exports and Imports during 1980–83

	1980	1981	1982	1983
	Exports to socialist countries (in million rubles)			
Socialist countries	2,202	2,558	2,747	3,150
CMEA Six	1,866	2,212	2,216	2,600
Bulgaria	231	385	439	660
Czechoslovakia	447	476	448	570
East Germany	459	496	598	528
Hungary	170	183	155	203
Poland	362	485	364	402
Romania	197	187	212	237
Other socialist countries*	336	346	531	550
	Exports to nonsocialist countries (in million dollars)			
Nonsocialist countries	5,670	6,540	8,200	7,990
Developing countries	5,570	6,440	8,100	7,890
Developed West	(100)	(100)	(100)	(100)
	Imports from socialist countries (in million rubles)			
CMEA Six	1,119	1,319	1,640	2,041
Bulgaria	252	312	413	479
Czechoslovakia	317	389	403	525
East Germany	170	220	284	350
Hungary	30	76	791	131
Poland	350	322	461	556
Romania	—	—	—	—
	Percent share of arms in total exports or imports			
Arms exports to the CMEA Six	8.9	9.1	8.4	8.9
Arms exports to other socialist countries	5.6	5.0	6.8	6.5
Arms exports to developing countries	52.7	54.2	57.8	55.6
Arms imports from the CMEA Six	5.9	6.2	6.7	7.4

*Cuba, North Korea, Mongolia, Vietnam, and Yugoslavia. During this period no arms were exported to China or Albania.

Source: Arms trade with socialist and nonsocialist countries—calculated as residual trade flows by subtracting the following items from total exports or imports: (i) all commodities identified in broad commodity breakdowns published in annual *Soviet Foreign Trade Yearbooks* (machinery; fuels and electric energy; ores, concentrates, and metals; chemicals, fertilizers, and rubber; wood and paper products; textile raw materials and semifabricates; food and food raw materials; industrial consumer goods); (ii) nonmetallic minerals (CTN 25);

Source (continued)

(iii) building materials (CTN 4); (iv) nonfood raw materials of agricultural origin (CTN 52 through 59); (v) live animals (CTN 6); (vi) aircraft repair (estimated, CTN 05193); and (vii) ship repair, printing services, other services (estimated, CTN 0 excluding CTN 05193).

Arms trade flows with individual East European countries—calculated on the basis of an analysis of unspecified commodity residuals in trade with individual countries (trade flows identified by country but not by commodity) and by comparing Soviet machinery export and import flows, which exclude arms, with mirror East European import and export flows, which include arms. (Note that the Soviet Union and Eastern Europe use quite different methodology to hide arms trade—whereas the Soviets hide arms in unspecified commodity residuals, which makes them easily identifiable, East European countries hide arms trade in overall machinery trade, making it much more difficult to separate military items from civilian/investment machinery. However, precisely because of the differences in Soviet and East European methodology with respect to recording arms trade, it is possible to calculate the size of arms trade between the Soviet Union and individual East European countries with comparative ease.)

Developments in Bulgarian Arms Exports, 1979–83

East European countries in general and Bulgaria in particular are extremely sensitive about releasing any information regarding certain types of foreign trade transactions. In the case of Bulgaria the areas most shrouded in secrecy are arms exports and exports and imports of crude oil and refined oil products. (Bulgaria also publishes no data on its arms imports, but it is not difficult to obtain a fairly reliable estimate of Bulgarian arms imports from the Soviet Union from mirror Soviet export statistics using the well-known "residual analysis." Since the Soviet Union supplies the dominant portion of total Bulgarian arms imports, the level of total Bulgarian arms imports can be reasonably estimated.) Fortunately, detailed unpublished information on Bulgarian exports in 1982 reveals interesting information about the level of both exports of arms and exports of crude oil and refined oil products, which represent reexports of Soviet, Libyan, Iranian, and a small amount of Iraqi oil in crude or refined form.

In particular, as is shown in the table below, in 1982 exports of arms represented the leading source of export earnings. They amounted to 990 million devisa leva and accounted for 9.1% of total Bulgarian export earnings in all countries. (It is difficult to state their level in dollar terms since arms were sold to the CMEA countries for inconvertible rubles as well to developing countries for hard currency, and we cannot obtain any meaningful dollar/ruble conversion rate for arms exports without having detailed information about unit ruble and unit dollar values for basic types of military hardware.) The second most important source of export revenue, accounting for 7.86% of total export earnings, was exports of crude oil and refined oil products. Their value amounted to 855 million

Centrally Planned Economies Current Analysis, Wharton Econometric Forecasting Associates, vol. 4, no. 58 (August 2, 1984), Jan Vaňous, ed.

Ranking of Bulgarian Commodity Exports According to Their Value in 1982

Rank	Commodity	Value in million devisa leva	Share in percent
	Total	10,880.0	100.0
1–25	Top 25 export items	5,922.2	54.43
1	Arms*	989.7	9.10
2	Crude oil and refined oil products**	854.7	7.86
3	Cigarettes	587.5	5.40
4	External computer memory equipment	353.5	3.25
5	Electric forklift trucks for moving goods	338.9	3.12
6	Motor forklift trucks for moving goods	279.1	2.56
7	Fresh grape wine	270.7	2.49
8	Oriental tobacco	243.4	2.24
9	Other pharmaceuticals	232.9	2.14
10	Electric conveyor transport equipment	186.0	1.71
11	Equipment for data processing	176.8	1.63
12	Wheat	166.2	1.53
13	Telephone switches/circuits	148.4	1.36
14	Spare parts for electric and motor forklift trucks	122.4	1.13
15	Soda ash	101.4	0.93
16	Heavy iron plate sheets over 3 mm thick	101.2	0.93
17	Electric energy	95.0	0.87
18	Toothpaste	93.7	0.86
19	Land improvement and irrigation equipment	93.0	0.86
20	Perfumes and cosmetics	91.8	0.84
21	Radiotelephones	86.4	0.79
22	Parts for commercial motor vehicles	83.2	0.76
23	Automatic telephone exchanges	79.7	0.73
24	Fruit juices and concentrates	74.0	0.68
25	Peripheral computer equipment	72.0	0.66
21	Radiotelephones	86.4	0.79
	All other items	4,957.8	45.57

*A *very small* portion of this may possibly be accounted for by exports of spare parts for automobiles.

**Resulting from reexports of Soviet, Libyan, Iranian, and Iraqi oil in crude or refined form.

Source: Official unpublished Bulgarian foreign trade statistics.

Developments in Bulgarian Exports of Arms, Road Vehicles, and Other Transport Equipment, 1979–83

	1979	1980	1981	1982	1983*
	To all countries (in million devisa leva)				
All items	601.5	823.6	1,037.3	1,254.1	n.a.
Arms	n.a.	n.a.	n.a.	989.7 **	n.a.
Road vehicles and other transport equipment	n.a.	n.a.	n.a.	264.4	n.a.
	To socialist countries (in million rubles)				
All socialist countries	342.3	396.7	474.5	564.2	n.a.
Soviet Union	234.0	266.9	321.4	373.4	n.a.
(Soviet arms imports)***	(175.4)	(252.0)	(312.0)	(413.0)	(479.0)
CMEA Five	102.9	123.5	134.3	184.5	n.a.
Czechoslovakia	23.1	28.2	34.1	47.7	n.a.
East Germany	32.6	37.5	63.0	76.6	n.a.
Hungary	17.5	26.9	21.0	22.1	n.a.
Poland	11.6	14.6	8.0	24.9	n.a.
Romania	18.0	16.3	8.2	13.2	n.a.
Other CPEs+	5.4	6.4	18.8	6.2	n.a.

To nonsocialist countries
(in million dollars)

All nonsocialist countries	182.0	353.9	490.6	547.5	375-455
Developed West	13.7	45.0	75.6	44.7	60
Developing countries	168.3	308.9	415.0	502.8	315-395
Africa	113.9	174.9	165.3	146.8	135
Algeria	52.6	95.3	94.1	61.1	55
Libya	9.7	77.1	69.1	64.9	60
Other countries	51.6	2.5	2.1	20.8	20.0
Central and South America	6.8	-	-	-	-
Asia	47.6	134.0	249.7	356.0	180-260
Iraq	21.1	54.7	218.6	322.2	150-230
Syria	5.8	5.1	10.1	23.9	15
Other countries	20.7	74.2	21.0	9.9	15

*Wharton CPE Service preliminary estimate.

**A *very small* portion of this may possibly be accounted for by exports of spare parts for automobiles.

***Wharton CPE Service estimate based on mirror Soviet import statistics.

+Albania, China, Cuba, North Korea, Mongolia, Vietnam, and Yugoslavia.

Note: The following dollar/devisa leva exchange rates were applied by the UN to convert data originally reported in devisa leva into dollars: \$1.1628 = 1 devisa leva in 1979, \$1.1494 in 1980, \$1.1669 in 1981, and \$1.0514 in 1982.

Source: The above statistics are official Bulgarian statistics for exports of engineering products in categories SITC 78 and 79 (based on SITC Rev. 2 classification). They are published annually in the *Bulletin of Statistics on World Trade in Engineering Products* by the United Nations.

devisa leva or about $877 million dollars. (We can state the dollar value of these exports since Bulgaria is known to sell virtually all oil and oil products only for hard currency.) The oil export figure of $877 million is very close to an estimate of total Bulgarian fuel exports to nonsocialist countries of $913 million in 1982 published in *Current Analysis*, No. 31 of May 7, 1984; the small discrepancy between the two estimates is explained by exports of electric energy to Turkey and a small amount of exports of other fuels to the West. According to our estimates, about 54% of revenue from oil exports reflected the value of reexports of oil from Libya, Iran, and Iraq, while the remaining 46% was accounted for by reexports of Soviet oil.

Careful inspection of detailed Bulgarian statistics on exports of machinery and transport equipment (SITC 7) supplied to the United Nations reveals that the Bulgarian statistical authorities have decided to allocate exports of arms to the categories SITC 78 and 79—road vehicles and other transport equipment. This is rather obvious given the fact that Bulgaria produces no passenger cars, only a small number of trucks, very few ships, and has no civilian aircraft industry of significance. Yet the official statistics show rather large and rapidly growing exports of "road vehicles and other transport equipment." (The reader who is aware of large Bulgarian production of forklift trucks and other loading and moving equipment is reminded that these products are classified in the category SITC 744—mechanical handling equipment. Therefore their exports cannot explain large exports of products in categories SITC 78 and 79.) Yet additional evidence that exports of arms are included in the category "road vehicles and other transport equipment" is reflected in the fact that the Bulgarian Central Statistical Office has decided to classify these exports in the CTN category 1919800—spare parts for automobiles. (CTN stands for CMEA Trade Nomenclature.) With no domestic automobile industry of significance, it is difficult to see how Bulgaria could be producing huge amounts of spare parts for automobiles.

As is shown in the table below, it appears that at least in 1982, exports of arms accounted for 78.9%, or nearly four-fifths of exports of arms and road vehicles and other transport equipment combined. In other words, actual exports of (civilian) road vehicles and other transport equipment amounted to only slightly more than one-fifth (21.1%) of these exports as claimed in reports to the United Nations and published in the annual *Bulletin of World Trade in Engineering Products*. Most genuine exports of road vehicles and other transport equipment were probably destined for the Soviet Union, the rest of Eastern Europe, and the developed West. The bulk of Bulgarian arms exports was destined for the Soviet Union, three developing countries—Algeria, Libya, and Iraq—and for other East European countries. Although it is not possible to separate exports of arms from exports of civilian road vehicles and other transport equipment in bilateral export transactions, the data on the developments of both exports combined for 1979–83 are revealing enough.

In particular, the data show quite clearly the rapid buildup of Bulgarian arms exports to the Third World—their value tripled between 1979 and 1982 and reached $400–500 million by 1982. Although a sharp drop in arms sales (between 20 and 40%) took place in 1983 because of a fall in sales to Iraq (possibly due to Iraqi payments problems and/or increased "competition" from the Soviets), in the longer run Bulgarian prospects for arms sales may be improving both within the Warsaw Pact and in the Middle East. The rapid buildup of the Bulgarian electronics industry in recent years—also documented by the high share of different types of communications and computing equipment in total Bulgarian exports—should enable Bulgaria to incorporate this technology into its arms production and gain a competitive edge over other East European countries (notably Czechoslovakia and Poland).

JAN VAŇOUS (UNITED STATES)

Soviet and East European Trade and Financial Relations with the Middle East*

I. Introduction

The analysis of Soviet and East European trade and financial relations with the Middle East should focus on the following three issues:

• the volume of oil purchased by the Soviet Union and Eastern Europe and the reasons for these purchases;

• sources of export revenue of the Soviet Union and East European countries in the Middle East and the reasons behind Soviet and East European efforts to increase export sales in this region;

• the role of the Middle East as a source of Soviet and East European hard-currency trade surplus as well as a source of credit to Eastern Europe.

For the purposes of this analysis, Eastern Europe consists of seven small centrally planned economies—Bulgaria, Czechoslovakia, East Germany, Hungary, Poland, Romania, and Yugoslavia. (The term centrally planned economies, or CPEs, will be used loosely in the sense that two of these economies—Hungary and Yugoslavia—are relatively decentralized.) Instead of including in our analysis all Middle East (and North African) countries, we

*This is an expanded version of the presentation at the "Middle East and Centrally Planned Economies Economic Outlook Conference" sponsored jointly by Wharton Econometrics and Standard Oil Company (Indiana) in Washington, D.C., October 10–12, 1983. The analysis was presented on October 11 in the course of a seminar on Soviet Bloc-Middle East Relations. *Centrally Planned Economies Current Analysis*, Wharton Econometric Forecasting Associates, vol. 3, nos. 76–78 (October 11, 1983).

shall concentrate only on six with which the Soviet Union and Eastern Europe maintain active trade and financial relations on a significant scale—Algeria, Egypt, Iran, Iraq, Libya, and Syria. (The term "six Middle East countries" will also be used loosely since Algeria and Libya should more appropriately be labeled North African countries.)

II. Soviet and East European Imports of Crude Oil from the Middle East

The statistics of Soviet and East European imports of crude oil from nonsocialist countries during 1975–83, which are presented in Table 1 in the Appendix, indicate that between 1975 and 1982 the seven CPEs covered in this study imported a total of 218 million metric tons (mmt) of crude oil from the oil-producing developing countries, mostly in the Middle East. Thus, on the average, Soviet and East European imports of Middle Eastern oil amounted to 27.2 mmt (545,000 barrels per day, or tbd), with the peak reached in 1979 at 33.9 mmt (678 tbd) and the lowest level running in 1975 and 1981 at 21.5 mmt (430 tbd). Whereas between 1975 and 1980, 44% of total Soviet and East European crude oil imports from oil-producing developing countries were accounted for by imports from Iraq, these imports collapsed in 1981–82 and are not expected to recover in the foreseeable future in view of the low overall level of Iraqi oil exports. Instead, rapid expansion took place in imports of crude oil from Libya, so that by 1982 these imports accounted for 37% of total CPE imports from oil-producing developing countries. In addition, imports of oil from Iran also registered steady growth since 1979, and in 1982 their share accounted for 29% of total CPE oil imports from oil-producing developing countries.

Contrary to widespread predictions by experts in the oil industry, government institutions, and academia offered in the late 1970s, the bulk of crude oil imported by CPEs from the Middle East since 1980 has not been used for domestic consumption. Over the past three years the relative dependence of Eastern Europe on Middle Eastern oil significantly declined. Not only did total CPE imports of oil from the Middle East decline sharply in 1981–82, but the share of reexported oil has also significantly risen. This is conveniently illustrated by data in Table 2 in the Appendix.

Table 2 presents information on *net* Soviet and East European exports (i.e., exports minus imports) of crude oil and refined oil products to nonsocialist countries. First, the data in Table 2 indicate that on net basis, East European oil imports from nonsocialist countries peaked at 14.9 mmt (298 tbd) in 1978 and then declined as low as 4.0 mmt (80 tbd) in 1981 before increasing to 7.3 mmt (146 tbd) in 1982. Second, among the eight CPEs analyzed, three groups of countries can be distinguished, namely:

- countries which reexport 100% of their imports of Middle Eastern oil—the Soviet Union, Bulgaria, Czechoslovakia, and Hungary;
- countries which consume all or a significant portion of imported Middle Eastern oil domestically—Yugoslavia belongs to the former category while Romania belongs to the latter category (Poland was also in this category during 1975–80);
- countries which reexport most of the imported Middle Eastern oil, but consume a small portion domestically—East Germany and Poland (during 1981–82).

One can only draw a single conclusion from the data in Table 2—with the exception of Romania and Yugoslavia, none of the other CPEs really need to import crude oil from the Middle East at the present time. Yet the fact is that these imports continue, and six out of eight CPEs—the Soviet Union, Bulgaria, Czechoslovakia, East Germany, Hungary, and Poland—are currently reexporting virtually all oil imported from the Middle East either in crude or refined form. It is then interesting to analyze the motivation of each of these six countries behind their imports of crude oil from the Middle East:

Soviet Union. None of the oil the Soviet Union imports from the Middle East—currently mostly from Libya and Iran—has ever landed in a Soviet port. In the case of Libya the Soviet Union receives oil as payment for deliveries of arms and reexports it to other countries. In particular, it is known that some of this oil is delivered to Yugoslavia in partial settlement of agreed Soviet oil deliveries to this country. Some Libyan oil was recently sold to the Finnish oil company Neste to be resold in third markets in order to reduce the current imbalance in Soviet-Finnish trade in Finland's favor. In the case of Iran it is believed that all of the Soviet imports of Iranian oil in 1981 and a portion of these imports in 1982 were swapped with Romania in a trilateral deal whereby the Soviet Union delivered certain goods (possibly including Soviet/Romanian munitions and some military hardware) to Iran, accepted payment in oil, re-exported the oil to Romania, and was in turn paid by Romania through extra deliveries of Romanian food, nonfood raw materials, and possibly some munitions/military hardware. The entire barter deal was denominated in hard currency with goods traded at prevailing "world market" prices.

Bulgaria. Bulgarian imports of oil from the Middle East have two explanations. First, Bulgaria's proximity to the Middle East stimulates the country's sales of food, consumer goods, and machinery in that region. Since the Soviet Union satisfies 100% of Bulgarian energy import needs, imports of oil from the Middle East would appear to reflect barter transactions and the need to accept oil as payment at least for a part of Bulgarian exports (especially during the present "weak" oil market). It is understood that, particularly in the case of Iran and Libya, Bulgaria is required to accept a portion of payment in oil and the rest in hard currency. This arrangement helps the Bulgarians to get an edge in sales to these two countries, although the quality of some of their exports is below that offered by alternative suppliers. However, these alternative suppliers may not be willing to accept barter transactions with a portion of payment in oil. Second, as in the case of Romania, Bulgaria may be refining Middle Eastern oil for profit—although this must have been difficult in recent years. Perhaps Bulgaria also stepped up imports of Middle Eastern crude oil in 1982 in order to partly offset the reduction in Soviet deliveries so as to achieve a high degree of utilization of domestic refining capacity—as we know from the Romanian experience, this may be done even though such a policy is not economical.

Czechoslovakia. In this case the sole reason for these imports is believed to be barter trade with Iran and Iraq in which some of the payment for Czechoslovak machinery goods is in the form of oil.

East Germany. Among all East European countries, only East Germany is in a situation where refining of the bulk of imported

Middle Eastern oil for reexport is always profitable. The reason for this is the cost-plus contract for substantial deliveries of gasoline, diesel fuel, and heating oil to East Berlin. Any fluctuation in the price of crude oil can be passed onto consumers in West Berlin. That is why East Germany is believed to have never reexported any Middle Eastern crude oil but always refines this oil and exports oil products to West Berlin, West Germany, and to a lesser degree also to West European countries (probably Austria, Switzerland, and Belgium).

Hungary. Hungary is unique in Eastern Europe in its recent innovative use of imported crude oil as a source of short-term credit for the financially strapped country. As we have indicated in *Current Analysis*, No. 65–66, August 31, 1983, in the case of Hungarian imports of Libyan crude oil, the bulk of this oil imported in 1982 and during the first half of 1983 was imported on credit (of up to 360 days) and immediately resold in Western Europe for cash. As a result, Hungary in effect was able to obtain substantial short-term Libyan loans—in excess of $200 million during the first six months of 1983—at what may well be a below-market implicit interest rate (we do not know for sure because we do not have exact information on the financing terms of the oil sale by the Libyans). In the case of Hungarian imports of Iranian oil, the Hungarian situation appears to be similar to that of Bulgaria. Hungary received Iranian oil as payment for its exports and by reselling oil in Western Europe ultimately obtains hard currency. The willingness of Hungary to enter into barter deals with Iran enables Hungary to gain a competitive edge and explains the rapid growth in exports of Hungarian goods to Iran in 1982.

Poland. Having virtually cut off all of its nonsocialist crude oil imports in 1981–82 because of the severe balance-of-payments crisis, Poland began to purchase Libyan oil during the first half of 1983 in addition to a smaller volume of Iranian oil. It is believed that imports of Libyan oil represent a payment for earlier deliveries of Polish goods in 1982, and this pattern will continue for some time as a result of a major Polish-Libyan barter deal.

Romania. Under pressure from the IMF Romania apparently curtailed somewhat its imports of Middle Eastern crude oil for refining and export to Western Europe last year. Most experts have concluded that a significant portion of this activity actually results in net hard-currency losses to the Romanian economy as product prices were too low to guarantee a positive refining margin over the price of imported crude. The Romanians have reportedly agreed to centralize all of these oil transactions under one oil company which will undertake imports of crude only if it can profitably sell products based on this oil. However, given the "creative" nature of Romanian economic accounting, whether Romania really makes money out of its refining for export continues to be unclear.

Yugoslavia. Of all East European countries Yugoslavia appears to have been the least active in reexporting Middle Eastern oil in crude or refined form. Most of the imported oil is consumed domestically. However, in mid-1983 Yugoslavia is known to have entered reexport activities for financial reasons. In order to liquidate all of its arrears to Western commerical banks under the rescheduling agreement, Yugoslavia resold some oil imported from the Soviet Union in Western Europe. However, this may well be only a temporary reexport transaction quite different from those undertaken by other East European countries which are generally of a permanent nature. It is likely that Yugoslavia will offset the reduction in stocks of Soviet crude by accelerated purchases of Middle Eastern oil during the second half of 1983 when the country's hard-currency balance-of-payments situation is expected to improve significantly.

To conclude, Soviet and East European imports of oil from the Middle East for reexport in crude and refined form to Western Europe are likely to continue so long as the oil market stays "soft." The weak oil market creates pressure to pay off certain financial obligations through deliveries of oil (such as in the case of Libyan oil deliveries to the Soviet Union to pay for earlier arms purchases) or offer oil in barter for East European goods. Depending on whether one is an optimist or a pessimist with respect to the outlook for the *real* price of oil, one should predict lower or higher (or at least sustained) deliveries of Middle Eastern oil to CPEs for reexport. If the world oil market hardens, it is quite possible that at least most of East European imports of Middle Eastern oil for reexport will cease. This will be a natural development as countries of the Middle

East will become more aware of many disadvantages of barter transactions and better terms of trade obtainable in straight cash deals.

(The reader interested in more detailed analysis of the pattern of Soviet and East European trade in crude oil and refined oil products is referred to Tables 3 and 4 in the Appendix. These two tables served as a source of data for net export figures for all oil in Table 2.)

III. Overall Pattern of CPE-Middle East Trade

The aggregate statistics for trade of eight CPEs with six key Middle Eastern countries—Algeria, Egypt, Iran, Iraq, Libya, and Syria—are presented in Tables 5 and 6 in the Appendix. The export statistics in Table 5 show that between 1975 and 1982 total CPE exports to these six countries increased from $5.3 billion to $15.9 billion in nominal terms, implying an average annual growth of nearly 17%. Soviet exports (including arms) increased from an estimated $3.1 billion in 1975 to $8.4 billion—a 15% average annual growth over the seven-year period. Exports by seven East European countries (including Yugoslavia) increased from $2.2 billion in 1975 to $7.5 billion in 1982—a 19% average annual growth during this period.

As indicated by data in Table 10 in the Appendix, the dominant portion of Soviet and East European exports to the Middle East is accounted for by machinery and equipment. Its share amounted to 65–66% both in 1975 and in 1982. Among CPEs the country most dependent on exports of machinery to the Middle East is the Soviet Union. For example in 1982, we estimate that arms accounted for 62% of total Soviet exports to these six countries while investment machinery and machinery with dual military-civilian use (such as trucks, aircraft, etc.) accounted for another 13% of these exports. Thus fully three-quarters of the total value of Soviet exports to these countries were machinery items. The share of machinery in total exports of the CMEA Six to the six Middle Eastern countries in 1982 amounted to 62% while that of Yugoslavia was around 29%.

In terms of importance Iraq is undoubtedly the largest recipient of Soviet and East European exports, accounting for almost 28% of total exports of CPEs to the six Middle Eastern countries studied which could be identified by destination in 1982. Regrettably, in the absence of unclassified information on the value of Soviet arms sales to individual Middle Eastern countries, it is difficult to assess the ranking of the remaining countries. Our educated quess is that in terms of volume, in recent years Libya has been the second largest buyer of Soviet and East European goods (when all arms purchases are taken into consideration), followed by Syria (especially in 1982–83), Iran, Egypt, and Algeria. The pattern of orientation of exports to the Middle East is fairly different among individual CPEs—the largest portion of the country's total export earnings from non-socialist trade is earned in the six Middle Eastern countries in the case of Bulgaria (43.0% in 1982), followed by Yugoslavia (30.0%), Romania (27.5%), the Soviet Union (21.1%), Hungary (20.2%), Czechoslovakia (15.4%), Poland (13.0%), and East Germany (10.8%).

The reasons for the relatively rapid expansion of East bloc exports to the six Middle Eastern countries—aside from the obvious political/strategic considerations in the case of the Soviet Union—are largely economic. Two East European countries—Romania and Yugoslavia—need to pay with these exports for their imports of crude oil for domestic consumption. The remaining countries view the Middle East as an attractive export market essentially for two reasons:

- The Soviet Union and Eastern Europe have encountered growing difficulties in expanding their exports of manufactures, particularly machinery and equipment, to the developed West because of Western economic recession and growing competition for relatively technologically backward machinery sold by the East bloc. However, in one area of machinery production—arms—the East has a comparative advantage and produces hardware of relatively good quality fairly cheaply because of huge economies of scale. Since this type of machinery cannot be sold in the West for obvious political/strategic reasons, the Middle East is the natural market for Soviet and East European arms given the abundance of political and military conflict and the availability of plentiful funds for arms purchases.
- Given the chronic hard-currency trade deficits with the devel-

oped West, most East bloc countries strive to earn substantial trade surpluses in developing countries, which are in turn used to offset the deficits in the former region. The bulk of these surpluses is earned in the Middle East—just the opposite situation from the pattern of trade of the developed West with the Middle East. In fact, since the Soviet Union and Eastern Europe (except for Romania and Yugoslavia) do not import almost any Middle Eastern crude oil for domestic consumption but for reexport, it is essentially true that from the viewpoint of the East bloc the entire export revenue in the Middle East amounts to a trade surplus.

The importance of the point that virtually the entire export revenue of the Soviet Union and five out seven East European countries in the six Middle Eastern countries amounts to a trade surplus cannot be overemphasized. Especially at a time of severe financial difficulties of most countries in the East bloc, the ability to secure nearly a $16 billion de facto trade surplus (in 1982) has helped to avoid even greater financial crisis. Even if from the viewpoint of Middle Eastern countries the sales of crude oil to the East bloc are just as good as sales anywhere else and the fact that this oil is reexported may not be of such great interest to them, the Middle East still has a large "conventional" trade deficit with the East bloc. As is indicated by data in Table 7 in the Appendix, in 1982 this deficit for the six Middle Eastern countries under study amounted to $8.5 billion, of which the Soviet Union accounted for $5.7 billion and Eastern Europe for the remaining $2.8 billion. With the exception of Romania, which registered a 1982 trade deficit with the six Middle Eastern countries estimated provisionally at $250 million, the remaining East European countries posted hefty surpluses—$933 million for Bulgaria, $615 million for Poland, $470 million for Czechoslovakia, $377 million for Yugoslavia, $321 million for East Germany, and $308 million for Hungary.

With regard to the East bloc imports from the Middle East, with the exception of Egypt virtually all of these imports reflect purchases of crude oil. Between 1975 and 1982 the total value of the East bloc imports from the Middle East increased from $3.4 billion to $7.4 billion, representing an average annual growth of somewhat less than 12%—a figure well below the 17% average annual growth of East bloc exports to this region. The relative importance of individual Middle Eastern countries as a source of East bloc imports almost exactly mirrors the distribution of East bloc imports of crude oil in physical terms, which has already been discussed above.

To summarize this section, if the trade of the East bloc with the Middle East is viewed in the framework of world trade, then it fits into this framework in the following fashion: Middle East purchases of East bloc goods are paid for partly by deliveries of oil and partly by surplus cash earned from oil sales in the developed West; East bloc reexports of Middle Eastern oil to the developed West augment the cash surplus and the entire trade surplus of the East bloc in the Middle East is used to offset the East bloc payments deficit in the developed West; the surplus the developed West earns in its payments transaction with the East bloc is then used to offset its own trade deficit in the Middle East.

IV. Soviet and East European Financial Relations with the Middle East

As we pointed out in Section III, for the Soviet Union and five out of seven East European countries (except Romania and Yugoslavia), virtually the entire export revenue earned in the Middle East effectively represents an export surplus which can be used to offset payments deficits in the developed West. However, Eastern Europe—but not the Soviet Union—also views the countries of the Middle East as an alternative supplier of credit. Regrettably there is an extremely limited amount of data on the financial exposure of the banks/government lending agencies of Middle Eastern countries in Eastern Europe. The bits and pieces that are known include the following:

• Direct exposure of banks/government lending agencies of Middle Eastern countries in two East European countries that have rescheduled their loans is not that large—in the case of Poland the outstanding borrowing from the Middle East amounted to $380 million at the end of 1982, and in the case of Romania the amount was $680 million in mid-1983. Most of the exposure is held by Iran, Iraq, Libya, and Kuwait. As yet no information has been released on the exposure of Middle Eastern countries in Yugoslavia—which is currently undergoing rescheduling of its 1983 debt payments—but it is thought to be comparable to or somewhat higher than the exposure in Romania.

• It is certain that total exposure of Middle Eastern banks/government lending agencies in Eastern Europe is much higher than the direct exposure. Middle Eastern financial institutions do most of their lending to Eastern Europe through banks in Western Europe (mostly in London and Paris). However, in terms of statistics from the Bank for International Settlements (BIS), this exposure is treated as British and French because of the place of registration/incorporation of these institutions. Pending direct cooperation from these institutions—which is a rather unlikely event—it is virtually impossible to obtain a reasonably accurate estimate of the total Middle Eastern banking exposure in Eastern Europe—the access to such information is limited to the Bank of England and Banque de France.

• Among the seven East European countries, three are known to be active in raising loans in or accepting deposits from countries in the Middle East—East Germany, Hungary, and Yugoslavia. Romania, which has borrowed a substantial amount in the Middle East in the past, is currently inactive in this area for obvious reasons, and this also applies to Poland. Neither Bulgaria nor Czechoslovakia is known to have been particularly active in trying to tap the Middle East for loans. According to reliable West European government information, East Germany raised substantial amounts of short-term loans in the Middle East over the past 12 months. The maturity of the bulk of these loans is reported to have been subsequently extended on the basis of an East German request for an unknown period. Hungary has been active in the past in accepting short-term deposits from the Middle East—in fact, the withdrawal of these deposits by Libya and/or Iraq (among other countries) during the first quarter of 1982 reportedly led to the Hungarian liquidity crisis, which required a bailout by the BIS. More recently the Arab Banking Corporation of Bahrain arranged a $200 million cofinancing for a World Bank-sponsored project (naturally, only a portion of it actually involves Middle Eastern funds).

• A more innovative approach to borrowing from the Middle East has been taken up recently by Hungary and Yugoslavia. It involves purchases of Middle Eastern oil on credit of up to 360 days. Especially in the case of Hungary, the reason for imports of crude oil from Libya are particularly interesting. As was pointed out above in Section II, all of the oil imported by Hungary from Libya (and possibly also Iran—but to a considerably smaller degree) on credit of up to 360 days was immediately resold for cash in Western Europe. Thus the purchase of Libyan oil was mostly a pretext to obtain a short-term Libyan loan. In our assessment, during the first six months of 1983, Hungary raised an equivalent of $200 million in short-term loans from Libya this way at what may well be a below-market implicit interest rate.

In the foreseeable future we expect some increase in Middle Eastern (Arab) lending activities in Eastern Europe. This reflects more active pursuit of Arab finance by East European bankers who can no longer tap "the usual sources" of loans to the degree available to them through early 1981. In addition, given the increased interest margins and substantial up-front fees, lending to Eastern Europe is probably more profitable now than ever before. Finally, given the payments difficulties of many countries in the Third World, which previously relied on loans from the Middle East, in relative terms the economic situation in Eastern Europe has been improving. As the risk of additional rescheduling is declining in the region, the combination of increased loan profitability and lower lending risk is bound to attract more Middle East financing to Eastern Europe.

Table 1

Imports of Crude Oil by Centrally Planned Economies from Non-Socialist Countries, 1975–83 (in thousand metric tons)

				Eastern Europe (CMEA Six)							
Year	All CPEs	CMEA seven	Soviet Union	Total	Bulgaria	Czecho-slovakia	East Germany	Hungary	Poland	Romania	Yugoslavia
1975	23,636	18,028	6,499	11,529	598	336	1,900	1,469	2,347	4,879	5,608
1976	28,271	23,017	6,425	16,592	817	766	2,024	1,060	3,450	8,475	5,254
1977	28,282	22,813	6,240	16,573	914	1,350	2,035	822	3,627	7,825	5,469
1978	35,983	29,704	8,490	21,214	1,342	865	2,165	1,463	3,247	12,132	6,279
1979	34,886	27,637	6,394	21,243	820	300	2,158	1,162	3,655	13,148	7,249
1980	31,397	25,286	3,564	21,722	627	459	2,865	836	3,247	13,688	6,111
1981	24,434	19,582	4,200	15,382	966	332	3,698	474	409	9,503	4,852
1982*	29,582	25,392	7,200	18,192	1,719	(450)	(4,000)	1,796	277	9,950	(4,190)
1983/ 1-6*	n.a.	n.a.	n.a.	n.a.	780	n.a.	n.a.	1,595	1,170	(4,650)	(2,250)
				From Oil-producing Developing Countries							
1975	21,539	15,944	6,499	9,445	598	291	1,900	1,469	478	4,709	5,595
1976	24,467	19,223	6,425	12,798	817	246	2,024	1,060	346	8,305	5,244
1977	24,518	19,049	6,240	12,809	914	750	2,035	822	633	7,655	5,469
1978	33,744	27,465	8,490	18,975	1,141	314	2,165	1,463	1,930	11,962	6,279
1979	33,942	26,737	6,394	20,343	820	—	2,158	1,162	3,235	12,968	7,205
1980	30,947	24,836	3,564	21,272	627	328	2,865	836	3,118	13,498	6,111
1981	21,479	16,627	4,200	12,427	966	215	(1,000)	474	409	9,363	4,852
1982*	27,292	23,102	7,200	15,902	1,719	(300)	(2,000)	1,796	277	9,810	(4,190)
1983/1-6*	n.a.	n.a.	n.a.	n.a.	780	n.a.	n.a.	1,595	1,170	(4,600)	(2,250)

					Of Which: From Iran						
1975	3,037	3,037	—	2,470	—	89	—	61	—	2,320	567
1976	4,250	4,250	—	4,250	417	—	—	263	—	3,570	—
1977	4,775	4,775	—	4,431	389	505	—	118	379	3,040	344
1978	4,782	4,782	—	4,243	750	165	—	125	783	2,420	539
1979	3,780	3,780	—	3,780	309	—	(70)	262	729	2,410	—
1980	4,590	4,590	—	4,362	188	263	(340)	417	494	2,660	228
1981	6,740	6,483	2,250	4,233	226	215	(70)	474	408	2,840	257
1982*	7,921	7,046	870	6,176	1,096	(300)	(420)	1,083	277	(3,000)	875
1983/1-6*	n.a.	n.a.	n.a.	n.a.	180	n.a.	n.a.	525	305	n.a.	690
					Of Which: From Iraq						
1975	12,856	8,394	5,304	3,090	139	202	1,454	1,205	—	90	4,462
1976	15,284	10,490	5,821	4,669	—	246	1,576	797	—	2,050	4,794
1977	13,724	9,119	4,675	4,444	153	245	1,072	704	—	2,270	4,605
1978	19,958	14,911	6,373	8,538	77	149	1,057	1,338	1,147	4,770	5,047
1979	20,274	14,452	3,623	10,829	107	—	1,095	900	1,877	6,850	5,822
1980	13,753	9,870	1,884	7,986	71	65	1,430	419	1,651	4,350	3,883
1981	2,796	1,400	—	1,400	—	—	—	—	—	1,400	1,396
1982*	3,507	2,267	80	2,187	67	—	(1,120)	—	—	(1,000)	1,240
1983/1-6*	n.a.	n.a.	n.a.	n.a.	—	n.a.	n.a.	—	—	n.a.	340
					Of Which: From Libya						
1975	1,421	953	—	953	113	—	—	—	—	840	468
1976	2,245	1,795	—	1,795	215	—	—	—	—	1,580	450
1977	2,939	2,439	1,031	1,408	284	—	224	—	—	900	500
1978	4,866	4,446	1,562	2,884	314	—	—	—	—	2,570	420
1979	6,530	5,714	2,771	2,943	404	—	(70)	—	569	1,900	816
1980	5,638	4,447	1,680	2,767	368	—	(480)	—	339	1,580	921

1981	4,979	4,010	1,700	2,310	740	—	(340)	—	—	1,230	969
1982*	10,149	8,669	5,900	2,769	556	—	—	713	—	(1,500)	1,480
1983/1-6*	n.a.	n.a.	n.a.	n.a.	600	n.a.	n.a.	1,070	865	n.a.	920
				Of Which: From Other Oil-Producing Developing Countries							
1975	4,225	4,127	1,195	2,932	346	—	446	203	478	1,459	98
1976	2,688	2,688	604	2,084	185	—	448	—	346	1,105	—
1977	3,080	3,060	534	2,526	88	—	739	—	254	1,445	20
1978	4,138	3,865	555	3,310	—	—	1,108	—	—	2,202	273
1979	3,388	2,821	—	2,821	—	—	(923)	—	60	1,838	567
1980	7,236	6,157	—	6,157	—	—	(615)	—	634	4,908	1,079
1981	6,964	4,734	250	4,484	—	—	(590)	—	1	3,893	2,230
1982*	5,715	5,120	350	4,470	—	—	(460)	—	—	(4,310)	(595)
1983/1-6*	n.a.	n.a.	n.a.	n.a.	—	n.a.	n.a.	—	—	n.a.	(300)
					From Developed West						
1975	2,097	2,084	—	2,084	—	45	—	—	1,869	(170)	13
1976	3,804	3,794	—	3,794	—	520	—	—	3,104	(170)	10
1977	3,764	3,764	—	3,764	—	600	—	—	2,994	(170)	—
1978	2,239	2,239	—	2,239	201	551	—	—	1,317	(170)	—
1979	944	900	—	900	—	300	—	—	420	(180)	44
1980	450	450	—	450	—	131	—	—	129	(190)	—
1981	2,955	2,955	—	2,955	—	117	(2,698)	—	—	(140)	—
1982	2,290	2,290	—	2,290	—	(150)	(2,000)	—	—	(140)	—
1983/1–6	n.a.	n.a.	—	n.a.	—	n.a.	n.a.	—	—	(50)	—

*Preliminary estimate.

Note: Figures in parentheses are educated guesses.

Source: Wharton Centrally Planned Economies Databank—Volume One: Energy Production and Trade Measured in Physical Units for 1960–82, June 1983, and other official data compiled by Wharton from Soviet and East European statistical sources.

Table 2

Net Exports of Crude Oil and Refined Oil Products by Centrally Planned Economies to Non-Socialist countries, 1975-83 (in thousand metric tons)

Year	All CPEs	CMEA seven	Soviet Union**	Eastern Europe (CMEA Six)							Yugoslavia
				Total	Bulgaria	Czecho-slovakia	East Germany	Hungary	Poland	Romania	
1975	−7,275	−1,704	—	−1,704	−8	234	83	−380	−1,825	192	−5,571
1976	−8,872	−3,758	—	−3,758	−247	−11	−393	280	−1,947	−1,440	−5,114
1977	−9,566	−4,988	—	−4,988	−94	−268	−675	592	−2,498	−2,045	−4,578
1978	−14,913	−9,256	—	−9,256	228	−303	−723	−290	−2,468	−5,700	−5,657
1979	−14,704	−7,876	—	−7,876	2,140	431	−433	−29	−3,316	−6,669	−6,828
1980	−9,942	−4,243	—	−4,243	3,013	771	−243	466	−2,263	−5,987	−5,699
1981	−4,023	895	—	895	2,454	618	−23	620	−378	−2,396	−4,918
1982*	−7,286	−3,196	—	−3,196	1,211	110	−421	259	−340	−4,015	−4,090

*Preliminary estimate.

**Re-exports of Middle Eastern crude oil cancel out with imports of crude oil from the Middle East.

Note: In the case of five East European countries—Bulgaria, Czechoslovakia, East Germany, Hungary, and Poland—a ***negative figure*** implies that exports of crude oil and refined oil products to non-socialist countries are less than imports of crude oil and refined oil products from these countries, i.e., some portion of imports from non-socialist countries is actually used domestically. A negative figure also implies strict observance of the contractual clause against re-exports (both in crude and refined form) of Soviet oil or exports of domestically produced oil (relevant particularly in the case of Hungary) except by special explicit permission from the Soviet Union (as in the case of Bulgaria during 1979-82).

A ***positive figure*** implies that exports of crude oil and refined oil products to non-socialist countries exceed imports of crude oil and refined oil products from these countries, i.e., no portion of imports from non-socialist countries is used domestically. A positive figure also implies that some Soviet oil is being re-exported (in crude or refined form) or domestically produced oil is exported (particularly in the case of Hungary). This may be taking place either in violation of the contractual clause against re-exports (both in crude and refined form) of Soviet oil or exports of domestically produced oil except by special explicit permission from the Soviet Union (possibly in the case of Czechoslovakia during 1979-82, and Hungary during 1976-77 and 1980-82) or in agreement with the Soviet Union (as in the case of Bulgaria during 1978-82).

Source: Calculated on the basis of data from Tables 3 and 4 below.

Table 3

Exports of Crude Oil and Refined Oil Products by Centrally Planned Economies to Non-Socialist Countries, 1975-83 (in thousand metric tons)

Year	All CPEs	CMEA seven	Soviet Union**	Eastern Europe (CMEA Six)							Yugoslavia
				Total	Bulgaria	Czecho-slovakia	East Germany	Hungary	Poland	Romania	
				Crude Oil and Oil Products							
1975	18,281	18,099	6,499	11,600	750	668	2,058	1,133	1,915	5,076	182
1976	20,894	20,640	6,425	14,215	710	831	1,657	1,369	2,608	7,040	254
1977	20,225	19,228	6,240	12,988	1,010	1,192	1,426	1,472	2,103	5,785	997
1978	22,721	21,846	8,490	13,356	1,710	748	1,465	1,230	1,766	6,437	875
1979	21,993	21,291	6,394	14,897	3,030	870	1,744	1,328	1,391	6,484	702
1980	23,139	22,607	3,564	19,043	3,740	1,323	2,778	1,442	2,054	7,706	532
1981	22,230	21,772	4,200	17,572	3,520	1,127	3,869	1,148	796	7,112	458
1982*	23,949	23,419	7,200	16,219	3,030	730	3,798	2,115	606	5,940	530

					Crude Oil						
1975	7,939	7,935	6,499	1,436	220	—	—	833	383	—	4
1976	8,107	8,107	6,425	1,682	450	246	—	986	—	—	—
1977	8,355	8,355	6,240	2,115	550	742	—	823	—	—	—
1978	10,660	10,600	8,490	2,170	900	313	—	957	—	—	—
1979	8,824	8,824	6,394	2,430	1,480	22	—	928	—	—	—
1980	6,893	6,893	3,564	3,329	1,740	205	—	881	503	—	—
1981	6,559	6,559	4,200	2,359	1,620	209	—	530	—	—	—
1982*	10,395	10,395	7,200	3,195	1,380	200	—	1,615	—	—	—
					Refined Oil Products						
1975	10,342	10,164	—	10,164	530	668	2,058	300	1,532	5,076	178
1976	12,787	12,533	—	12,533	260	585	1,657	383	2,608	7,040	254
1977	11,870	10,873	—	10,873	460	450	1,426	649	2,103	5,785	997
1978	12,061	11,186	—	11,186	8[illegible]0	435	1,465	273	1,766	6,437	875
1979	13,169	12,467	—	12,467	1,600	848	1,744	400	1,391	6,484	702
1980	16,246	15,714	—	15,714	2,000	1,118	2,778	561	1,551	7,706	532
1981	15,671	15,213	—	15,213	1,900	918	3,869	618	796	7,112	458
1982*	13,554	13,024	—	13,024	1,650	530	3,798	500	606	5,940	530

*Preliminary estimate.
**Only re-exports of Middle Eastern crude oil are reported for the Soviet Union.

Table 4

Imports of Crude Oil and Refined Oil Products by Centrally Planned Economies from Non-Socialist Countries, 1975-83 (in thousand metric tons)

Year	All CPEs	CMEA seven	Soviet Union**	Eastern Europe (CMEA Six)							Yugoslavia
				Total	Bulgaria	Czecho-slovakia	East Germany	Hungary	Poland	Romania	
				Crude Oil and Oil Products							
1975	25,556	19,803	6,499	13,304	758	434	1,975	1,513	3,740	4,884	5,753
1976	29,766	24,398	6,425	17,973	957	842	2,050	1,089	4,555	8,480	5,368
1977	29,791	24,216	6,240	17,976	1,104	1,460	2,101	880	4,601	7,830	5,575
1978	37,634	31,102	8,490	22,612	1,482	1,051	2,188	1,520	4,234	12,137	6,532
1979	36,697	29,167	6,394	22,773	940	439	2,177	1,357	4,707	13,153	7,530
1980	33,081	26,850	3,564	23,286	727	552	3,021	976	4,317	13,693	6,231
1981	26,253	20,877	4,200	16,677	1.066	509	3,892	528	1,174	9,508	5,376
1982*	31,235	26,615	7,200	19,415	1,819	620	4,219	1,856	946	9,955	4,620
				Crude Oil							
1975	23,636	18,028	6,499	11,529	598	336	1,900	1,469	2,347	4,879	5,608
1976	28,271	23,017	6,425	16,592	817	766	2,024	1,060	3,450	8,475	5,254

1977	28,282	22,813	6,240	16,573	914	1,350	2,035	822	3,267	7,825	5,469
1978	35,983	29,704	8,490	21,214	1,342	865	2,165	1,463	3,247	12,132	6,279
1979	34,886	27,637	6,394	21,243	820	300	2,158	1,162	3,655	13,148	7,249
1980	31,397	25,286	3,564	21,722	627	459	2,865	836	3,247	13,688	6,111
1981	24,434	19,582	4,200	15,382	966	332	3,698	474	409	9,503	4,852
1982*	29,582	25,392	7,200	18,192	1,719	450	4,000	1,796	277	9,950	4,190
					Refined Oil Products						
1975	1,920	1,775	—	1,775	160	98	75	44	1,393	5	145
1976	1,495	1,381	—	1,381	140	76	26	29	1,105	5	114
1977	1,509	1,403	—	1,403	190	110	66	58	974	5	106
1978	1,651	1,398	—	1,398	140	186	23	57	987	5	253
1979	1,811	1,530	—	1,530	120	139	19	195	1,052	5	281
1980	1,684	1,564	—	1,564	100	93	156	140	1,070	5	120
1981	1,819	1,295	—	1,295	100	177	194	54	765	5	524
1982*	1,653	1,223	—	1,223	100	170	219	60	669	5	430

*Preliminary estimate
**Only imports of Middle Eastern crude oil intended for re-exports are reported for the Soviet Union.
Source: Wharton Centrally Planned Economies Databank—Volume One: Energy Production and Trade Measured in Physical Units for 1960-82, June 1983.

Table 5

Exports of Centrally Planned Economies to Six Most Important Trade Partners in the Middle East, 1975-83 (in million dollars)

				Eastern Europe (CMEA Six)							
Year	All CPEs	CMEA seven	Soviet Union	Total	Bulgaria	Czecho-slovakia	East Germany	Hungary	Poland	Romania	Yugoslavia
				Total for Six Middle Eastern Countries (Algeria, Egypt, Iran, Iraq, Libya, Syria)							
1975	5,333	5,078	3,150**	1,928.1	294.4	375.3	261.6	187.0	292.8	517.0	255.4
1976	5,918	5,619	3,450**	2,168.6	321.2	376.3	(302.4)	224.2	345.1	599.4	299.6
1977	7,887	7,433	5,000**	2,432.7	407.2	424.1	264.7	240.4	343.2	753.1	454.6
1978	9,184	8,684	5,950**	2,734.3	552.0	472.7	(330.3)	286.1	337.7	755.5	499.6
1979	9,784	9,236	6,300**	2,935.6	552.2	469.2	(367.6)	342.0	401.5	803.1	548.4
1980	10,833	10,026	5,900**	4,126.1	870.6	670.2	(505.3)	429.5	581.3	1,069.2	806.5
1981	14,224	12,910	7,050**	5,859.6	1,295.1	704.8	(621.4)	605.7	528.4	2,104.2	1,314.7
1982	15,903	14,397	8,450**	5,947.0	1,374.8	(630.0)	(848.6)	767.6	676.0	(1,650.0)	1,506.3
1983/1-6	n.a.	n.a.	n.a.	n.a.	563.1	n.a.	n.a.	301.7	288.4	n.a.	(693.0)

					Algeria						
1975	280.4	277.7	155.7*	122.0	8.0	8.1	20.1	14.4	35.5	35.9	2.7
1976	366.0	351.1	174.3*	176.8	21.2	10.6	(32.6)	27.2	43.8	41.4	14.9
1977	465.9	443.4	167.5*	275.9	44.2	20.7	23.6	46.6	57.1	83.7	22.5
1978	489.6	447.4	129.2*	318.2	96.8	19.0	(56.1)	43.5	37.8	65.0	42.2
1979	525.5	477.4	125.3*	352.1	71.9	28.6	(71.1)	41.4	41.3	97.8	48.1
1980	656.2	586.5	142.7*	443.8	119.8	39.6	(103.3)	56.2	48.9	76.0	69.7
1981	668.9	538.6	157.7*	380.9	105.4	40.3	(70.2)	69.0	44.2	51.8)	130.3
1982	n.a.	n.a.	182.3*	n.,a.	86.7	n.a.	(100.0)	95.7	46.0	n.a.	216.6
1983/1-6	n.a.	n.a.	n.a.	n.a.	43.5	n.a.	n.a.	48.2	14.2	n.a.	(78.0)
					Egypt						
1975	735.7	685.3	363.2*	322.1	30.3	77.0	86.6	21.2	33.1	73.9	50.4
1976	610.3	537.7	265.0*	272.7	27.5	69.8	(70.3)	10.2	25.2	69.7	72.6
1977	709.2	592.0	275.9*	316.1	26.0	87.0	74.7	10.3	37.1	81.0	117.2
1978	675.8	542.1	215.8*	326.3	19.7	60.0	(53.8)	14.2	45.9	132.7	133.7
1979	718.3	605.8	193.5*	412.3	27.3	41.8	(62.0)	24.0	36.9	220.3	112.5
1980	939.2	781.6	266.1*	515.5	25.4	89.0	(48.0)	25.2	61.5	266.4	157.6
1981	1,053.6	870.6	339.7*	530.9	28.7	72.9	(53.0)	40.5	43.0	292.8)	183.0
1982	n.a.	n.a.	301.0*	n.a.	11.2	97.5	(50.0)	35.4	43.9	n.a.	169.6
1983/1-6	n.a.	n.a.	n.a.	n.a.	3.8	n.a.	n.a.	11.2	21.7	n.a.	(90.0)

					Iran						
1975	790.3	774.7	390.2*	384.5	53.4	52.6	11.7	42.9	60.7	163.2	15.6
1976	787.9	764.1	289.0*	475.1	59.2	85.4	(14.2)	53.2	76.4	186.7	23.8
1977	1,106.7	1,085.7	575.5*	510.2	59.2	91.5	21.0	59.1	67.4	212.0	21.0
1978	1,156.2	1,123.3	633.2*	490.1	83.2	77.9	(27.8)	54.4	63.7	183.1	32.9
1979	811.2	788.0	415.2*	372.8	59.0	54.6	(29.8)	35.9	64.0	129.5	23.2
1980	1,267.6	1,185.7	399.3*	786.4	145.8	76.5	(75.0)	134.8	111.2	243.1	81.9
1981	1,677.3	1,553.9	569.4*	984.5	160.2	64.9	(135.0)	125.6	84.5	414.3	123.4
1982	n.a.	n.a.	795.0*	n.a.	211.9	n.a.	(217.3)	223.5	84.8	n.a.	191.9
1983/1-6	n.a.	n.a.	n.a.	n.a.	98.6	n.a.	n.a.	94.0	57.8	n.a.	(129.0)
					Iraq						
1975	984.3	864.4	380.0*	484.4	83.9	94.9	104.5	77.8	57.9	65.4	119.9
1976	976.7	873.3	453.1*	420.2	60.8	84.1	(88.9)	85.9	69.0	31.5	103.4
1977	898.5	721.4	381.3*	340.1	38.5	77.5	71.0	73.0	63.4	16.7	177.1
1978	1,602.3	1,447.2	985.8*	461.4	92.5	64.1	(109.2)	96.5	66.0	33.1	155.1
1979	2,139.4	1,909.3	1,302.6*	606.7	84.9	106.3	(111.2)	145.1	94.3	64.9	230.1
1980	1,918.1	1,611.6	729.0*	882.6	143.8	159.9	(139.3)	120.5	127.7	191.4	306.5
1981	3,955.3	3,376.0	1,260.6*	2,115.4	364.0	185.8	(214.7)	217.5	160.3	973.1	579.3
1982	n.a.	n.a.	1,343.9*	n.a.	521.7	n.a.	(276.0)	271.9	258.9	n.a.	719.5
1983/1-6	n.a.	n.a.	n.a.	n.a.	189.5	n.a.	n.a.	95.7	99.2	n.a.	(292.0)
					Libya						
1975	509.2	447.8	26.1*	421.7	103.3	87.7	3.5	18.8	91.3	117.1	61.4
1976	524.4	458.6	21.5*	437.1	131.1	44.2	(18.2)	11.5	118.3	113.8	65.8
1977	637.2	536.7	28.2*	508.5	209.2	33.8	3.5	25.1	103.3	133.6	100.5
1978	869.8	750.0	75.8*	674.2	209.0	133.9	(3.8)	57.9	111.3	158.3	119.8
1979	1,006.8	902.9	240.2*	662.7	259.1	113.1	(5.0)	41.8	129.7	114.0	103.9

1980	1,314.4	1,150.1	251.7*	898.4	371.1	148.6	(25.0)	47.3	194.6	111.8	164.3
1981	1,882.0	1,610.4	264.4*	1,346.0	572.3	205.4	(50.0)	98.1	175.1	245.1	271.6
1982	n.a.	n.a.	304.5*	n.a.	505.3	n.a.	(75.0)	81.3	230.7	n.a.	178.7
1983/1-6	n.a.	n.a.	n.a.	n.a.	218.4	n.a.	n.a.	38.6	93.0	n.a.	(89.0)
					Syria						
1975	336.0	330.6	137.2*	193.4	15.5	55.0	35.2	11.9	14.3	61.5	5.4
1976	589.5	570.4	183.7*	386.7	21.4	82.2	(78.2)	36.2	12.4	156.3	19.1
1977	635.0	618.7	136.8*	481.9	30.1	113.6	70.9	26.3	14.9	226.1	16.3
1978	672.0	656.1	192.0*	464.1	50.8	117.8	(79.6)	19.6	13.0	183.3	15.9
1979	763.8	732.4	203.4*	529.0	50.0	124.8	(88.5)	53.8	35.3	176.6	30.6
1980	884.1	857.6	258.2*	599.4	64.7	156.6	(114.7)	45.5	37.4	180.5	26.5
1981	916.7	889.6	387.7*	501.9	64.5	135.5	(98.5)	55.0	21.3	127.1	27.1
1982	n.a.	n.a.	290.3*	n.a.	38.0	n.a.	(130.3)	59.8	11.7	n.a.	(30.0)
1983/1-6	n.a.	n.a.	n.a.	n.a.	9.3	n.a.	n.a.	14.0	2.5	n.a.	(15.0)

*Excluding the bulk of Soviet exports of arms: see footnote ** for more detail.

Excluding exports of arms to the Middle East not identified by country of destination estimated by Wharton at $1,700 million in 1975, $2,050 million in 1976, $3,450 million in 1977, $3,700 million in 1978, $3,800 million in 1979, $3,850 million in 1980, $4,050 million in 1981, and $5,250 million in 1982. It should be noted that the value of total Soviet arms exports (sales) to the Middle East is higher than the above figures since sales of certain type of semi-military equipment (such as trucks with dual civilian and military use) are reported in Soviet bilateral export figures. In recent years, 20-25% of Soviet exports of arms to individual Middle Eastern countries are identifiable by country of destination. The remaining 75-80% of total Soviet arms exports to the Middle East is hidden in the so-called "LDC export residual" in aggregate Soviet trade statistics.

Figures in parentheses are Wharton estimates. In the case of East Germany, except for years 1975 and 1977, official statistics on trade with individual Middle Eastern countries are available only in the form of total trade turnover, i.e., the sum of total exports and imports. Through painstaking reconstruction, Wharton was able to separate export and import transactions for the remaining years under study—these are tentative estimates, but probably quite accurate.

Note: Official Soviet and East European foreign trade statistics.

Table 6

Imports of Centrally Planned Economies from Six Most Important Trade Partners in the Middle East, 1975-83 (in million dollars)

				Eastern Europe (CMEA Six)							
Year	All CPEs	CMEA seven	Soviet Union	Total	Bulgaria	Czecho-slovakia	East Germany	Hungary	Poland	Romania	Yugoslavia
				Total for Six Middle Eastern Countries (Algeria, Egypt, Iran, Iraq, Libya, Syria)							
1975	3,403.4	2,867.6	1,670.6	1,197.0	83.0	167.0	244.8	195.6	111.7	394.9	535.8
1976	3,401.2	2,878.8	1,440.1	1,438.7	105.0	133.5	(263.0)	173.9	108.2	655.1	522.4
1977	3,581.1	2,986.3	1,514.5	1,471.8	120.4	248.9	250.3	126.3	93.0	632.9	594.8
1978	4,242.7	3,556.6	1,578.3	1,978.3	142.3	121.0	(260.3)	197.2	225.7	1,031.8	686.1
1979	5,743.4	4,725.9	1,592.5	3,133.4	153.4	106.2	(306.4)	226.4	488.1	1,852.9	1,017.5
1980	7,501.7	6,115.6	1,614.9	4,500.7	200.2	160.5	(642.2)	250.3	598.1	2,649.4	1,386.1
1981	5,925.4	4,769.0	2,001.3	2,767.7	314.8	108.1	(219.2)	159.9	136.0	1,829.7	1,156.4
1982	7,407.8	6,278.8	2,729.0	3,549.8	441.5	(160.0)	(528.0)	459.6	60.7	(1,900.0)	1,129.0
1983/1-6	n.a.	n.a.	n.a.	n.a.	188.5	n.a.	n.a.	379.6	270.3	n.a.	(463.0)

					Algeria						
1975	350.0	329.7	186.7	143.0	16.6	11.8	0.8	28.5	39.1	46.2	20.3
1976	138.2	137.4	78.1	59.3	3.6	4.3	(2.0)	6.8	40.9	1.7	0.8
1977	110.9	109.4	53.5	55.9	14.7	6.5	5.5	9.4	11.4	8.4	1.5
1978	196.7	184.7	75.1	109.6	2.6	6.1	(37.0)	9.9	3.5	50.5	12.0
1979	188.6	187.2	52.2	135.0	2.8	4.0	(5.0)	9.6	13.0	100.6	1.4
1980	394.6	287.0	96.3	190.7	2.6	4.6	(60.0)	11.5	3.7	108.3	107.6
1981	394.2	146.3	117.2	29.1	3.1	4.8	(5.0)	11.8	4.0	0.4	247.9
1982	n.a.	n.a.	63.5	n.a.	2.2	n.a.	(34.0)	5.8	4.4	n.a.	86.6
1983/1-6	n.a.	n.a.	n.a.	n.a.	1.4	n.a.	n.a.	3.8	1.1	n.a.	(3.0)
					Egypt						
1975	1,021.8	1,002.5	621.4	381.1	38.0	99.5	97.2	18.4	55.7	72.3	19.3
1976	737.8	716.7	438.8	277.9	29.0	75.0	(90.4)	24.8	30.4	28.3	21.1
1977	697.5	674.9	392.3	282.6	15.2	127.7	82.2	14.0	26.1	17.4	22.6
1978	523.4	484.9	289.7	195.2	10.8	45.8	(73.3)	21.2	17.1	27.0	38.5
1979	649.8	608.9	302.7	306.2	13.4	81.3	(87.6)	28.5	31.6	63.8	40.9
1980	748.6	690.5	325.0	365.5	18.5	41.6	(45.0)	19.4	25.5	215.5	58.1
1981	711.2	591.6	372.1	219.5	11.2	19.7	(35.9)	18.2	23.5	111.0	119.6
1982	n.a.	n.a.	416.0	n.a.	8.3	46.8)	(49.0)	15.7	0.3	n.a.	47.7
1983/1-6	n.a.	n.a.	n.a.	n.a.	3.7	n.a.	n.a.	12.3	4.7	n.a.	(14.0)

					Iran						
1975	634.5	572.3	316.3	256.0	1.9	24.7	6.2	30.2	13.7	179.3	62.2
1976	781.0	774.7	300.7	474.0	39.3	22.2	(13.6)	64.4	31.5	303.0	6.3
1977	928.6	887.0	384.6	502.4	41.8	71.7	13.7	29.2	50.9	295.1	41.6
1978	922.0	859.7	348.8	510.9	81.9	46.5	(18.0)	34.1	88.1	242.3	62.3
1979	801.9	800.3	208.9	591.4	51.2	5.1	(15.0)	58.9	99.5	361.7	1.6
1980	1,325.9	1,261.9	116.2	1,145.7	56.3	69.3	(91.1)	120.9	117.5	690.6	64.0
1981	1,929.7	1,844.9	653.6	1,191.3	69.4	62.1	(48.3)	126.2	108.3	777.0	84.8
1982	n.a.	n.a.	259.9	n.a.	260.3	n.a.	(130.0)	239.8	56.0	n.a.	230.4
1983/1-6	n.a.	n.a.	n.a.	n.a.	42.3	n.a.	n.a.	107.8	62.1	n.a.	(148.0)
					Iraq						
1975	1,106.8	718.0	451.1	266.9	11.8	16.5	115.1	115.0	1.5	7.0	388.8
1976	1,352.2	904.2	494.0	410.2	6.2	21.3	(135.0)	74.6	0.9	172.2	448.0
1977	1,327.0	854.8	435.6	419.2	16.2	23.5	100.0	68.4	2.5	208.6	472.2
1978	1,928.3	1,403.2	600.4	802.8	8.2	14.8	(99.0)	125.6	115.9	439.3	525.1
1979	2,817.8	1,978.8	500.8	1,478.0	17.5	5.1	(151.0)	122.7	253.1	928.6	839.0
1980	3,064.7	2,169.6	398.2	1,771.4	18.1	22.5	(316.0)	95.6	357.1	962.1	895.1
1981	765.6	376.9	5.4	371.5	2.6	1.9	—	2.6	0.2	364.2	388.7
1982	n.a.	n.a.	25.1	n.a.	19.2	n.a.	(280.0)	3.3	—	n.a.	344.9
1983/1-6	n.a.	n.a.	n.a.	n.a.	—	n.a.	n.a.	3.4	—	n.a.	(78.0)

					Libya						
1975	125.8	81.9	—	81.9	10.9	—	—	—	0.3	70.7	43.9
1976	209.3	164.0	—	164.0	21.1	—	(—)	—	0.5	142.4	45.3
1977	301.8	246.2	104.4	141.8	29.8	—	20.9	—	—	91.1	55.6
1978	493.2	446.7	156.3	290.4	33.4	—	(—)	—	—	257.0	46.6
1979	1,020.5	888.1	427.5	460.6	65.7	—	(10.8)	0.3	89.6	294.2	132.4
1980	1,433.8	1,177.3	442.9	734.4	97.1	—	(127.1)	0.3	93.8	416.1	256.5
1981	1,478.1	1,178.6	502.9	675.7	216.6	—	(99.0)	0.4	—	359.7	299.5
1982	n.a.	n.a.	1,550.3	n.a.	146.2	n.a.	(—)	193.2	—	n.a.	409.4
1983/1-6	n.a.	n.a.	n.a.	n.a.	140.0	n.a.	n.a.	248.7	202.4	n.a.	(215.0)
					Syria						
1975	164.5	163.2	95.1	68.1	3.8	14.5	25.5	3.5	1.4	19.4	1.3
1976	182.7	181.8	128.5	53.3	5.8	10.7	(22.0)	3.3	4.0	7.5	0.9
1977	215.3	214.0	144.1	69.9	2.7	19.5	28.0	5.3	2.1	12.3	1.3
1978	179.0	177.4	108.0	69.4	5.4	7.8	(33.0)	6.4	1.1	15.7	1.6
1979	264.8	262.6	100.4	162.2	2.8	10.7	(37.0)	6.4	1.3	104.0	2.2
1980	534.1	529.3	236.3	293.0	7.6	22.5	(3.0)	2.6	0.5	256.8	4.8
1981	646.6	630.7	350.1	280.6	11.9	19.6	(31.0)	0.7	—	217.4	15.9
1982	n.a.	n.a.	414.2	n.a.	5.3	n.a.	(35.0)	1.8	—	n.a.	(10.0)
1983/1-6	n.a.	n.a.	n.a.	n.a.	1.1	n.a.	n.a.	3.6	—	n.a.	(5.0)

Note: Figures in parentheses are Wharton estimates. In the case of East Germany, except for years 1975 and 1977, official statistics on trade with individual Middle Eastern countries are available only in the form of total trade turnover, i.e., the sum of total exports and imports. Through painstaking reconstruction, Wharton was able to separate export and import transactions for the remaining years under study—these are tentative estimates, but probably quite accurate.

Source: Official Soviet and East European foreign trade statistics.

Table 7

Trade Balances of Centrally Planned Economies with Six Most Important Trade Partners in the Middle East, 1975-83 (in million dollars)

Year	All CPEs	CMEA seven	Soviet Union	Eastern Europe (CMEA Six)							
				Total	Bulgaria	Czecho-slovakia	East Germany	Hungary	Poland	Romania	Yugoslavia
				Total for Six Middle Eastern Countries (Algeria, Egypt, Iran, Iraq, Libya, Syria)							
1975	1,930	2,210	1,479	731.1	211.4	208.3	16.8	−8.6	181.1	122.1	−280.4
1976	2,517	2,740	2,010	729.9	216.2	242.8	(39.4)	50.3	236.9	−55.7	−222.8
1977	4,306	4,447	3,485	960.9	286.8	175.2	14.4	114.1	250.2	−120.2	−140.2
1978	4,941	5,127	4,372	756.0	409.7	351.7	(70.0)	88.9	112.0	−276.3	−186.5
1979	4,041	4,510	4,708	−197.8	398.8	363.0	(61.2)	115.6	−86.6	−1,049.8	−469.1
1980	3,331	3,910	4,285	−374.6	670.4	509.7	(−136.9)	179.2	−16.8	−1,580.2	−579.6
1981	8,299	8,141	5,049	3,091.9	980.3	596.7	(402.2)	445.8	392.4	274.5	158.3
1982	8,495	8,118	5,721	2,397.2	933.3	(470.0)	(320.6)	308.0	615.3	− (250.0)	377.3
1983/1-6	n.a.	n.a.	n.a.	n.a.	374.6	n.a.	n.a.	−77.9	18.1	n.a.	(230.0)

Table 8

Share of Six Middle Eastern Countries in Total Non-Socialist (Dollar Area) Exports and Imports of Centrally Planned Economies, 1975-83

				Eastern Europe (CMEA Six)							
Year	All CPEs	CMEA seven	Soviet Union	Total	Bulgaria	Czecho-slovakia	East Germany	Hungary	Poland	Romania	Yugoslavia
				Percentage Share in Exports							
1975	n.a.	n.a.	24.0	n.a.	31.3	15.8	9.7	10.7	7.1	17.9	11.9
1980	n.a.	n.a.	16.8	n.a.	23.8	14.8	(9.6)	10.8	7.8	16.9	16.7
1982	n.a.	n.a.	21.1	n.a.	43.0	15.4	(10.8)	20.2	13.0	27.5	30.0
				Percentage Share in Imports							
1975	n.a.	n.a.	9.5	n.a.	5.5	6.1	6.5	7.4	1.6	13.1	9.3
1980	n.a.	n.a.	5.0	n.a.	9.8	3.6	(9.3)	5.4	7.1	33.2	13.2
1982	n.a.	n.a.	7.7	n.a.	17.2	4.4	(8.3)	11.1	1.6	41.3	13.0

Source: Wharton calculation on the basis of official Soviet and East European foreign trade statistics.

Table 9

Trade Balances of Six Middle Eastern Countries with Eastern Europe Including Yugoslavia, 1975-82 (in million dollars; based on mirror East European trade statistics)

Year	Six countries	Algeria	Egypt	Iran	Iraq	Libya	Syria
1975	−450.7	38.6	27.9	−81.9	51.4	−357.3	−129.4
1976	−507.1	−131.6	−46.3	−18.6	334.6	−293.6	−351.6
1977	−820.7	−241.0	−128.1	12.8	374.2	−411.6	−427.0
1978	−569.5	−238.8	−226.3	50.2	711.4	−457.0	−409.0
1979	666.9	−263.8	−177.7	197.0	1,480.2	−173.6	−395.2
1980	954.2	−215.2	−249.5	341.4	1,477.4	−71.8	−328.1
1981	−3,250.2	−234.2	−374.8	168.2	1,934.5	−642.4	−232.5
1982	−2,019.9	n.a.	n.a.	n.a.	n.a.	n.a.	n.a.

Source: Wharton calculation on the basis of data presented in Tables 5 and 6 above.

Table 10

Exports of Machinery and Equipment (SITC 7 including arms) by Centrally Planned Economies to Six Most Important Trade Partners in the Middle East, 1975-83 (in million dollars)

				Eastern Europe (CMEA Six)							
Year	All CPEs	CMEA seven	Soviet Union	Total	Bulgaria	Czecho-slovakia	East Germany	Hungary	Poland	Ro-mania***	Yugo-slavia
				Total for Six Middle Eastern Countries (Algeria, Egypt, Iran, Iraq, Libya, Syria)							
1975	3,440	3,354	2,384**	970.5	111.2	216.4	192.4	104.8	175.7	170.0	85.8
1976	3,997	3,892	2,729**	1,163.1	123.0	238.9	205.9	124.4	183.7	287.2	104.8
1977	5,678	5,490	4,189**	1,301.3	127.7	270.9	204.8	105.7	196.9	395.3	187.7
1978	6,236	6,062	4,663**	1,398.5	174.1	301.7	240.7	122.3	185.4	(374.3)	174.8
1979	6,520	6,332	4,942**	1,390.0	126.3	314.8	254.5	111.4	208.2	(374.8)	188.3
1980	7,252	6,971	4,841**	2,130.4	272.6	438.0	359.8	147.1	373.9	(539.0)	281.0
1981	(9,010)	(8,579)	(5,036)**	3,542.6	493.0	571.4	463.5	253.2	383.8	(1,377.7)	431.6
1982	(10,494)	(10,051)	(6,376)**	(3,675.0)	(583.0)	(510.0)	(642.0)	(346.0)	(514.0)	(1,080.0)	(443.0)
				Algeria							
1975	88.8	86.7	52.3*	34.4	1.3	0.9	11.7	6.3	5.4	8.8	2.1
1976	166.5	166.2	98.6*	67.6	10.9	2.8	15.9	12.4	3.0	22.6	0.3
1977	211.7	209.6	75.3*	134.3	30.0	9.9	21.1	26.5	6.0	40.8	2.1
1978	244.3	227.0	62.1*	164.9	79.0	7.8	28.1	18.5	9.6	21.9	17.3
1979	224.9	214.4	69.2*	145.2	56.5	4.5	33.8	13.8	15.7	20.9	10.5
1980	298.7	269.3	58.6*	210.7	103.7	10.8	52.2	12.8	19.6	12.2	29.4
1981	(337.8)	(252.6)	(24.0*)	228.6	100.5	32.0	49.9	12.3	24.5	9.4	85.2
1982	n.a.	n.a.	(63.0)*	n.a.	(83.0)	n.a.	(71.0)	(17.0)	(17.0)	n.a.	(142.0)

					Egypt						
1975	296.2	272.3	109.9*	162.4	18.3	34.5	53.9	15.5	25.2	15.0	23.9
1976	254.2	218.9	73.7*	145.2	12.2	36.9	46.8	5.7	13.9	29.7	35.3
1977	329.3	283.4	108.0*	175.4	7.9	44.8	53.2	3.6	23.0	42.9	45.9
1978	325.6	275.4	101.1*	174.3	8.0	33.1	36.1	5.6	26.1	65.4	50.2
1979	330.7	290.3	80.8*	209.5	10.7	24.2	42.7	7.8	19.2	104.9	40.4
1980	372.2	305.4	91.4*	214.0	5.0	40.5	33.1	15.5	20.1	99.8	66.8
1981	(459.0)	(364.9)	(130.0)*	234.9	5.9	40.2	36.3	20.5	23.7	108.3	94.1
1982	n.a.	n.a.	(121.0)*	n.a.	(2.0)	(54.0)	(34.0)	(14.0)	(19.0)	n.a.	(87.0)
					Iran						
1975	425.4	419.8	257.5*	162.3	3.9	24.1	4.9	11.7	36.6	81.1	5.6
1976	410.1	404.6	187.0*	217.6	4.2	48.6	6.7	13.9	42.0	102.2	5.5
1977	452.4	447.7	228.2*	219.5	3.4	52.2	11.2	13.4	34.9	104.4	4.7
1978	405.1	396.5	217.5*	179.0	2.8	30.9	12.8	11.1	29.4	(92.0)	8.6
1979	307.8	303.6	178.4*	125.2	2.0	21.0	21.3	8.8	7.1	(65.0)	4.2
1980	405.1	392.0	136.4*	255.6	14.1	18.6	62.1	22.9	15.9	(122.0)	13.1
1981	(623.4)	(604.4)	(175.0)*	(429.4)	18.7	18.2	115.4	44.8	25.3	(207.0)	19.0
1982	n.a.	n.a.	(141.0)*	n.a.	(25.0)	n.a.	(186.0)	(80.0)	(23.0)	n.a.	(30.0)
					Iraq						
1975	534.5	497.8	191.0*	306.8	47.7	50.1	94.1	59.6	40.9	14.4	36.7
1976	558.9	530.3	237.5*	292.8	30.4	60.6	71.5	68.7	54.2	7.4	28.6
1977	545.7	477.6	257.0*	220.6	9.1	51.1	52.7	49.3	52.8	5.6	68.1
1978	778.0	720.1	422.9*	297.2	50.4	32.8	84.1	61.2	58.7	(10.0)	57.9
1979	883.3	803.9	464.6*	339.3	29.2	67.0	80.8	72.9	69.4	(20.0)	79.4
1980	1,027.0	916.8	305.9*	610.9	63.8	113.7	108.8	71.3	113.3	(140.0)	110.2
1981	(2,188.9)	(2,045.2)	(299.0)*	(1,746.2)	267.9	163.9	155.3	142.5	146.6	(870.0)	143.7
1982	n.a.	n.a.	(373.0)*	n.a.	(385.0)	n.a.	(200.0)	(178.0)	(240.0)	n.a.	(124.0)

					Libya						
1975	220.1	203.6	0.8*	202.8	37.8	73.9	0.8	5.2	59.3	25.8	16.5
1976	223.0	192.3	0.0*	192.3	60.4	32.5	0.5	1.2	63.5	34.2	30.7
1977	297.1	232.5	10.6*	221.9	72.9	22.7	0.9	1.3	71.0	53.1	63.6
1978	365.5	329.7	53.1*	271.6	27.0	108.6	0.7	16.6	55.7	(63.0)	35.8
1979	511.5	465.4	223.6*	241.8	20.9	102.3	1.8	0.6	70.2	(46.0)	46.1
1980	750.9	694.0	244.2*	449.8	79.7	129.6	0.7	10.8	184.0	(45.0)	56.9
1981	(916.8)	(829.8)	(249.0)*	580.8	87.0	201.8	17.8	20.7	155.5	(98.0)	87.0
1982	n.a.	n.a.	(300.0)*	n.a.	(80.0)	n.a.	(35.0)	(17.0)	(210.0)	n.a.	(57.0)
					Syria						
1975	175.7	174.7	72.9*	101.8	2.2	32.9	27.0	6.5	8.3	24.9	1.0
1976	334.1	329.7	82.1*	247.6	4.9	57.5	64.5	22.5	7.1	91.1	4.4
1977	392.2	389.9	60.3*	329.6	4.4	90.2	65.7	11.6	9.2	148.5	2.3
1978	417.9	412.9	101.4*	311.5	6.9	88.5	78.9	9.3	5.9	(122.0)	5.0
1979	462.6	454.9	125.9*	329.0	7.0	95.8	74.1	7.5	26.6	(118.0)	7.7
1980	548.5	543.9	154.5*	389.4	6.9	124.8	102.9	13.8	21.0	(120.0)	4.6
1981	434.3	431.7	(109.0)*	322.7	13.0	115.3	88.8	12.4	8.2	(85.0)	2.6
1982	n.a.	n.a.	(123.0)*	n.a.	(8.0)	n.a.	(116.0)	(40.0)	(5.0)	n.a.	(3.0)

*Excluding the bulk of Soviet arms exports to individual Middle Eastern countries. The reported figures include only exports of investment machinery and equipment and exports of military machinery with potential dual use (such as military trucks which could also be used for civilian transport).

**Including the estimated value of arms sales not reported in official bilateral Soviet trade statistics with individual Middle Eastern countries.

***In the case of Romania, the machinery classification corresponds to CMEA category CTN 1 rather than SITC 7.

Note: All figures in parentheses are Wharton estimates.

Source: 1975-81 (except for Romania): Economic Commission for Europe, United Nations, *Bulletin of Statistics on World Trade in Engineering Products*, annual. In the case of Romania, the data not enclosed in parentheses are official unpublished statistics.

SASHA GROZDANOVA (BULGARIA)

Trade and Economic Relations between Bulgaria and the Arab Countries

Under the conditions of international detente, the developing countries have come to play a growing role in international economic relations, and their influence in dealing with a number of important problems in the world economy and politics has become stronger.

The resolute demands of many of the developing countries for a reorganization of international economic relations and the active struggle they are conducting against imperialist exploitation are supported by the Soviet Union and the other countries of the socialist community. Friendly relations, based on mutual advantage, a respect for sovereignty, and noninterference in internal affairs, are being created on this basis between the CMEA and the developing countries. These relations are, moreover, not based on class solidarity, since most of the developing countries have embarked on the capitalist path, and only a few of them have a socialist orientation. Rather, these are relations of a new type, characterized by international support and assistance shown by the socialist countries to the developing nations.

Bulgaria maintains especially active and multifaceted economic ties with the Arab countries.[1] This is due to a number of factors: the policies of our country with regard to this group of countries, historically evolved traditions, geographic proximity, convenient transportation, a complementarity of economic structures, etc.

"T''rgovsko-ikonomicheskite otnosheniia na b''lgariia s arabskite strani," *V''nshna t''rgoviia*, 1981, no. 9, pp. 7–10. Translated by Michel Vale.

Trade relations play an important role in the ties between the People's Republic of Bulgaria and the Arab countries. In the last few years (1979 to 1980) more than half of our trade with the developing countries and about 4% of our total trade was with this group of nations. Our trade volume with the Arab countries rose from 123 millions levs in 1970 to 936.2 million levs in 1980.

Bulgaria has especially active relations with the progressive Arab regimes. Trade with Libya, Iraq, Algeria, and Syria accounts for 77% of our total trade with the Arab world. For example, in 1979 Libya was our tenth most important trading partner, with a volume of 280.8 million levs, while our trade in 1980 with Iraq amounted to 137.9 million levs, with Algeria 104.7 million levs, and with Syria 61.8 million levs, which placed these countries among the ten most important trading partners of Bulgaria among the developing countries.

An analysis of the structure of trade between Bulgaria and the Arab countries in the past decades gives an impression of a quite pronounced tendency toward increase in the relative proportion of means of production, or capital goods, in exports to these countries. In 1978 machinery and equipment accounted for over 50%, which is quite important for the industrialization of Arab countries, for their socioeconomic development, and for international economic relations in general. But the growth rate of our machinery and equipment exports to the Arab countries still lags behind the rate and volume of their imports of this type of product. Some of the other countries (Algeria and Iraq) have in recent years begun to organize their own production of this type of machinery (tractors, metal-working machinery, etc.), which ultimately will reduce their imports of them. At the same time, competition from the developed capitalist countries[2] has been increasing, and the requirements of the Arab countries with regard to the quality and technical level of imported machinery and equipment have also increased.

The structure of Bulgarian exports of machinery and equipment is relatively varied. The principal exports are metal-working machinery, farm equipment, lifting and transport equipment, and power and electrotechnical machinery and equipment. The largest orders of metal-working machinery go to Iraq and Syria. In the future the

Arab countries expect to increase their import of metal-working machinery independent of their own efforts to expand their own production of such technology. The relative proportion of high precision and highly specialized machinery in particular will increase.

The Arab countries will continue to rely on imports to meet their needs for lifting and transport machinery. For example, in 1979 Bulgaria delivered to Iraq, Lebanon, and Egypt 214 electric trucks, 177 motor vehicles, and 88 electric hoists. Our exports are well received in these countries, but lately they have increasingly frequently met with competition from the capitalist countries, especially Japan.

The Arab world has an especially great interest in Bulgarian farm machinery. The market for tilling machinery, irrigation equipment, and harvesting machinery is especially promising. Bulgaria exports various types of power and electric machinery and equipment to the Arab countries.

The increase in the relative share of Bulgarian machinery and equipment in the imports of Arab countries is due to the process of industrialization going on in these countries, and that is ultimately dependent on a rational and efficient utilization of the advantages that participation of any country in the international division of labor provides.

The share of the Arab countries in Bulgarian imports from the developing countries is also considerable. Initially it consisted exclusively of agricultural products: rice, oils, citrus fruits, cotton, etc. Our country is a promising and stable market for the sale of traditional agricultural products from these countries. But Bulgaria is not only an importer but also an exporter of certain types of agricultural raw material and foods to the Arab countries. These products, many of which are traditional, make up about 17% of our exports to these countries. This is one more bit of evidence of the fundamentally new approach of our country to the problems that the Arab countries are facing, including the food problem.

In the last few years we have also imported finished products and semifinished products from the Arab countries. The industrialization that is taking place in the Arab countries gives reason to believe that this process will continue to grow considerably in the future. More and more frequently, the percentage of finished products is specified when long-term trade agreements are signed. Thus, in the program for long-term cooperation between Bulgaria and Iraq, the import of tape recorders, fluorescent lamps, cloth, and shoes from Iraq is specified. We can reasonably expect that the processing industry, which is developing at a rapid pace in the Arab countries, will be providing new and even more interesting goods for export. Products from the chemical industry, a few types of instruments, etc., produced in the Arab countries are turning up more and more frequently on our markets.

Importation of raw materials from the Arab countries is growing rapidly. They comprise about 80% of our imports from these countries. Some considerable changes have also taken place in their structure. The share of raw materials of an industrial nature is increasing. Imports of petroleum and mineral raw materials, phosphates, ores, and metals are increasing most rapidly. The Arab world is the second largest supplier of oil to Bulgaria, after the USSR. Our ties with Libya, Algeria, and Iraq are most promising.

The imports of oil and mineral raw materials should also continue to grow due to the expansion of the production of these materials, and this requires the development of new deposits and the installation of additional productive capacities. The Arab countries do not have sufficient experience, and many of them do not have sufficient means, to achieve such goals independently. The cooperation provided by Bulgaria in searching for and developing natural resources is considerable and is in accordance with mutual interests. In Algeria, Tunisia, Syria, Morocco, and Iraq, Bulgarian geological teams are exploring for deposits, designing ore fields, and compiling geological maps. Our assistance in production, financing, and scientific and technological matters for developing certain sources of raw materials will ensure that the exports of these materials to our country will continue to grow.

In addition to an increase in the trade volume between Bulgaria and the Arab countries, other more progressive forms of economic relations are also developing. Cooperation in technical assistance is an example of a higher stage of development of these relations.

In the past few years a form of economic cooperation that is comparatively new for our country has also grown. This is the export of turnkey projects to countries in this region. The principal importers are Iraq, Syria, Algeria, and Libya. Bulgaria primarily provides projects for the foodstuffs industry: canned goods factories, citrus fruit greenhouses, light industry firms, factories for the production of electric motors, assembly lines, etc.

Our country has also furnished Iraq with the canned goods plants in Bakuba, Numania, Khair, and Shaklava, and a plant for starch and dextrin. The delivery of fodder plants, fruit juice plants, fruit greenhouses, and a poultry farm is scheduled.

The export of whole units of equipment for mines and concentrating plants has also been quite successful. Thus an orefield and a concentrating plant for phosphates have been constructed and equipped in Syria, while equipment for developing iron ore deposits has been delivered to Algeria, etc.

The activity of our country in this area helps to promote the all-round development of certain branches of industry in the Arab countries. This comprehensive technological assistance has a very considerable effect, and its development in the future should be expanded. For Bulgaria it is an important means for increasing the export of machinery and raw materials, and at the same time it secures the import of some raw materials, semifinished products, and finished products.

Another important area of external economic relations being developed by our country with the Arab countries is the designing and building of various types of projects. Highways, airports, bridges, public buildings, reservoirs, and irrigation systems are being designed and built. The first such projects were in Syria: a grain storage silo, the Rastan and Makharde reservoirs, etc. Two airports with all the ancillary equipment and buildings were designed and built by Bulgarian construction organizations. The municipal airport at Baghdad, the sports stadium in Tunis, the sport complexes in Tripoli and Bengazi, the airport at Sebkha, the sewage system in Tripoli, and a good number of the polyclinics and hospitals in Libya have been built by Bulgarian builders.

Construction projects by Bulgaria in the Arab countries have concentrated mainly on projects of a representative character, aimed at improving the infrastructure and directly tied in with economic development. These are projects that help strengthen the public sector of the economy in the Arab countries and establish the foundations for the development of new sectors of industry.

Scientific and technological cooperation with the Arab countries is also developing in a positive direction. As a result of the long years of colonial enslavement, illiteracy in these countries was widespread, while specialists were extremely few in number, and educated mainly in the former metropolises. With the rapid progress of industrialization in the Arab countries, they are experiencing an acute need for skilled scientific cadres and specialists. They can be obtained from the developed capitalist countries. But since this is a part of the neocolonial policies of these countries, the Arab nations are seeking other sources for such aid. This creates objective conditions for a rapid increase in the scale of scientific assistance provided by the socialist countries. Such assistance differs fundamentally from that provided by the West. Bulgaria and the other socialist countries do not pursue covert objectives when they send their specialists or accept Arab youth in their educational institutions to educate them. Thousands of Bulgarian scientists and specialists are providing assistance in these countries in agriculture, industry, transportation, and public health. We have been sending our specialists since the late '50s. Bulgarian specialists are working in Syria, Kuwait, Iraq, Morocco, and elsewhere. Bulgaria sets up educational establishments in Arab countries, sends teachers, and receives students learning a speciality or doing graduate work. In the last few years the number of youth from Arab countries receiving an education in our country has increased rapidly. These students are mainly from Algeria, Yemen, Lebanon, and Iraq. This process will grow since the need for specialists is increasing steadily, as a consequence of the accelerated industrialization in the Arab countries.

Cooperation between Bulgaria and the Arab countries will continue to develop and deepen in the future. Friendly visits at the highest party and state levels will promote this. The Theses of the Twelfth Congress of the Bulgarian Party stressed once again the readiness of our country to "pursue a line of accelerated development of external economic relations with the developing countries," a readiness and willingness to support the "struggle of the Arab peoples against imperialism, Zionism and reaction. . . ."[3]

Of course, a number of problems arise in the process of deepening and expanding economic relations between Bulgaria and the Arab countries. Dealing with these problems is rendered more difficult by the variety of political regimes in the Arab countries, the frequent internal contractions culminating in armed conflict, and the political instability of the region.

Problems are also created by the close economic ties with the imperialist countries that were built up during the period of colonialism. We must also improve the quality of our goods to the level of international standards, so that they will be suited to the specific climatic conditions of the Arab world, etc. In addition there are the Arab countries' ambitious programs for economic development, in which accelerated construction of factories is envisioned in the textile and foodstuffs industries, machinery construction, and metallurgy; Bulgaria could considerably increase its exports of turnkey factories since it has industrial experience and personnel.

A traditional element in our cooperation with the Arab countries is the export of agricultural technology. For further growth, what is necessary now is the organization of high-level technical servicing of exported machinery and equipment. Good service and a regular supply of spare parts are of utmost importance for improving Bulgaria's reputation as an exporter of machinery and an additional factor in boosting sales.

A major problem is filling orders to the Arab countries on time and improving our advertising activity. We must also devote more attention to the study of Arab markets and cheaper and more effective transport routes.

There are also problems in our imports from Arab countries. The extreme underdevelopment of some Arab countries and their negligible export potential (with the exception of oil) cause a number of difficulties. Some countries are trying to achieve a balance in their trade turnover with Bulgaria, which is especially important for them. They try to meet their payments for imports with matching exports; but because of their limited export possibilities, they place deliberate limits on our exports.

The rapid growth of the oil-processing industry in the Arab world has created possibilities for increasing the import of petroleum products. Deliveries of our goods would require matching deliveries of raw material important for resolving some of our raw material problems.

One of the principal factors contributing to the deepening of our relations with the Arab world is socialist economic integration. Through it productive forces are steadily improving, and the productivity of social labor is rising. This means an increase in export opportunities for Bulgaria.

The achievements of the CMEA countries in developing their national economies exert an attraction on the young independent countries. As a confirmation of this interest, in 1975 the first agreement on cooperation was signed between the CMEA and an Arab country, namely Iraq. The purpose was the development of multilateral economic cooperation along with a broadening and deepening of contacts on a bilateral basis.

Joint coordinated participation of CMEA countries takes place in construction work, the supplying of turnkey projects, and geological explorations in the Arab countries. Bulgaria and the USSR have already completed a number of joint projects: phosphate mines in Jordan, Morocco, and Tunisia, a plant for the production of artificial fertilizer, sulphur, and phosphoric acid in Iraq. In Algeria natural resources are being developed with the joint efforts of Soviet, Bulgarian, and Romanian specialists. Bulgaria, Romania, Czechoslovakia, and the GDR have built and equipped three projects in the phosphate extraction industry in Syria.

But the question of broader specialization and cooperation in production between the CMEA and Arab countries remains unresolved. One of the main reasons for this is the tremendous industrial backwardness of the Arab world.

An improvement in the mechanism of cooperation plays an important role in stimulating various forms of foreign economic relations. An organizational and legal mechanism for regulating these relations has been developed. It provides for bilateral agreements between governments for trade, economic, and scientific and technological cooperation and cooperation in constructing specific projects. Agreements of a new type, resulting from the adoption of long-term programs, are also concluded. These secure a stable basis for the development of mutual economic ties and constitute a factor for stabilizing the economies of the Arab countries. Bulgaria has set up mixed intergovernment commissions with most of these countries. These commissions set up working groups, sections, and subcommissions in which well-known specialists participate. This helps to maintain the interests of these countries and serves as an instrument for agreeing on joint measures.

All-round economic and scientific and technological cooperation with the Arab countries and a policy aimed at supporting their struggle to achieve political and economic independence objectively strengthen the positions of the antiimperialist front in the interests of detente and create the means for a fundamental restructuring of contemporary international economic relations, so that in the future we can also expect a deepening of these relations. This is one of the effective ways to encourage the Arab countries to choose the path of progressive social change.

Notes

1. The Arab countries are: Algeria, Bahrain, Egypt, Iraq, Yemen, Jordan, the People's Republic of Yemen, Kuwait, Qatar, Libya, Lebanon, Mauritania, Morocco, the United Arab Emirates, Oman, Sudan, Saudi Arabia, Syria, Somalia and Tunisia. According to UN data, in 1978 the population of the Arab countries increased to almost 145 million, on a territory covering 14 million square kilometers on the two continents of Asia and Africa. About 55% of the world's oil reserves and one-sixth of its natural gas reserves have been discovered on the territory of the Arab countries.
2. For example, in the past few years the developed capitalist countries have become major trading partners of Egypt, Tunisia, and Morocco.
3. *Robotnichesko delo*, April 10, 1981.

A. KOZOLAEV (USSR)

Cooperation of the CMEA Countries with Syria

The CMEA countries, in accordance with their policy of peaceful coexistence, and in the interests of social progress, are deepening their trade and economic relations with other states, regardless of their social system, on the principles of equality, mutual advantage, and respect for sovereignty. Special attention is given in this to the expansion of trade and to economic and scientific and technical interaction with the developing countries.

The cooperation of the CMEA countries with Syria is contributing to the development of key sectors of its economy, of decisive importance for the economic independence and an increase in the well-being of the people. These sectors are mainly industry and power, transport and communications, irrigation and water projects, agriculture, and the training of native-born skilled personnel.

The assistance given to Syria by the countries of the socialist community helps to strengthen the state sector. The vast majority of the products in contemporary branches of industry are produced by enterprises constructed in the state sector with CMEA participation: these include 100% of the oil and phosphorus-containing raw material extracted and processed, the production of nitrogen fertilizers, more than 80% of the electric power developed, etc.

The Soviet Union occupies a leading place in this cooperation. After the first agreement was signed between the USSR and Syria on economic and technical cooperation (1957), 38 important industrial

---

Russian text © 1984 by "Nauka" Publishers. "Sotudnichestvo stran-chlenov SEV s Siriei," *Ekonomicheskoe sotrudnichestvo stran-chlenov SEV*, 1984, no. 2, pp. 67-69. Translated by Michel Vale.

projects were built and started up by the joint efforts of Soviet specialists. These included the hydroelectric power plant on the Euphrates River, the largest in the Near East, including a dam 58 meters high and over 4 kilometers long, a power plant of 800,000 kilowatts, and a water reservoir of 12 billion square meters. The importance of the Euphrates hydroelectric complex for Syria's economy is tremendous: each year the power station generates 3.0 billion kilowatt hours and covers 60% of the country's entire need for electric power; the artificial lake will eventually irrigate over 600,000 hectares of arid lands around the hydroelectric project, doubling the area of irrigated lands in the country.

Soviet organizations are helping design and construct 220-kilowatt and 2,600-kilometers-long high-voltage lines. Most of them, about 2,120 kilometers, have already been built. These lines enabled the large industrial centers of the country, including the cities of Damascus, Aleppo, Homs, and oil-extracting areas in the northeast of the country, to be provided with cheap electric power and also let power be exported to Lebanon and Jordan.

On the calculation of specialists, the costs of building the hydroelectric complex have been completely paid off merely from the use of the electric power generated by the Euphrates power plant.

A modern petroleum-extracting industry in Syria has been created and is developing with the economic and technical assistance of the Soviet Union. Six deposits have begun operations in the northeast of the country, and more than 100 million tons of oil have been extracted. We should point out that the geological prospecting was done by Western companies, in particular the firm Concordia, which concluded that there were no industrial reserves of oil in Syria and broke off their prospecting. Soviet specialists not only demonstrated the presence of this extremely valuable raw material deep under the earth in Syria but helped to set up oil fields and to extract oil.

The USSR is giving technical aid in transport construction: a modern system of railroads has been created practically from scratch in the country. At present there are 1,280 km railroads in operation. In 1980 the line between Kamyshla and Latakia, running over 758 kilometers and connecting the rich agricultural and petroleum fields in the northeast of the country with the seaport of Latakia, was commissioned. Roads from the phosphate fields near Palmyra to the seaport Tartus, through the cities of Mhin-Homs-Accari, extending 285 kilometers, have been temporarily activated. A railroad was laid on the Damascus-Homs line (208 km). The USSR has supplied Syria with modern mainline and switching locomotives, cars, platforms, and cisterns.

Soviet organizations participated in the expansion of the seaport of Latakia from 1.6 million to 3 million tons of freight turnover per year; it is ultimately planned to increase this figure to 7 million tons. In 1981 a breakwater was completed, the first project for reconstruction of the port.

A major irrigation project and the development of new lands, mainly near the Euphrates hydroelectric unit, are being undertaken through the combined efforts of the USSR and Syria. This will make it possible to increase the area of irrigated lands by approximately 15%. A pumping station with a capacity of 36 cubic meters per second was put into operation in 1979 for irrigating 21,000 hectares of land from the Euphrates reservoir. More than 16,000 hectares of land have already been prepared for development; the sowed area under wheat, sugarbeet, cotton, and other crops made up about 10,000 hectares.

The USSR and Czechoslovakia helped build the first nitrogen fertilizer plant near Homs Lake, with a capacity of 150,000 tons of ammonium and calcium nitrate per year.

Economic cooperation of the CMEA countries contributes to the comprehensive development of entire sectors of the country's economy.

Soviet geologists have found phosphorite deposits with total reserves of about one billion tons, including three large ones near Palmyra. Bulgaria, Poland, and Romania are participating in the construction of plants for the mining and exploitation of these deposits. A factory for the production of tertiary superphosphate, with capacity of 450,000 tons per year, was built with the help of Romanian organizations in Homs.

A large petroleum-processing refinery with a capacity of 5.2 million tons per year was built in Homs with the participation of

Czechoslovakia; Romania helped build another refinery in Banias with a capacity of 6 million tons of petroleum per year. These refineries completely cover the domestic needs of the country for petroleum products.

As a result of cooperation with the CMEA countries, Syria has stopped importing petroleum and, in fact, has begun to sell it on the world market. Oil has become the main source of the foreign currency earnings of the country. It covers about 70% of the earnings from exports.

Syria is the first Arab country in which the extraction and processing of oil reserves take place without the participation of the monopolies. Completely new branches of industry, the petroleum-processing and the petroleum-extracting industries, are totally within the state sector and play an extremely important role in the country's economy.

Czechoslovakia has also helped build a tire factory in Ham with a capacity of 600,000 tires per year, two middle-wave radio stations, two sugar plants in Homs and Ham, two shoe factories in Damascus and Homs with a total capacity of 1,500 pairs of shoes per day, a textile factory in Idlib that processes 10.6 thousand tons of cotton, a weaving factory in Latackia with a capacity of 20 million meters of cloth per year; the erection and expansion of thermoelectric power plants are also objects of cooperation. In 1983 another sugar plant was completed in Deir-ez-Zore with a capacity of processing 4,000 tons of sugarbeets per day.

The GDR has helped build four cement plants, a large workshop for repairing farm equipment, a cotton fabric factory in Khasek with a capacity of 75,000 spindles, and 10 flour mills with a total capacity of 2,500 tons per day. The construction of another three cement plants is being completed in Tartus, Adra, and Mysylme. Electric power lines are being built on a large-scale basis to electrify the Syrian countryside. Two cattle farms are being organized. The GDR also provides complex medical equipment in considerable quantities for rural clinics, hospitals, and medical centers.

Polish specialists have participated in the construction of a small caliber sheet steel plant in Ham with a capacity of 110,000 tons of sheet steel and wire per year, a foundry in Aleppo with a capacity of

6,000 tons of cast iron per year, and two large slaughterhouses in Damascus and Aleppo (2,400 head of cattle per day in each).

Hungary has helped to build a tire factory, an electric bulb factory, and a central telephone exchange in the city of Damascus. Three canned goods plants have been completed in Idlibe, Deir-ez-Zore, and Haseka, with assembly lines for the processing of vegetables, and nine petroleum storage tanks. Together with Soviet organizations, Hungary has participated in the construction of a plant in Aleppo for reinforced concrete blocks and centrifugal supports.

Bulgaria has helped to build two cement plants and a grain elevator with a capacity of 35,000 cubic meters in the port of Latakia. The construction work has been completed on the most difficult (mountain) part of the railroad from the Oronta River to Latakia (90 kilometers). Much has been done by Bulgarian specialists to set up the "Asharna" irrigation system to water 20,000 hectares and the Makharda and Rastan reservoirs.

About 250 industrial enterprises and other projects are being built in cooperation with the CMEA countries in Syria, and of them over 200 are already in operation.

The countries of the community have given the Syrian government long-term credit under favorable conditions for paying for deliveries of complex equipment, design work, and other services. The credits are usually paid off through the export of traditional goods, especially cotton, as well as oil, phosphorus-containing raw materials, and products of domestic industry. The demand for these goods in the CMEA countries is growing steadily.

The CMEA countries provide Syria with considerable help in solving its acute problem of training native personnel for industry, the energy sector, transport, agriculture, science, and culture. Trained workers and specialists are being taught directly in the process of construction, assembly, and operation of industrial enterprises, as well as in educational establishments set up with the help of the CMEA countries.

At present there are more than 1,600 specialists from the fraternal countries working in Syria who are providing technical assistance and transmitting their rich experience and knowledge.

Syrian leaders estimate that the construction of the Euphrates hydroelectric complex has become a real place of learning. Several hundred workers in different areas of specialization have been trained here. The educational center for training skilled workers in Aleppo for the Euphrates hydroelectric project has graduated more than 3,000 skilled workers in 26 areas of specialization. They are currently working at various construction projects throughout the country.

The number of Syrian students studying in colleges, universities, and secondary schools in the CMEA countries is growing. On January 1, 1983, 4,300 Syrian citizens were studying in colleges, universities, and secondary specialized schools in the CMEA countries. Over 6,700 Syrians have received education in them. The CMEA scholarship fund was created in the 1974/75 school year. From 1974 to 1982, 200 Syrian citizens with CMEA scholarships were admitted to colleges and universities in the countries of the socialist community, and 60 of them have already received their diplomas.

The broad cooperation of the CMEA countries with Syria is promoting the rapid movement of this country along the path of progress toward acquiring economic independence, is helping to solve current socioeconomic problems, and is raising the living standards of broad layers of the population.

V. IVANENKO (USSR)

Twenty Years of Soviet-Iranian Economic and Technical Cooperation

Twenty years have passed since the first agreement on economic and technical cooperation between the USSR and Iran was signed; this agreement laid the foundations for broad economic ties between the two countries in major sectors of the economy.

Our country has always tried to build its economic relations with Iran on the basis of a good neighbor policy, mutual advantage, and balanced accounts. The twenty years of history of broad economic and technical cooperation between the two countries is testimony to this.

The first Soviet-Iranian agreement provided for cooperation in the construction of two dams with hydroelectric power stations on the Araks River dividing the two countries, a sturgeon fish-breeding plant on the Sefidrud River to replenish the reserves of sturgeon in the Caspian Sea, and eleven grain elevators.

This agreement was followed by a number of others which stipulated an arrangement between the governments of the USSR and Iran for cooperation in the construction in Iran of a large number of industrial and other facilities playing an important role in strengthening the economic potential of that country.

 "20 let sovetsko-iranskogo ekonomicheskogo i tekhnicheskogo sotrudnichestva," *Vneshniaia torgovlia*, 1984, no. 1, pp. 24–27. Translated by Michel Vale.

The author is Responsible Secretary of the Standing Soviet-Iranian Committee on Economic Cooperation.

Indeed, even the mere enumeration of the projects and endeavors in which the USSR and Iran have cooperated (there are about 160 of them, more than a hundred of which have begun operation or are now completed) is testimony to the importance they have for strengthening Iran's national economy, providing employment for the population, developing vitally important sectors of the economy and the country's export potential, training national cadres, etc.

Among these projects are the only ferrous metallurgy plant in Iran with a full industrial cycle, namely, the Isfahan metallurgical factory with a capacity of 550,000 tons of steel per year; the coal and raw material base of the factory at the Chogart iron ore mine, a number of coal mines, and coal concentrating plants; the machinery factory in Araks with a capacity of 25,000 tons of products per year; hydroelectric power equipment on the border river Araks; 23 schools and institutions of learning with 6,500 places for training specialists in various areas; 48 grain elevators with a total capacity of over one million tons of grain, and two large thermoelectric power stations in the city of Akhvaz with a capacity of 1,260,000 kilowatts and in the city of Isfahan with a capacity of 800,000 kilowatts.

The Soviet Union has helped and will continue to help Iran in setting up these projects by providing modern complete equipment and machinery and materials and by sending Soviet specialists to Iran. The Soviet Union has granted Iran credits on advantageous terms for the construction of some projects. An important aspect of cooperation is the fact that Iran pays off these credits not in hard currency, as it is forced to do in economic relations with Western countries, but by supplying Iranian goods, in particular gas between 1970 and 1980, and at present crude oil.

The largest project of Soviet-Iranian economic and technical cooperation is the Isfahan metallurgical factory with its coal and raw material base. Iran had for decades purchased practically all the metal products it needed abroad, and hence it was natural that it should want to create its own metallurgical industry. The Iranians' repeated requests for assistance from the monopolies of the Western countries foundered on the unwillingness of the latter to lose a stable market for disposing of their own metal output in Iran. The former Chancellor of the FRG, L. Erhard, once declared that he preferred to see Iran a "country of roses and nightingales" and not an industrially developed country.

The principal "argument" for the negative attitude of the imperialist countries toward the idea of creating an Iranian national metallurgical industry was the fact that Iran had neither iron ore nor the coking coal necessary for producing steel. Many expeditions and "authoritative conclusions" of foreign experts in metallurgy cost the Iranian government some goodly sums of money but came not one step further toward the development of a real plan for creating a national metallurgical industry.

Only the Soviet Union responded with sympathy to the appeals of its neighbor. In January 1966 a Soviet-Iranian agreement on economic and technical cooperation was signed; Soviet organizations were to collaborate technologically with Iran in the construction of a metallurgical combine with a capacity of 500,000–600,000 tons of steel per year near the city of Isfahan, a machinery factory, and the northern part of the trans-Iranian gas pipeline, which ran from the deposits in the southern part of the country to the Soviet-Iranian border near Astara.

The designing of the industrial complex of the Isfahan metallurgical complex, with its coal and raw material base, so important for Iran, was done by the Soviet planning institutes "Gipromez," "Giprokoks," "Giproruda," and others. This project was constructed with the cooperation of the All-Union Association "Tiazhpromeksport," which furnished modern metallurgical equipment to the construction site and sent Soviet specialists to Iran as advisers. The plant's coal base was set up with the technical cooperation of the All-Union Association "Tsvetmetpromeksport."

Despite the pessimistic forecasts of some specialists in the Western countries about the lack of iron ore reserves and coking coal in Iran, Soviet geologists sent to Iran by the All-Union Association "Tekhnoeksport," together with their Iranian colleagues, succeeded in finding iron ore deposits sufficient to last for decades of operation of the metallurgical plant.

The construction of the Isfahan metallurgical plant and its necessary coal and raw material base caused a revolution not only in Iran's industry but also in the ideas of many Iranians about other nations, helped to increase employment and create new railroads and highways, and led to the development of housing construction and a growth in the number of skilled national cadres.

The Isfahan metallurgical plant began operation in March 1973. Thanks to the Iranian workers, who assiduously mastered the metallurgical industry, which was new for them, and to the broad experience of their Soviet mentors, the planned capacity of the Isfahan metallurgical plant was reached within a very short period, even by international standards. The plant began to produce an output on the designed scale within the very next year.

In its ten years of operation the Isfahan metallurgical plant has produced 5.6 million tons of steel, testimony to the high quality of Soviet metallurgical equipment installed in this facility.

The output of the metallurgical plant, especially rolled metal for construction, has a broad market in Iran and has made it possible to reduce considerably the hard currency expenditures which Iran had to shoulder from importing rolled steel from capitalist countries. According to statements by the leadership of the Iranian national steel foundry company, the plant has already paid back the funds invested in its construction twice over and is now operating above planned capacity. The construction of a second-generation plant whose capacity will be about 2 million tons of steel per year is currently nearing completion. When it begins operation, Iran will be able more fully to meet its own needs in metal products. The coal and raw material base of the plant is also being expanded at the same time.

The importance of this circumstance should be stressed since the operation of the Isfahan metallurgical plant is practically independent of raw material resources and materials from abroad. Soviet designers also included the construction of repair shops in the plant so that various types of metallurgical equipment could be repaired on the spot without having to rely on foreign firms.

A few months before the Isfahan metallurgical plant, the Araks machinery factory, built with the technical cooperation of the All-Union Association "Prommasheksport," began operations. This factory for heavy machinery construction, the largest in Iran, produces various goods for the needs of Iran's developing industry. For example, one can now see in Iran building cranes made in this factory. A considerable portion of the equipment for the coal mines at the Isfahan metallurgical plant were also manufactured in this factory.

Cooperation in energy also occupies an important place in Soviet-Iranian economic relations.

The hydroelectric unit "Araks," built with the technical cooperation of the All-Union Association "Tekhnopromeksport" on the Araks River, the border between the two countries, has made it possible not only to irrigate tens of thousands of hectares of fertile land that had previously not had enough water but also to provide electrical energy to the border regions of Iran and the USSR. The hydroelectric power station at the "Araks" hydro unit, which is the property of both the USSR and Iran, has been operating for more than ten years to the benefit of both countries. The two countries will also cooperate in the building of two more hydraulic power units on this river: namely, "Khodaaferin" and "Gyz-Galasa." Turbines with a total capacity of 280,000 kilowatts will be installed in these hydroelectric plants. The reservoirs formed by the dams will contain 2.4 billion cubic meters of water, which will provide additional irrigation to large areas on both banks of the river.

The thermoelectric power station "Ramin" (near Akhvaz) is being built in southern Iran; it will be the largest in this area and is being built by the All-Union Association "Tekhnopromeksport" under contract. Two power plants with a capacity of 315,000 kilowatts have begun operations, and the assembly of two other plants is still going on. Work on the construction of the thermoelectric power plant near the city of Isfahan is being carried on across a broad front. The All-Union Association "Tekhnopromeksport" is building the plant under contract. After it begins operations, the power plant will provide energy to the major industrial area of Iran forming around the city of Isfahan. The start of these projects will not only provide an impetus for the development of industry but will also help raise employment of the population in these areas and increase the number of industrial workers.

Soviet organizations are providing Iran with technical cooperation in developing transportation as well. At Iran's request, specialized Soviet vessels have regularly deepened the waters of the Iranian ports Enzeli and Noushakar on the Caspian Sea.

The economic cooperation between our countries has promoted the development of Iran's railroad network. Thus, for example, the railroad from Kerman to Isfahan was constructed especially to provide the Isfahan metallurgical plant with coking coal and iron ore and was later extended to Teheran.

Because of the growing number of Soviet export and transit goods from Europe to Iran, as well as Iranian freight to Europe, at the end of the '60s the Iranians requested the Soviet government to provide technical assistance in the electrification of the railroad from Djulfa at the Soviet-Iranian border to Tebriz.

The work on the construction of the first and so far only electrified railroad in Iran was done by the All-Union Association "Tekhnostroieksport" under contract, and this section began operations at the end of 1982. The electrification of the railroad, which runs over very rugged country, made it possible to raise the speed of trains considerably, so that goods turnover has already increased by one-third.

One of the most important areas of economic cooperation between our countries is the training of Iranian national cadres.

The monopolies of the Western countries, which build mainly assembled industrial enterprises in Iran in which many operations do not require a skilled labor force, are not so eager to train national cadres in Iran. On the contrary, they explicitly or implicitly obstruct this.

Not only do Soviet organizations provide technical assistance in the construction of large industrial projects in Iran, they have also at the same time begun to train national cadres—workers, technicians, and engineers necessary both for the construction and the operation of these projects. Practically every construction project in which Soviet organizations participate is a special school for Iranian builders and workers. The experience and assistance of Soviet specialists has been very necessary and timely for them. Over 100,000 Iranian workers have already been trained by this method of on-site learning in the construction and operation of these projects.

Thirteen centers of learning have been constructed in Iran with the technical assistance of the Soviet Union; these now train skilled workers and technicians in 47 different areas of specialization. Usually the graduates of these educational institutions work in the construction and operation of projects built with Soviet-Iranian economic and technical cooperation. These centers of learning, built with the technical assistance of Soviet organizations (the All-Union Association "Tekhnoeksport"), are known not only in Iran but also abroad. In particular, students from India and Pakistan have studied at the Isfahan metallurgical center of learning. Around 23,000 Iranian technicians and skilled workers have been trained in the years past in these centers of learning. Another ten centers are currently being built in Iran with the technical assistance of the USSR.

One of the traditional areas of cooperation between the two countries is in the building of grain elevators. The first grain elevators in Iran were constructed with the technical assistance of Soviet organizations before World War II. These elevators are still in operation.

At present Soviet organizations are working with the Iranians to build and put into operation 48 grain elevators with a total capacity of over one million tons of grain. This constitutes more than half of Iran's existing elevator and storage capacity.

The largest and most modern elevator in the Middle East, in Meshkhed, with a capacity of 113,000 tons, is one of those built with the help of the All-Union Association "Sel'khozpromeksport" which have recently begun operations. Grain elevators constructed in Iran with the technical assistance of this association have helped to improve the storage of grain.

The All-Union Association "Tsvetmetpromeksport" built the northern part of the trans-Iranian gas pipeline as well as eight compressor stations on the gas pipeline leading from the southern oil deposits in Iran to the Soviet-Iranian border near Astara. It is difficult to overestimate the importance of this project for the development of Iran's economy.

Until recently the gas by-product extracted with oil was burned on the spot. The Western monopolies that had extracted oil in Iran literally threw to the winds one of the most important natural riches of the country. Once the trans-Iranian gas pipeline was built, Iran was able not only to use this gas for everyday purposes and the needs of industry but also to pay for the services of Soviet organizations in the technical assistance they offered to Iran by supplying this gas to the USSR. Soviet credits to Iran were also paid off by gas supplies. From 1970 to 1980 over 73 billion cubic meters of gas were supplied to the USSR. Iranian officials have stated that the supplies of Iranian gas to the USSR made it possible, for example, to pay back the capital investment in the construction of the Isfahan metallurgical plant with its coal and raw material basis three times over.

We should point out that the Soviet Union holds steadfastly to the principle of mutual advantage in its economic relations with its southern neighbor. Our country has never anywhere, including in Iran, sought nor will it seek excessive profits. The USSR has never made its economic aid to Iran contingent on any political demands. All enterprises constructed in Iran with the aid of Soviet organizations are the property of the Iranian people and work for their good.

The standing Soviet-Iranian Committee for Economic Cooperation created in June 1968 is an important and effective instrument for accomplishing the tasks of reinforcing and developing economic and trade relations between our countries. The Committee has met nine times, and in these meetings questions having to do with the present state and the prospects for the development of economic and trade relations between the USSR have been examined, concrete questions concerning cooperation in the construction and operation of particular projects which have been or are being constructed in Iran with the technical assistance of the Soviet Union have been discussed, and corresponding recommendations have been developed for raising their economic effectiveness.

The "Basic Directions of Economic and Social Development of the USSR in 1981–85 and until 1990" provide for "the development on a long-term and egalitarian basis of mutually advantageous exchange of goods and comprehensive economic and scientific and technological and other relations between the Soviet Union and the developing countries, as well as continuing to provide economic and technical assistance to these countries in the construction of industrial enterprises, power plants, and agricultural and other projects that promote and reinforce their economic and political independence."

This also applies in full measure to the Islamic Republic of Iran.

The Soviet Union and Iran have favorable prospects for the further development of comprehensive cooperation, especially in the economic domain. Mutual respect of sovereignty, noninterference in one another's internal affairs, and mutual advantage are the principles which guide the Soviet state in its economic relations with other countries; and by observing these principles unswervingly, the Soviet Union will help make this favorable prospect a reality.

Lawrence H. Theriot and JeNelle Matheson (United States)

Soviet Economic Relations with the Non-European CMEA: Cuba, Vietnam, and Mongolia

CUBA

I. Introduction

When assessing bilateral Soviet relations with the countries of Eastern Europe, analysts generally accept an inherent linkage of political and economic factors. In contrast, such a linkage has not been sufficiently considered in analysis of Soviet relations with the non-European CMEA countries. Moscow's ties with Cuba, Vietnam, and Mongolia have traditionally been dealt with only in a political context. The implications for the future of Soviet economic relations with its non-European client states have largely been ignored.

Cuba's close association with the USSR, dating back some 20 years, has grown since the early 1970s to a pervasive Cuban economic dependence and close political identification. The North Vietnamese-Soviet economic connection existed prior to 1975. However, only recently has it begun to assume a more longer-term and economic-political rather than military-supportive nature. Therefore the evolution and interaction of Cuba's economic-political ties with Moscow may offer insights into the future course of Soviet relations with unified Vietnam. Moreover, Cuba's experi-

Soviet Economy in a Time of Change, vol. 2, October 10, 1979 (Washington, D.C.: GPO, 1979).

The authors are with the Office of East-West Policy and Planning, Department of Commerce. This is a staff research note. It should not be construed as a statement of Commerce Department policy.

ence may also have implications for Soviet relations with a number of other developing countries, especially in Africa.

Cuba and Vietnam: Early Soviet Ties Follow Similar Patterns

Cuba in 1959 and Vietnam in 1975 witnessed the establishment (or consolidation) of revolutionary, communist governments. In both instances the U.S. reaction was political disengagement followed shortly by a complete economic embargo. In both instances the United States also urged other Western governments to take similar actions, although with only limited success.

Faced with severe economic dislocations from restricted trade ties with the West, both Cuba and Vietnam sought emergency economic support. The Soviet Union has proven to be a willing benefactor. Moscow's pattern, clearly demonstrated in Cuba, involved a quick response with essential economic support while slowly developing political ties that would eventually yield benefits of support from its Havana client. On the other hand, Cuba's leaders then (and probably Vietnam's today) apparently assumed they could accept Soviet assistance as necessary for survival while continuing to exercise autonomy in pursuing their self-perceived interests.

However, extensively isolated from the noncommunist trading community, a small nation's economic dependence on a major power like the USSR inevitably grows; its autonomy in foreign policy is reduced, and some degree of subservience to Soviet global interests becomes unavoidable. For example, Cuba apparently supported the Soviet invasion of Czechoslovakia in 1968 only with great reluctance. More recent developments in Southeast Asia and Africa may be further demonstrations of Soviet economic dependence influencing the foreign policies of their client states.

Only time will tell whether Hanoi and possibly others in Africa will follow Cuba's path of economic and, ultimately, political dependence on Moscow. However, the economic factors underlying Moscow's relations with its developing country clients could impose significant costs and therefore limitations on both sides. We believe analysis of these factors has been seriously neglected.

This paper assesses the development and current status of Soviet economic relations with Cuba and Vietnam. It focuses on the costs the Soviets have incurred and are likely to continue to incur, as well as on the benefits they have or expect to derive. Mongolia is also dealt with briefly as an example of virtually total economic dependence on the USSR.

While the course of Vietnamese-Soviet economic relations seems to be paralleling the Cuban experience in some aspects, there are also fundamental differences which may prove important. Soviet economic ties with some of the emerging African governments are excluded from consideration because they are in the infancy of development. Nevertheless the patterns the Soviets have established with Cuba and possibly Vietnam could be an indication of the future course of Soviet relations with some African countries.

II. Brief History of Cuban-Soviet Economic Relations

Aid to the New Revolution

After Fidel Castro assumed the post of Cuban Prime Minister in January 1959, the historically pervasive U.S. economic presence in its island neighbor began to unravel rapidly. In August 1960 U.S. oil refineries were nationalized for refusing to process Soviet-supplied crude. Relations continued to deteriorate as the U.S. reduced, then eliminated entirely its import quota for Cuban sugar, and Havana nationalized all U.S.-owned properties (the value later appraised at $1.8 billion). The United States responded by embargoing all trade except shipments of food and medicines, which were also barred in 1962. The trade embargo was mutlilateralized in 1964 by the Organization of American States, and Cuba's trade ties with the Western Hemisphere were severed, with the exception of Mexico and Canada.

As the dominant U.S. position in the Cuban economy declined, ties with the Soviet Union grew apace. The February 1960 visit by Soviet Premier Mikoyan, which resulted in signing of a Bilateral Trade and Clearing Agreement, proved to be a decisive turning point. The USSR extended MFN tariff status and agreed to annual purchases of a minimum of one million tons of sugar and to supply Cuba's needs for petroleum and refined products. Oil was a key economic support item since Cuba was (and is today) 95% dependent on imports for its petroleum needs, and Havana had been cut off from its traditional suppliers, Venezuela and the United States.

The highly advantageous nature of Cuba's trade relations with the Soviet Union was set early, with sugar prices set at subsidized levels more favorable than world market prices. The USSR also allowed partial payment (initially 80%) to be made in Cuban goods rather than hard currency.

Actual trade volumes substantially exceeded agreed goals, as the Soviets imported half of Cuban sugar production (3.345 million tons in 1961) and supplied more than 2 million tons of petroleum and products. Clearly the Soviets were acting as Havana's economic friend in need. As two-way U.S. trade declined precipitously from $1.1 billion to $20 million between 1958 and 1962, the Soviet share rose from virtually nil to $630 million.

Strains Develop as Economic Ties Grow

Rapidly expanding economic ties between the Soviets and Cuba were not without strains. Soviet capitulation to U.S. pressure and failure to consult Cuban leaders in removing MRBMs during the 1962 crisis dramatically demonstrated to Havana that Soviet solidarity with the Cuban revolution had strict limits. Moreover, Moscow worried that its economic aid was being wasted by the often erratic economic management of the Cuban leadership. In 1962 the revolutionary government initiated an economic development policy that sharply reversed the traditional Cuban emphasis on agriculture in favor of forced industrialization. The goal was to eliminate Cuba's dependence on sugar, which had come to be identified as the essential source of Cuba's colonial domination by the United States.

There were other political frictions as well. Castro's strident nationalism, direct support of revolutionary factions in Latin America, his disdain for the old-line, Moscow-oriented Cuban Communist Party (the PSP), and his cultivation of ties with the PRC all gave the Soviet leadership some pause and engendered suspicion about

Cuba's true motives and interests.

Continued erratic economic management epitomized by yet another reversal of policy to reemphasize sugar production ultimately forced Moscow to exert its economic leverage. By restricting oil deliveries, the Soviets effectively demonstrated the extent of Cuba's economic dependence.

The pervasive dominance of the Soviet Union in the Cuban economy is usually dated from 1970, after the disastrous attempt, personally identified with Castro, to produce 10 million tons of sugar (annual production had been averaging about 5.4 million tons). Although Cuba managed to produce 8.5 million tons of sugar in 1970, the economy was nearly wrecked as the industry and service sectors were seriously neglected to concentrate all available resources on the sugar harvest. This economic disaster was also a political setback for Castro, who even made a public offer to resign. However, once again the generous hand of Soviet economic assistance was available, and a long-term bilateral agreement on economic, scientific, and technical cooperation was signed in 1970, thereby providing another milestone in the entrenchment of Soviet economic ties. Subsequent joint commission meetings led to extensive Soviet assistance in many key economic sectors.

Most importantly, the Soviets helped maintain and modernize Cuba's sugar industry, which today accounts for a substantial part of overall economic activity and 85% of Cuba's export earnings. The Soviets also pledged assistance for the nickel industry, at the time Cuba's only important nonagricultural export industry. As an island economy now almost completely dependent on long-distance trade routes, Cuba's maritime fleet and ports badly needed expansion and improvements which the Soviets also supplied. Soviet boats and crews formed the nucleus of a Cuban fishing fleet that has since become one of the examples of real success in economic cooperation. Cuba's total fish catch has grown from 22,000 tons in 1958 to 185,000 tons in 1977. The Soviets also began to supply infrastructure investments, mainly irrigation systems, needed for a viable citrus industry.

Bilateral economic negotiations in 1972 were another important milestone in the evolution of Cuban ties with the USSR. Cuba, under continued Soviet presssure to rationalize its economic management and adopt orthodox central planning, became a full member of the CMEA. Havana thereby agreed to permit close coordination (and unavoidably some degree of control) of its economic development plans within the communist bloc. The number of technical advisers in Cuba's economic management structure rose dramatically—especially Soviets, but other East Europeans as well. In its induction into the CMEA, Cuba was also afforded special developing member status, making it eligible for preferential treatment in its trade relations with the more developed European CMEA members. Economic aid, which had consisted almost exclusively of Soviet assistance, was now multilateralized, at least to some extent.

Involvement of Soviet specialists in economic planning increased sharply in 1973 in preparation for Cuba's first comprehensive five-year plan for the 1976–80 period. Concurrent with its increased control over Cuban economic planning, Moscow restructured $4.5 billion of outstanding Cuban debts, allowing repayment (in sugar) to begin in 1986 and forgiving all interest accrued prior to 1972. Moscow also extended bilateral credits for balancing the 1973–75 trade account and offered a 1.1 billion ruble credit line for financing industrial development during the 1976–80 plan. Assistance was to be concentrated in developing industrial uses for agricultural by-products. An additional 270 million ruble loan was extended for modernization of textile, nickel, and electric power plants. This new display of Soviet generosity coincided with a visit to Havana by General Secretary Brezhnev, the first Soviet chief of state to visit Cuba.

More important for the future, the Soviet Union shifted the nature of its economic aid from direct loans to indirect subsidies through heavily preferential trade prices. Beginning in 1973, the Soviets agreed to pay a minimum 12 cents a pound for sugar and $5,540 a ton for nickel, compared to then current world prices of 7.4 cents and $3,500.

However, what was to prove to be Moscow's most important economic concession came during subsequent negotiations for the 1976–80 plan, when it agreed to link prices paid for Cuban sugar to a basket of prices charged for Soviet exports, including oil and other products. Starting from a high base sugar price of 30 cents (then current market prices were the highest in history and peaked briefly at 66 cents in late 1974), Havana was assured the price paid for its sugar would increase to match any increased cost of Soviet products, including oil. This was of crucial importance since after 1974 Soviet oil prices were set to rise for all CMEA members in accordance with a five-year moving average of world oil prices. The terms of trade between the two most important products in Cuban-Soviet trade (that is, sugar and oil) were therefore fixed for the five-year plan to 1980.

The increased control gained over Cuban economic planning proved much less effective than Moscow had probably expected. While the rigors of comprehensive planning, patterned on the Soviet model, imposed severely needed managerial discipline on Cuba's domestic and foreign trade sectors, plan goals proved overly optimistic primarily because the key economic variable, predicted world sugar prices, was set too high. Having overestimated hard currency earnings from record high sugar prices in 1974, Cuba in 1975 reverted to incurring large deficits in its hard currency trade. As sugar prices remained low throughout 1975 and 1976, Cuba was forced to renegotiate import contracts, delay receiving some $300 million in imports, and postpone or cancel numerous development projects tied to imports.

In a September 1976 speech Castro announced an austerity policy and increased rationing of consumer goods, and he signaled a sharp cutback in hard currency imports. From a record high level of $1.6 billion in 1975, imports from the noncommunist countries declined to $1.3 billion in 1977, a sharp decline in real terms adjusted for the continued high level of Western inflation.

Havana thus clearly demonstrated that when it has the hard currency capability to do so, it will reorient its trade to noncommunist countries. In 1975 Cuba obtained 46% of its global imports from the noncommunist West, compared with a more normal 30% in the early 1970s. However, when the five-year plan proved unrealistic and the new-found prosperity only transient, Cuba was forced to return to dependence on its Soviet benefactors. The basic economic fact of overreliance on sugar remained largely unchanged since the early 1970s, when Soviet planning technicians had assumed much of the responsibility for charting Cuba's economic future. The highly attractive subsidized terms of trade once again proved to be Havana's most important insurance policy. For Moscow any anticipations that the cost of supporting Cuba had peaked now proved illusory.

In 1977 trade with the Soviet Union accounted for 62% of Cuba's global two-way trade, compared to 52% in 1970. Adding East European and Asian trading partners, communist countries accounted for three-fourths of Cuba's 1977 trade turnover (see Table 1).

In sharp contrast with continued large deficits in hard currency trade, Cuba has been able to achieve surpluses with the communist countries since 1975, not coincidentally the year when the USSR switched economic aid from direct loans to subsidized trade prices.[1]

The composition of Cuban trade with the Soviet Union is what would be expected between a major industrial power and its developing country client. Cuban exports are dominated by sugar, which comprised 92% of total exports by ruble value in 1977. (Sugar deliveries totaled 3.8 million tons[2] or 54% of total Cuban production in 1978.) Nickel accounted for 6.5% of 1977 exports, while other products in declining order of importance were rum, cigarettes, and citrus fruit (see Table 2).

Half of Soviet exports to Cuba are concentrated in raw materials and capital equipment. Petroleum and refined products accounted for 23% of the total ruble value of 1977 Soviet exports, while machinery and transport equipment amounted to 27%. A variety of agricultural chemicals, food products, and durable consumer goods, including appliances, made up the remainder (see Table 3).

In addition to the Soviets, Cuba also enjoys preferred prices from its Eastern European trading partners who currently pay 22 cents per pound for sugar. Again, payment is in soft currency at prices agreed in bilateral negotiations. Since little is known about the pricing of Eastern European exports to Cuba, it is impossible to determine the real net gains to Cuba.

III. Cuban Economic Dependence: Soviet Costs

Having surveyed the evolution of Cuban economic dependence on

Table 1

Cuban Foreign Trade by Major Area, Selected Years (In Millions of U.S. Dollars)

	1957	1974	1975	1976	1977[1]
Total exports, f.o.b.	818	2,618	3,597	3,186	3,553
Communist countries	42	1,536	2,415	2,427	2,998[2]
U.S.S.R.[2,3]	(42)	(981)	(2,011)	(2,027)	(2,521)
Non-Communist countries	776	1,082	1,207	759	571
Total imports, c.i.f.	895	2,648	3,575	3,658	4,188
Communist countries	2	1,629	1,957	2,250	2,836
U.S.S.R.[3]	([4])	(1,240)	(1,531)	(1,800)	(2,267)
Non-Communist countries	893	1,019	1,656	1,408	1,352
Balance	−77	−30	+22	−472	−635
Communist countries	40	−93	458	177	146
U.S.S.R.	(42)	(−259	(480)	(227)	(254)
Non-Communist countries	−117	+63	−449	−649	−781

Source: Cuban data.
[1]Estimated.
[2]Does not include above planned sugar exports to U.S.S.R. for hard currency totalling 2,650,000,000 tons since 1975.
[3]Inconsistencies with totals in tables 2 and 3 result from irreconcilable differences between Cuban and Soviet data sources.
[4]Negligible.

Table 2

Soviet Imports from Cuba
(Million Rubles and Quantities)

Product	1974		1975		1076		1977	
	Rubles (millions)	Quantity	Rubles (millions)	Quantity	Rubles (millions)	Quantity	Rubles (millions)	Quantity
Naptha[1]	0.287	20.6	1.0	20.8	n.a.	n.a.	n.a.	n.a.
Metal ores and concentrates[1]	81.053	n.a.	74.4	n.a.	94.3	n.a.	117.4	n.a.
Sugar[1]	611.2	1,856.0	1,344.3	2,964.0	1,397.8	3,068.0	1,675.4	3,652.0
Citrus[1]	4.1	21.1	3.0	16.2	4.3	22.2	5.3	27.9
Of which:								
Bananas[1]	.4	1.4	.3	.4	.1	.2		
Grapefruit[1]	2.7	1.62	2.3	13.6	2.9	16.7	3.7	21.7
Oranges[1]	.9	3.6	.4	.9	1.3	5.2	1.5	5.9
Liqueurs[2]	.6	33.5	2.1	129.6	1.9	120.4	1.0	63.7
Rum[2]	5.4	319.1	9.4	550.1	11.6	679.5	8.9	522.9
Cigarettes[3]	9.3	2.4	8.6	2.3	6.9	1.8	6.1	1.8
Cigars[4]	3.2	13.9	3.1	3.2	1.7	8.8	1.8	9.7
Books[4]	.1		.2		.2		.2	
Stamps	1.1		1.2		1.1		.9	
Total	716.2		1,447.7		1,520.8		1,817.2	

***Source**: Vneshniaia torgovlia SSSR.*
[1]Thousand metric tons.
[2]Thousand decaliters.
[3]Billion units.
[4]Million units.

the Soviet Union, we turn to assessing the costs to the Soviets of continuing to underwrite the Cuban economy and conversely the economic benefits that accrue to Cuba.

Subsidized Terms of Trade: Oil

Since 1974 the key mechanism for Soviet economic aid has been subsidized trade prices through a linkage of export and import prices; that is, as Soviet prices for exports to Cuba increase, the prices the Soviets pay for Cuban products increase in tandem, guaranteeing maintenance of the Soviet subsidy. The economic subsidies involved, while more hidden, nonetheless are real and are most dramatically important in terms of oil and sugar.

Oil constitutes about 23% by value of total Soviet exports to Cuba. In 1977 the Soviet Union exported 9.2 million tons of petroleum and refined products to Cuba at an estimated crude oil equivalent price of $7.40 a barrel, compared to the available world market price of about $12.50. The oil subsidy to Cuba therefore totaled $328 million in 1977, and the equivalent opportunity cost to the Soviet of lost hard currency export earnings equaled $840 million.

Soviet oil prices to Cuba have apparently risen in accordance with the floating intra-CMEA price mechanism in effect since 1974. However, Cuba appears to be continuing to enjoy an oil price significantly more favorable than that charged by the Soviets to Eastern Europe. Deliveries of oil products are expected to total an estimated 9.6 million tons during 1979 and possibly 10 million tons in 1980, about 11% of expected overall Soviet shipments to all CMEA member countries. During the 1981–85 plan the USSR is also expected to build Cuba's third oil refinery. When completed, annual refinery capacity will rise from the present 6.5 to 9 million tons per year, possibly resulting in an increase of Soviet crude exports to as much as 9 million tons, while shipments of refined products decline sharply. Lost Soviet hard currency earnings on crude deliveries alone would then total $955 million in 1980 if world oil prices remain at current levels or $1.1 billion if world prices rise just 10%. Clearly the cost to the USSR of supplying Cuban oil needs can only increase over time.

Table 3

Major Soviet Exports to Cuba, 1974–77 (In Millions of Rubles)

	1974	1975	1976	1977
Machines, equipment, means of transport	229.5	278.1	366.5	447.3
Of which:				
Generating equipment	13.3	32.5	25.9	29.2
Hoisting gear	11.5	12.8	12.9	17.4
Road-building equipment	11.8	11.9	19.5	19.3
Tractors, agricultural machinery	41.0	49.2	66.1	38.7
Trucks and parts	35.2	37.5	45.8	57.5
Aircraft	6.6	5.5	14.5	42.6
Oil and oil products	135.8	248.2	288.2	375.2
Rolled ferous metal	22.4	28.1	38.2	49.1
Rolled nonferous metal	9.4	9.4	12.7	n.a.
Chemical products	15.6	16.9	12.0	12.2
Nitrogen fertilizers	10.4	15.0	26.5	36.4
Sawn lumber	23.7	24.8	20.5	25.7
Cotton fiber	22.5	18.7	23.7	24.0
Grain (except groats)	55.6	62.6	62.8	91.9
Canned meat	61.3	17.5	22.0	18.8
Milk products	8.4	9.2	10.7	12.3
Fish and fish products	17.7	20.1	16.6	21.6
Flour	38.1	62.7	67.2	67.3
Vegetable oils (edible)	22.5	28.1	26.5	33.6
Consumer goods	33.0	37.2	46.6	53.6
Subtotal	646.3	876.6	1,040.7	126.9
Total (including other items):				
Million rubles	926.1	1,141.3	1,351.1	1,634.9
Million dollars[1]	1,221.8	1,587.3	1,823.6	2,224.5

Source: *Vneshniaia torgovlia SSSR.*

Sugar

Cuba's matching product under the preferential trade price mechanism is sugar. In 1975 the Soviets agreed to a base price of 30 cents per pound for preplanned annual Cuban sugar exports. As already noted, this base price was linked to a basket of Soviet export prices including oil. As a result, in 1978, to compensate for oil price increases, Cuban sugar deliveries were priced at about 40 cents per pound, compared to the available free market price of 8 cents.[3]

This arrangement resulted in a sugar subsidy to Cuba of about $2.4 billion last year. In addition to the volume of sugar purchases agreed to in annual bilateral trade protocols, the Soviets have periodically bought extra sugar from Cuba to make up shortfalls in their own production and/or to relieve Cuba of surpluses unsalable on the free world market. Payment is in hard currency at existing world prices. These preplanned exports totaled 2.7 million tons between 1974–78, earning Cuba about $800 million in hard currency.

While most agricultural specialists believe the Soviets actually needed the extra Cuban sugar for domestic consumption, the possibility cannot be fully discounted that some part of the hard currency shipments are another form of indirect subsidy. If correct, such purchases represent another instance (together with oil) where economic assistance to Cuba costs the Soviets hard currency either directly (as in payment for sugar) or as an opportunity cost (as in lost earnings from oil deliveries which could be sold on the world market). In addition other known instances of indirect hard currency aid include Canadian wheat and flour, which the Soviets buy for delivery to Cuba. Minimum annual shipments have been 800,000 tons, averaging $120 million in value 1974–77. Cuban corn imports from Argentina and rice, ostensibly from the USSR, may also be covered by a similar Soviet purchase mechanism.

Nickel

Since 1973 the USSR has also paid a preferential price for Cuban nickel. By 1977 that price had been increased to $6,075 per ton, compared to the then current world market price of about $4,500 per ton. Although the nickel price is not linked to the cost of Soviet imports, increases are allowed to match any rise in the world price. Cuban subsidies from nickel thus totaled an estimated $38 million in 1978.

Soviet Aid: Totals and Significance

Overall Soviet economic aid to Cuba is estimated to have totaled the

Table 4

Soviet Economic Assistance to Cuba (In Equivalent Millions of U.S. Dollars)

	1961–74	1975	1976	1977	1978
Balance of payments aid	4,417	150	150	205	225
Trade and development aid	3,781	115	115	175	190
Interest charges	292	0	0	0	0
Other invisibles	344	35	35	35	35
Total repayable aid	4,417	4,567	4,717	4,922	5,147
Subsidies	1,155	901	1,357	1,772	2,713
Sugar subsidy	695	590	977	1,428	2,435
Petroleum subsidy	0	290	362	328	240
Nickel subsidy	91	31	18	16	38
Total grants	1,155	2,056	3,413	5,185	7,898
Total economic aid	5,572	6,623	8,130	10,107	13,045

equivalent of about $13 billion since 1960. Some 40% has been in the form of bilateral loans which will be repaid interest-free over a 25-year period beginning in 1986. The remaining 60% consist of subsidies in the trade of sugar, petroleum, and nickel which are not repayable (see Table 4).

While Cuba has achieved significant economic progress, especially since 1971, the importance of Soviet assistance can hardly be overemphasized. The combined flow of Soviet aid (repayable and subsidy grants) is estimated to have totaled the equivalent of $2.9 billion in 1978. In other words, Soviet assistance equaled nearly one-fourth of Cuba's estimated $12 billion GNP and the equivalent of about $300 per capita in economic support.

By way of contrast, the maximum likely Cuban gains from any resumption of trade ties with the United States would be substantially less important than Soviet assistance at present levels. Expected two-way U.S.-Cuban trade is unlikely to exceed $700 million.[4] Moreover, the bulk of both exports and imports with the United States would be diverted from existing trade flows with other Western countries and would not represent net additions to Havana's hard currency trade.

Consequently, with its continued inherent weakness as basically a monoculture sugar-based economy, Cuba is likely to remain very dependent on Soviet aid for the foreseeable future. Some of the important remaining questions are: What will the future cost be to the Soviet Union, and how long will it be willingly incurred?

Hard Currency vs. Soft Currency Costs

First an important caveat: Care must be taken in assessing Soviet economic relations with Cuba using U.S. dollars as a unit of account. Soviet-Cuban bilateral trade is essentially a barter exchange of Cuban sugar, nickel, tobacco, and citrus for a variety of Soviet products, including oil. Exchange prices computed from Cuban or Soviet data are not indicative of hard currency flows; rather, they are soft currency prices used for valuing the volume of goods exchanged under bilateral trade protocols. Prices are set by political negotiation and do not necessarily reflect real economic value or cost of alternative supply sources. The real economic benefits to Cuba and the equivalent cost to the USSR depend on the terms of trade in real terms that result from these negotiations. Consequently, calculating the subsidy element by comparing soft currency value of trade flows with prevailing hard currency world prices gives only a general indicator of the value of Soviet subsidies to Cuba. Moreover, the relative gains to Cuba from imported Soviet manufactured goods (and thus the costs to USSR) depend on alternatives available to each on hard currency world markets.

The Soviets may be charging high prices in supplying Cuba capital goods and equipment which, because of quality or service deficiencies, are not readily salable on the world market. If that is the case, in the exchange for Cuban sugar which is either consumed domestically or reexported for hard currency, what is apparently only a subsidy to Cuba in fact also accrues as a real economic benefit to the USSR. Who gains the most is impossible to determine.

Future Cost of Subsidies

The cost of the sugar-for-oil exchange to the USSR will continue to rise as the world price of oil increases and the differential increases between the Soviet offered price for Cuban sugar and the stagnant world sugar price. Even if the International Sugar Agreement (the ISA is designed to raise free market prices by better balancing supply and demand) operates effectively, little upward movement is expected in world sugar prices for the foreseeable future.

Moreover, in 1978 deliveries to Cuba of oil and refined products represented 13% of total Soviet exports to the Eastern European members of CMEA.[5] If Soviet oil production levels off and declines as expected in the mid 1980s, the calculus of economic and political costs of continuing to supply and subsidize Cuba, at the possible expense of Eastern Europe, will confront Soviet planners with difficult decisions.

Continuing to supply wheat and flour (and possibly rice and corn) purchased in the West for hard currency could add another drain on Soviet financial resources.

However, the future costs of the sugar subsidy are less clear. If Moscow continues to purchase substantial amounts of sugar for hard currency, that will of course represent a direct hard currency cost. If the USSR proves more willing to accept long-term reliance on Cuba for a substantial portion of its sugar consumption needs and diverts available land resources to alternative crops rather than increasing beet production, assured access to Cuban sugar would be an advantage. However, with the soft currency sugar price linked to oil and therefore high above expected world market levels, the subsidy will continue to be very costly.

The benefits of an assured market for nearly half its sugar production are clearly of immense importance to Cuba. Regardless of the quality or price of goods received in exchange (except for oil and other "hard goods," for example, grains where the benefit is unambiguous), without the Soviet market Cuba could not dispose of its current sugar production (except at severely depressed prices) in face of stagnant world demand and increased competition from sugar substitutes such as corn sweeteners.

If the ISA continues to limit Cuban sugar exports to the world market, the Soviet market would become increasingly important were Havana to actually pursue its announced goal of 8.5 million tons of sugar annually by 1980. However if, as some observers expect, Cuba actually increases production only slightly above the 7 million tons produced last year, then Cuban dependence on sugar exports to the USSR will have peaked in 1978. If an effectively operating ISA means a larger Cuban hard currency export quota (possibly up to 2.8 from the current 2.5 million tons), then the trend to increased reliance on the USSR sugar market would reverse. However, continued Soviet purchases of half Cuba's sugar crop insures its predominant importance will continue.

Industrial Equipment and Know-How

In addition to subsidies from the sugar, nickel, and oil-trading exchange, the Soviets have provided large amounts of economic aid as technical assistance and equipment in developing other Cuban industries. By year end 1977 the USSR reportedly had remodeled or built 150 Cuban industrial facilities and was engaged on 200 installations. A partial listing of facilities built or under construction either wholly or in part with Soviet-supplied goods and know-how includes:

Fertilizer plant.
Modernization of two existing oil refineries.
New 3,000-ton-capacity oil refinery.
Fuel storage tank farms.
Two oxygen plants.
Modernization of steel plant.
Expansion of machine-building plant.
Modernization of two nickel plants.
New 30,000-ton nickel plant.
A 440-megawatt nuclear powerplant.
Thermoelectric plants.
Long-distance high powerlines.
Unified national electric grid.
Reconstruction of 21 sugar mills.
Ground satellite station.
Railways and rolling stock.
Ships and port facilities.

Because of its importance to Cuba as a potential hard currency earner, Soviet aid in nickel has been and continues to be especially significant. With Soviet help, production at the two formerly U.S.-owned facilities at Nicaro and Mao Bay is being expanded from 37,000 to 47,000 tons. A third facility capable of 30,000 tons of output, currently under construction at Punta Gorda with Soviet assistance, is scheduled for completion in 1982.

The experience of Punta Gorda is generally characteristic of Soviet-Cuba joint development projects. Originally scheduled to open in 1980, coordination problems between enterprises and lack of Soviet priority in supplying required equipment, particularly if hard currency expenditure is needed, have caused extensive delays. In apparent deference to Cuban requests, at one point the Soviets solicited participation by Western engineering firms capable of supplying more efficient technology than available from the USSR or in the older existing Cuban plants. However, the Soviets subsequently reversed direction and apparently decided to replicate the existing 20-year-old nickel plant rather than use hard currency to purchase more efficient up-to-date Western design and equipment. This demonstrates once again that Soviet assistance to Cuba is likely to be strictly limited where scarce hard currency resources are required.

A fourth nickel plant which would increase Cuban production to 100,000 tons is to be built with multilateral CMEA assistance during the 1981–85 plan. However, even more difficult multilateral coordination problems are likely to result in substantial delays.

One Soviet project of major significance is construction of a 440-megawatt nuclear power station near Cienfuegos in southwestern Cuba. This first Soviet-supplied nuclear power station in the Western Hemisphere is to be followed by a second 440-megawatt unit. This commitment to supply Cuba with nuclear power is at least indirect confirmation that the Soviets are aware of the ever growing opportunity cost of supplying Cuban energy needs. However, with the anticipated delays, nuclear power can be at best only a partial answer. If completed as planned by 1985 (very doubtful), the first unit could supply 17% of Cuba's anticipated electrical power generation. Thus nuclear energy will not begin to mitigate the Cuba oil drain until the 1990s, while Soviet crude oil production shortages are expected to be crucial in the early to mid-1980s.

Industrial development assistance projects can involve direct and indirect costs to the Soviets in at least three ways. First, there are the opportunity costs of resources invested in Cuba where the anticipated economic return consists only of sugar imports at subsidized prices over the very long-term future (sugar deliveries are the accepted means for payment of Cuban debts to all communist countries).

Second, for some industrial projects, such as the Punta Gorda nickel plant, Soviet cooperation may require provision of some technologies and equipment available only in the West for hard currency. While the Soviet Union is less reluctant to invest soft currency or "soft goods" in Cuba for a return of sugar, it is clearly more reluctant to supply either Western goods purchased for hard currency or its own "hard goods" (that is, those marketable in the West).

Third, most all CMEA countries face similar long-term economic problems, including: Insufficient energy resources and dependence on Soviet supplies, extremely limited supplies of goods that can be exported for hard currency, and widespread needs for Western technology to upgrade and expand domestic industry. In addition to continued pressure from Havana for additional resources, the Soviets also constantly must face similar demands from much of Eastern Europe—and since 1975, from Vietnam. Furthermore, other developing countries (for example, Angola and Ethiopia) are apparently considering various forms of economic association with the CMEA. Their needs for investment resources will predictably be massive. Faced with its own ever growing domestic demand for scarce investment resources, the Soviet Union can be expected to attempt to press other more developed members of the CMEA, such as the GDR and Poland, to bear a larger portion of the cost of assisting Cuba and any other less developed countries which may join the CMEA bloc. However, with problems of their own, Eastern Europe can be expected to resist extending economic aid beyond token amounts and become increasingly dissatisfied with the heavy subsidies enjoyed by Cuba. This could force the Soviets to spend political capital within the CMEA structure to maintain Cuba's preferential trade status intact.

There may also be a direct cost to the USSR. When the Eastern Europeans must provide valuable "hard goods" to Cuba, they may demand reductions in their obligation to supply equivalent volumes to the USSR.

Debt Management

Managing its external debt is an additional area of economic assistance for Cuba that involves important direct and indirect costs to the Soviets. Direct Soviet soft currency ruble credits to Cuba since the 1960s total 5.1 billion. Repayment will commence after 1986 on an interest-free basis. An additional 1.1 billion rubles made available since 1975 is repayable after 1983 in sugar. The actual cost to the USSR of soft currency debt to Cuba is incalculable, depending as it does on the pricing of long-term sugar deliveries as repayment. However, the interest-free feature suggests a net loss in real terms to the USSR. In fact, some observers believe Cuba's debt will never be repaid in more than token amounts and will ultimately be largely written off by the Soviets.

In addition to direct soft currency Soviet loans, since 1974 Cuba has maintained membership in the CMEA banks, the International Bank for Economic Cooperation (IBEC) and the International Investment Bank (IIB).[6] IBEC provides hard and soft currency loans for development projects in member countries. Although no concrete data is available, Cuba is known to have drawn loans from both institutions. Hard currency credits could total up to several hundred million dollars.

Since decisions in CMEA organizations presumably require unanimous approval and since all CMEA countries face chronic shortages of hard currency, approval of loans to Cuba probably require substantial lobbying by CMEA's most influential member, the Soviet Union. Again, political capital has to be used on Cuba's behalf.

In addition to soft and hard currency debts to the USSR and CMEA banks, Cuba's hard currency debt to the West has accumulated rapidly from an estimated $580 million in 1973 to $2.2 billion by year end 1977. However, Cuba is rarely if ever included in Western assessments of either CMEA or Soviet debt. Havana has used credits from governmental export finance programs and commercial banks to finance $1.8 billion in hard currency trade deficits, accumulated over the 1975–77 period. Cuba has been able to maintain a reasonably favorable credit rating with international banks that account for $870 million or 40% of outstanding debt at the end of 1977. This has been possible in spite of its continued poor economic outlook and controversial foreign policies in Africa at least in part because many bankers presume the existence of a Soviet financial "umbrella" which serves as the ultimate guarantee behind Havana's debts. But the "umbrella" also means the Soviet Union bears a contingent liability for Cuban debts in addition to its own $11 billion outstanding hard currency debt and perhaps a similarly perceived "umbrella" liability for $43 billion of debt held by East Europe and the CMEA banks.

Furthermore, indications are that Cuba is currently funding its hard currency debt on an extremely short-term basis. In mid-1978 fully 70% of Eurocurrency bank claims on Cuba consisted of trade credits and interbank deposit accounts with maturities of less than 6 months. Havana's cash flow position is therefore particularly vulnerable to changes in international money market conditions and banks' confidence in its creditworthiness. The necessity for additional direct Soviet hard currency aid for Havana to service its Western debts therefore cannot be ruled out.

This contingent liability for Cuban debts is clearly a negative influence on the Soviet's own international credit standing. That influence would surely increase if bankers perceived that Moscow was assuming responsibility for current and future hard currency debts of additional economic clients such as Vietnam, Angola, or Ethiopia.

Military Assistance: The Economic Impact

The Soviets have supplied Cuba with military equipment worth an estimated $1.5 billion since 1960. This too entails some opportunity costs for the Soviets. Prior to 1974 Soviet military equipment and assistance to Havana had leveled off. Although Cuban forces were slowly upgraded, equipment was always defensive in nature and several generations old. However, successes in support of Soviet policies in Angola and Ethiopia may well have strengthened Cuba's bargaining position with the USSR for more sophisticated military equipment and training.

Domestic pressures in Cuba for expanded and improved military forces are likely to mount for two reasons: First, the relative importance of the military establishment in the Cuban leadership has been bolstered by African successes. Second, in contrast to the European members of CMEA, Cuba's labor force is growing rapidly. However, the civilian economy, dominated by agriculture, is likely to prove increasingly incapable of providing new Cuban technocrats (products of an impressive educational system) with the industrial employment they expect. This seems likely to add some pressures to expand the military to absorb at least part of the surplus young labor force.

Although the amounts of military equipment supplied have been very small relative to Soviet stocks, anything supplied Cuba is then unavailable for direct supply to other potential client states. Alternative demands for Soviet military aid have been notably substantial of late. For example, some $1 billion of equipment was rapidly shipped to Ethiopia in 1978 and unknown amounts to Vietnam in 1979. Furthermore, deliveries of military hardware appear to coincide with involvement of Cuban combat troops. Any repeat of the massive arms deliveries made to Ethiopia and Angola in some other area of conflict where Cubans might become involved could mean an increased drain of Soviet resources necessarily devoted to military assistance. Since available investment resources are always tight, the Soviet civilian economy can ill afford such additional drains.

Supplying Cuba's military with equipment also involves a degree of political risk to the Soviets because of the 1962 bilateral understanding with the United States that offensive, strategic type (never clearly defined) equipment would not be supplied.

IV. Gains to the Soviet Union from Economic Support of Cuba

This paper has concentrated on the evolution of direct and indirect costs to the Soviet Union of maintaining its economic support of Cuba. The costs have clearly been substantial, and prospects are that maintaining Cuba as a client state in the manner to which Havana has recently become accustomed will no doubt become increasingly costly.

It is an irony of history that the Soviets have almost exactly replaced the United States as Cuba's dominant benefactor and most pervasive economic influence. The costs have indeed been high. We will now attempt to assess the nature of the return on its investment Moscow has derived from Cuba.

Economic Returns

While the net flow of economic resources has clearly been overwhelmingly in Cuba's favor, the USSR has been able to extract some reciprocal economic benefits. However, given the very limited assortment of Cuban products, the choices have indeed been slim.

Principally important is sugar. At the current level of supply (3.8 million tons for the 1977–78 crop year), Cuba supplies about one-fourth of total Soviet consumption. With its notorious weather patterns, the availability of Cuban sugar also provides the USSR assurance against a serious sugar beet crop failure. Nevertheless, the Soviets have continued their own efforts to expand sugar beet production, which if successful would diminish the need for Cuban imports. Of course, faced with a surplus of domestic and imported sugar at some future point, the Soviets could always sell the excess on the free world market. However, such sales could rebound against Cuba, whose exports to the USSR are excluded from its ISA quota on the understanding that Soviet imports will not be reexported and disrupt the free world market.

The USSR currently imports 18,000 tons of nickel annually or about half of Cuban production. In addition, one-half the production of the new Punta Gorda plant, when completed, is committed to repay Soviet construction assistance. As the world's largest producer of nickel, the Soviets have no serious need for Cuban nickel, but it is one of the few "hard goods" available and can free domestic production for exports. Cuba also exports refractory grade chromite ore to the USSR (possibly 30,000 tons each year), and small quantities of tobacco products and rum are also exported. However, none of these products supplies essential needs.

In recent years the Cubans have sharply expanded production of one product that can surely satisfy a genuine Soviet demand—citrus. Production has increased steadily to 200,000 tons in 1976, and plans call for producing 250,000 tons in 1980. Soviet imports of Cuban citrus have risen sharply to about 60,000 tons. Because investment in transport, packaging, and quality control has lagged, fresh Cuban citrus is generally not competitive on the world markets. However, it is most welcome by insatiable Soviet consumers.

One additional possible future Cuban export to the USSR has received little attention: labor. In sharp contrast with the leveling off of the Soviet labor force (and the rest of the CMEA as well), Cuba faces a 2.8% growth through 1987. Recently Cuba has begun to emphasize export of technical assistance embodied in its workers. At present at least 10,000 Cuban "gastarbeiters," including doctors, nurses, construction workers, and sugar engineers, are employed in several developing countries, generating possibly as much as $50 million in hard currency earnings for Havana. The most ambitious projects are in Iraq and Libya.

Although in the past thousands of Cubans have received technical training and education in the USSR, that flow could reverse in the years ahead if Cuba, like the East Europeans, is required to contribute directly to Soviet development projects in return for continued access to Soviet raw materials. Havana's contribution, however, could only be labor.

Political Returns

In conclusion, there has been some, albeit disproportionately small, economic return on the massive Soviet investments in Cuba. More visible, and perhaps more valuable, have been the political returns. While political issues are largely beyond the scope of this paper, it is important to point out that Soviet political gains from its Havana connection have recently become significant. Although Havana earlier may have been somewhat useful in support of Soviet foreign policy goals, especially in the UN and the nonaligned movement, Cuba has only recently been able to aid Moscow's objectives in a tangible way. The willingness of Cuban leaders to commit their combat forces in direct support of Soviet political objectives (first demonstrated in Angola) clearly provides the Soviets with foreign policy options unavailable earlier.

It is also beyond the scope of this paper to add to the large volume of existing analysis on the issue of Cuban autonomy or Soviet control in Africa or to speculate about future Soviet political benefits from its Caribbean client. Rather, the purpose has been simply to illustrate the evolutionary process which ultimately has led to a pervasive Cuban economic dependence on the USSR. Viewed over the last 20 years, that economic dependence has clearly been matched by an ever-increasing degree of Soviet influence, and possibly even some control over Cuban foreign policy goals and objectives.

In the second part we will analyze the development of Soviet economic relations with the Socialist Republic of Vietnam (SRV) since 1975 in order to discern any possible parallels with the Cuban experience.

VIETNAM

I. Introduction

Although the USSR has maintained relations with the Socialist Republic of Vietnam (identified as North Vietnam prior to 1975) since 1945, the evolution of that relationship into something resembling a closely knit economic-political alliance is a recent development. In fact, prior to 1975 North Vietnam managed, with varying degrees of success, to garner support from the Soviet Union and China while pledging allegiance to neither. Amid persistent rumors of a tilt in its relationship in favor of the Soviet Union, North Vietnam retained its economic and political ties with the People's Republic of China. With reunification of the country in 1975, the newly established Government of the Socialist Republic of Vietnam (referred to throughout the paper as Vietnam or the SRV) sought to strengthen its economic relationship with the West as well. After what appeared to be a promising start in moderating the Sino-Soviet influence in its economic development, Vietnam's relations with both China and the USSR changed suddenly in mid-1978. Since then it appears that Vietnam's political and economic ties with the USSR have been expanding rapidly, in a manner not unlike the evolution of Soviet-Cuban relations in the early 1970s.

II. Brief History of Soviet-Vietnamese Economic Relations

Prior to 1955 Soviet attitudes and actions toward Vietnam were tied to Soviet interests in Western Europe. As a result, the Soviet role in Vietnam between 1945 and 1954 was nonsupportive at best, despite the establishment in 1945 by Ho Chi Minh of a Communist-led independent government in Vietnam. Because Soviet actions before 1954 supported the French Communist party's interest rather than Ho Chi Minh's nationalistic goals, North Vietnam turned to China and the United States for assistance. However, the United States and the USSR supported France in its attempts to regain control over Vietnam. China, on the other hand, responded to Ho Chi Minh's request for support by recognizing his government in 1950 and sending in arms, supplies, and advisers in 1952. After the Geneva agreement in 1954, the USSR became more supportive of the North Vietnamese government and began developing economic ties through trade and aid. Between 1955 and 1964 the USSR supplied North Vietnam with over $400 million in nonmilitary aid, more than 40% of North Vietnam's nonmilitary aid receipts. China also provided approximately $350 million in aid, while the Eastern European countries contributed $200 million. (See Table 5 for figures on aid to the SRV.)

Just as early Soviet involvement in Vietnam was determined largely by USSR-European relations, Soviet interest in Vietnam after 1960 was linked to its rivalry with China. Between 1965 and 1975 this rivalry was temporarily downplayed as both countries assisted North Vietnam in its fight against a common foe—the United States.

Table 5

Aid to Socialist Republic of Vietnam[1]
(In Millions of U.S. Dollars)

	1955–64[2]	1965–75[2]	1976–80 (estimate)[3]
Total	993	4,304	5,613
Communist countries	993	4,116	3,831
U.S.S.R.	440	1,778	2,500
People's Republic of China	352	1,491	600[4]
Eastern Europe	201	844	719
Cuba	—	3	12
Non-Communist	n.a.	188	1,155

[1]Prior to 1975, was Democratic Republic of Vietnam or North Vietnam.
[2]*Source*: Citibank N.A., "Vietnam: An Economic Study," Hong Kong, September 1976.
[3]*Source*: Office of Economic Research, Central Intelligence Agency.
[4]Estimated Chinese aid receipts up to cutoff in mid-1978.

During the 1965–75 period the USSR poured more than $1.8 billion of nonmilitary aid into North Vietnam, paralleling its Cuba pattern. Like Cuba, North Vietnam also received fraternal support valued at some $840 million from the Eastern European countries. At the same time, North Vietnam enjoyed an option never fully exploited by Cuba. It received considerable amounts of aid from China. Between 1965 and 1975 Chinese aid is estimated to have reached $1.5 billion.

In the two decades following the French departure from Vietnam, the USSR also supplied Hanoi with $300 to $500 million annually in military aid, whereas Chinese military aid during that period averaged roughly $35 million per year.

By 1975 Soviet economic influence in North Vietnam had become extensive. Of 220 projects scheduled for construction under agreements between Moscow and Hanoi, over 160 were in various stages of completion. As in Cuba, projects extended to every sector of the North Vietnamese economy and included Soviet aid in constructing dams and hydroelectric stations, flour mills, port facilities, highways and railroads, and various industrial facilities.

After 1975, with the United States out of the picture, the Sino-Soviet rivalry resurfaced, and the struggle for influence in Vietnam intensified. Being more highly industrialized, the Soviets appeared to have a greater capacity to provide economic assistance than China, struggling with its own massive development problems. Fresh from similar negotiations in Havana, in 1975 the Soviets signed an agreement with Hanoi for economic and technical assistance. Under terms of the agreement the Soviets pledged to send technical experts to Vietnam and to provide economic, scientific, cultural, and technical training for Vietnamese personnel, as well as technical assistance for a number of major projects in Vietnam. More importantly, as it had with Cuba, Moscow extended MFN and substantial credits to Vietnam for the purchase of Soviet heavy industrial equipment, agricultural inputs, transport facilities, raw materials, oil, and food. Although no details are available on the negotiated terms of trade, it is probable that Vietnam was accorded preferences similar to those granted Cuba, with prices for Soviet oil and food set at subsidized levels compared to world market prices and at least partial payment allowed in Vietnamese goods rather than hard currency.

The 1975 bilateral assistance agreement was followed a year later by a similar agreement for construction of 40 industrial enterprises and other projects during 1976–80, including an iron and steel plant and a petroleum refinery and petrochemical complex. Clearly the USSR was prepared to compete with China to become Vietnam's most important economic benefactor over the long term. Whatever Moscow's motives, however, Vietnam appeared unwilling to become economically dependent on any one nation. Rather, following Cuba's example in its efforts after 1973 to renew ties with the United States and other hemispheric neighbors, beginning in 1976 the SRV leadership sought to strengthen and expand its relations with any developed country capable of assisting it to rebuild its economy. Diplomatic overtures were made to many Western nations, including the United States and ASEAN countries, with the hope of reestablishing commercial relations that had been severed during long years of conflict. But Vietnam seemed even more flexible and pragmatic than Cuba in seeking to broaden its economic contacts. Joining multilateral organizations such as the IMF, the World Bank,[7] and the United Nations, Hanoi opened up new sources of aid. As a result, Vietnam's aid and trade patterns began to change somewhat, just as Cuba's did in 1974–75. Of the $5.6 billion in aid and credit pledged to Vietnam for the 1976–80 period, over 20% ($1.2 billion) was committed by noncommunist sources. Noncommunist aid to North Vietnam between 1971 and 1975 is estimated at $440 million, over 50% of that in grant aid.

Vietnam's trade diversified as well (see Table 6). While North Vietnam conducted over 55% of its trade with the USSR during the 1970–75 period, compared to only 11% with the noncommunist countries, in 1977, 42% of its trade was with the USSR and 43% with noncommunist countries. The biggest change occurred in Vietnam's imports from the West. With access to new sources of aid, Vietnam was able to expand imports from the West. Whereas the USSR supplied North Vietnam with 50% of its total import needs in 1974, compared to only 13% from the noncommunist countries, by 1976 the Soviet share had dropped to 42%, while the noncommunist share had risen to nearly 39%. Similarly, buoyed by record high sugar prices in 1974–75, Cuba diversified and expanded its economic ties with noncommunist nations. However, when sugar prices subsequently declined, Cuba was forced to reorient its trade even more heavily to its Eastern communist trading partners.

Although Vietnam's attempts in 1975 and 1976 to chart an independent course were displeasing to Moscow, the Soviets could not exercise the same economic leverage they had used in Cuba in 1968 to redirect economic planning and insure support for their invasion of Czechoslovakia. In contrast with Cuba, Vietnam was more successful, at least temporarily, in avoiding continuously increasing dependence on Moscow. For one thing, the SRV was still receiving substantial aid from China, including 20% of its petroleum needs. Moreover, Vietnam was able to draw on new noncommunist sources of aid which promised significant assistance for its development goals in the long term. (Cuba also had access to official bilateral export credits after 1974, but its rapidly growing debt from continued hard currency trade deficits prevented Havana from using more than half of the available credit lines.) And finally, the Vietnamese economy was considerably more diversified than the Cuban economy, providing Vietnam more trading options.

Table 6

Socialist Republic of Vietnam[1] Foreign Trade by Major Area, Selected Years (In Millions of U.S. Dollars)

	1970	1974	1975[2]	1970–75	1976[2]	1977[2]
Total exports, f.o.b.[3]	46.6	127.1	142.5	514.0	232.3	347.7
Communist countries	32.8	83.5	96.9	366.8	122.0	220.0
U.S.S.R.	(18.6)	(57.3)	(66.4)	(243.4)	(85.9)	(176.5)
Non-Communist countries	13.8	43.6	45.6	147.2	110.3	127.5
Total imports, c.i.f.[3]	293.8	429.1	492.1	1,993.8	744.9	956.6
Communist countries	285.3	372.1	367.3	1,769.1	448.8	522.4
U.S.S.R.	(185.0)	(253.8)	(220.6)	(1,121.4)	(313.9)	(372.9)
Non-Communist countries	8.5	57.0	124.8	224.7	293.1	434.2
Trade balance	−247.2	−302.0	−349.6	−1,479.8	−509.6	−608.9
Communist countries	−252.5	−286.6	−270.4	−1,402.3	−326.8	−302.2
U.S.S.R.	(−166.4)	(−196.5)	(−154.2)	(−878.0)	(−228.0)	(−196.4)
Non-Communist countries	+5.3	−13.4	−79.2	−774.5	−182.8	−306.7

[1]Prior to 1975 was Democratic Republic of Vietnam or North Vietnam.
[2]Estimate based on available data for Vietnam's trade with CMEA nations.
[3]Totals are somewhat understated since data on SRV trade with some non-Communist countries are unavailable.

While some political strains appeared in the Soviet-Vietnamese relationship, Moscow remained steadfast in its economic support of Vietnam. In fact, 1976 saw an increase in Soviet equipment exports to the SRV, largely as part of the Soviet commitment to assist Vietnam with some major programs, most notably in the agricultural, oil and gas drilling, and mining-construction areas. The USSR also increased its agricultural exports to Vietnam in 1976. As indicated in Table 7, the value of Soviet wheat exports to the SRV doubled between 1975 and 1976, while raw cotton exports tripled. Since the USSR is a net importer of grains, it seems likely that (as in the case of Cuba) the Soviets supplied Vietnam with Western wheat, thereby helping the SRV offset agricultural production shortfalls. (Although some Western wheat found its way to Vietnam, Soviet grain shipments also included some poor quality Soviet wheat.) China also assisted Vietnam in meeting its food needs by giving 500,000 tons of rice in 1976.

Soviet assistance notwithstanding, by early 1977 it was evident that Vietnam's economic development program was in trouble and five-year plan goals would not be met. This coincided with indications that Cuba's economic performance would also seriously miss five-year plan goals. The Vietnamese leadership redoubled its efforts to obtain badly needed capital and technology from all available sources. Keeping one foot in the Soviet camp, Vietnam tried to woo Western investors by unveiling a new investment code in April 1977. (Similarly, in 1975 Cuba announced that foreign direct investment was acceptable "in principle.") The code, the most liberal ever promulgated by a Communist government, was greeted with enthusiasm and optimism in the West. Unfortunately, it yielded no concrete investments in the SRV. Moreover, by the end of 1977 it was clear that despite some progress in individual industrial sectors, Vietnam's overall economic performance had been dismal. Poor weather, insect damage, lack of fertilizers, bureaucratic mismanagement, and resistance by farmers in the South to producing more than subsistence levels of grain left Vietnam 1.5 million tons short of grain needed to feed its populace. However, just as it had increased support of Cuba when sugar prices plunged in 1975, the Soviets supplied sufficient economic aid to allow its client to mud-

Table 7

Major Soviet Exports to the SRV, 1974–77 (In Millions of Rubles)

Description	1974	1975	1976	1977
Machines, equipment and means of transportation	82.3	70.0	102.9	120.3
Of which:				
Metalworking machine tools	1.2	1.8	1.9	4.1
Power generating equipment	6.2	8.3	5.4	6.8
Electrotechnical equipment	1.7	1.2	.7	.8
Mining equipment	3.8	5.0	7.0	11.5
Drilling equipment	7.1	4.2	6.6	8.4
Of which:				
Hydrological drilling	.7	.1	.3	1.2
Oil drilling	6.0	3.5	5.9	6.7
Material handling equipment	1.0	.8	1.3	1.0
Construction equipment	3.1	2.7	2.5	.04
Construction equipment parts	.9	.2	.5	.5
Agricultural and forestry equipment	4.0	2.1	5.1	4.5
Irrigation and reclamation equipment	1.1	3.3	.5	.9
Tractors	3.3	1.6	6.4	2.8
Tractor parts	1.3	1.8	1.8	3.8
Other agricultural equipment	.9	1.0	2.2	2.3
Diesel locomotives	.7	.8	.8	1.6

Trucks	9.2	3.8	7.8	8.3
Truck parts	4.0	3.4	4.4	5.6
Airplanes and related equipment	9.6	1.6	9.7	5.7
Cable and wire	2.4	1.9	1.6	2.6
Equipment for chemical industry	.2	.1	1.0	2.9
Petroleum and petroleum products	11.3	14.2	14.4	27.8
Rolled ferrous metals	9.4	7.2	8.4	11.0
Of which: Sheet steel	5.6	2.6	n.a.	n.a.
Cotton (raw)	3.9	5.5	16.8	18.9
Wheat flour	42.4	16.3	16.9	20.0
Wheat	—	7.5	23.1	25.7
Rice	6.1	—	—	—
Cotton cloth	3.6	4.8	7.0	.3
Chemical products	.8	.9	1.2	1.0
Ammonia sulphate	2.9	3.2	2.2	4.2
Lumber products	—	1.0	1.4	1.3
Medicines	.6	.7	3.0	2.9
Subtotal	163.4	131.4	197.5	268.4
Other	28.9	27.3	35.0	5.8
Total:				
Million rubles	192.3	158.7	232.5	274.2
Million dollars[2]	253.8	220.6	313.9	372.9

Source: Vneshniaia torgovlia SSSR.

[1]Data for scrapers only. 1977 data for other types of construction equipment not available. Soviet scraper exports to SRV in 1976 valued at 300,000 rubles.

[2]Ruble-dollar conversion factors used: 1974—0.758; 1975—0.719; 1976—0.741; 1977—0.735.

dle through. In 1977 Vietnam imported the equivalent of $62 million in wheat and wheat flour from the USSR and $40 million in Western grain. While a large portion of the Western grain was probably shipped under aid agreements, it is virtually certain that the USSR supplied Vietnam with agricultural products on extremely favorable soft currency terms.

Vietnam's poor economic performance in 1977 was one of a series of events which together clearly signaled a turning point in the SRV's economic and political relations with the Soviet Union. On the political side, maintaining China as an alternative ally and benefactor became increasingly unfeasible. In early 1978 Vietnam's conflict with Cambodia, which had been smoldering since 1975, finally erupted into full-scale war. The USSR immediately aligned with the SRV, while China (with its own interests in Cambodia) remained officially neutral. Sino-Vietnamese relations continued to deteriorate, however, and by February China and Vietnam were engaged in skirmishes along their common border. The Vietnamese decision in March 1978 to fully nationalize the private commercial sector in the south (long the domain of resident Chinese) resulted in a mass exodus of Chinese from Vietnam and ultimately precipitated a complete Sino-Vietnamese split. In summer 1978 China canceled its $300 million a year aid program to Vietnam, including 80 known aid projects.

Faced with continuing delays in agricultural self-sufficiency, potential loss of Western aid due to both political issues and absorption problems, a rising hard currency trade deficit, and the ever increasing military drain on already scarce resources, Vietnam acceeded to Soviet pressure and in June 1978 joined the CMEA. According to Soviet officials, the CMEA will take over most of the abandoned Chinese projects and will provide preferential prices for Vietnam's major export products. Once again the Cuban pattern (that is, CMEA membership and subsidies) is apparently being followed.

Moreover, as with Cuba after 1973, Moscow was able to tighten its economic grip on Vietnam, since membership in the CMEA carries with it the responsibility to coordinate five-year plans. Thus, although degrees of coordination vary, the Soviet Union is likely to have an important role in planning Vietnam's future economic development.

Soviet-Vietnamese ties were strengthened even further with the signing of a Treaty of Friendship and Cooperation in November 1978 binding the two countries more closely together against their now common foe—China. This treaty was immediately followed with economic and technical agreements that when fully implemented will sharply increase Soviet aid to Vietnam. Under terms of the economic and technical agreement, the USSR agreed to help improve strategic railroads between Hanoi and Haiphong and between Hanoi and Ho Chi Minh City. (Cuba's main rail line has been entirely rebuilt with Soviet equipment and aid.)

The importance of Soviet aid was underscored in 1978 when Vietnam suffered a disastrous crop failure, its third in a row. Unable to acquire the 2.9 million tons needed to make up for domestic production shortfalls as gifts or loans from other countries, and able to pay for only a small quantity of imports, the SRV turned to the USSR, its traditional supplier of emergency food aid. Although no figures are available, it is virtually certain that Moscow, as it has several times with Cuba, again came to the rescue with substantial amounts of grain.

In January 1979, perhaps bolstered by Soviet political and military support implied by the Friendship and Cooperation Treaty, Vietnam invaded Cambodia. When China then retaliated by invading the SRV, the Soviet commitment to Vietnam was severly tested, reminiscent of the situation it faced during the 1962 Cuban missile crisis.

Although it is clearly premature to assess the political implications of very recent events on Soviet-Vietnamese relations, it is certain that Vietnam is under even greater economic pressure now than before, while its options are narrower than ever. Invading Cambodia has meant condemnation and counterinvasion by China, as well as widespread disapproval in the noncommunist West. Like Havana after the 1970 sugar disaster, Hanoi would now appear to have very limited options. If the Soviets follow their pattern in Cuba and accept the role of Vietnam's principal economic benefactor, the costs to the USSR will surely continue to increase. Moreover, as was the case in Cuba in the early 1970s, what the Soviets expect in return is very difficult to foresee at this point.

III. Vietnamese Economic Dependence—Soviet Costs

Like Cuban dependence, Soviet economic support of Vietnam involves direct and indirect costs that though primarily economic are also political.

As with Cuba, bilateral trade is probably the most important mechanism of Soviet economic support in Vietnam. The economic costs to the Soviets of trade with Vietnam derive primarily from the low subsidized sale prices of important Soviet goods such as oil and grain. The SRV, like Cuba, undoubtedly enjoys such subsidies by virtue of its "developing country" status in the CMEA. Unfortunately, in examining these costs we are hampered by an almost complete lack of information on SRV-Soviet terms of trade. Unlike Cuba, the SRV has never been very specific about the nature of its bilateral ties with the Soviet Union.[8] Hence the scope of this analysis is necessarily limited.

The Soviet subsidy is particularly important in Soviet-SRV oil trade. However, without specific information on the terms of trade, it is impossible to precisely determine the extent of this subsidy. Nevertheless, from available trade data we are able to approximate the volume and price of Soviet petroleum product exports to the SRV. (Soviet petroleum exports to Vietnam are predominantly gasoline and other fuels.) Between 1965 and 1975 Soviet deliveries of petroleum and refined products totaled approximately 3 million tons (equivalent to $132 million by value). Although volume figures are not available, the ruble value of Soviet petroleum deliveries to the SRV in 1976 reached the equivalent of $19.5 million and in 1977 jumped sharply to $37.8 million, bringing the total value of Soviet petroleum exports to Vietnam for the 12-year period to the equivalent of nearly $190 million. Depending on the amount of hard currency paid by Vietnam for petroleum products (we know that at least some of the deliveries are paid for that way), the total cost to the Soviet Union of supplying Vietnam with petroleum products from 1965 through 1977 could be equivalent to as much as $180 million, or more.

What is clear from the available data, however, is that the "price" per ton (in equivalent U.S. dollars) charged by the USSR for its oil product deliveries to the SRV has recently declined somewhat, in sharp contrast to rising world prices for crude. Between 1965 and 1969 the Soviet price per ton of petroleum products shipped to Vietnam remained fairly steady (roughly equivalent to $41 per ton), in line with prevailing world market prices for crude. After declining slightly to the equivalent of $38 per ton in 1970 and 1971, the price rose to $54 per ton in 1972 and $58 per ton in 1973, probably reflecting Soviet adjustments for the jump in world crude prices. However, as Soviet-Vietnamese economic relations broadened in 1974 and 1975, Soviet oil export prices apparently began to drop, despite steady increases in world market prices. In 1974 the value of Soviet petroleum product exports to Vietnam (in equivalent U.S. dollars) was $51 per ton. The trend continued downward in 1975 and 1976, when Soviet petroleum exports to Vietnam were valued at $44 per ton. In 1977 the value of these exports rose to $54 per ton. While this was below world market and intra-CMEA prices, it was exactly the same "price" charged by the Soviets for their petroleum exports to Cuba in 1977.

Soviet exports to Vietnam of wheat, flour, and rice also entail economic burdens in the form of direct costs. Since at least some, and probably most, grain is supplied on a soft currency basis (as in Cuba) or gratis as emergency food aid, the Soviets as net grain importers must incur a hard currency cost to purchase grain from Western sources. Soviet grain exports to Vietnam between 1965 and 1977 totaled 289 million rubles (equivalent to $365 million), 86 million rubles in 1976–77 alone. Hence the cost to the USSR has been roughly equivalent to $365 million, less whatever the SRV has paid for in hard currency. Table 7 presents major Vietnamese imports from the USSR between 1974 and 1977.

Aside from hard currency costs, the Soviet Union incurs other costs from its technical assistance program. Through the numerous agreements noted earlier, the Soviets have committed themselves to providing equipment and trained personnel to assist Vietnam in various projects. In 1975 the number of Soviet technicians in Vietnam was estimated at 2,000 and has certainly increased since then. If the CMEA takes over most of the abandoned PRC projects, as is its declared intention, it will mean sending in additional technicians, at least some of them from the USSR. In view of the worsening manpower shortage in the Soviet Union, supplying skilled technicians to Vietnam could be increasingly costly.

The problem may be even more acute in technical areas which have a high development priority in the Soviet Union. A prime example is oil and gas exploration. In July 1978 Hanoi and Moscow agreed on measures to build up Soviet technical assistance in oil and gas prospecting. This is one area where the Soviets would be particularly hard pressed to divert skilled technicians from domestic projects to work in Vietnam.

Perhaps more important for long-term Soviet interests are potential political costs associated with continued economic support of Vietnam. The SRV is not the only CMEA member country with a critical need for Soviet oil, equipment, and technical manpower; other CMEA nations are also supplied with varying amounts of these scarce resources. The massive economic assistance program for Cuba is a significant example. Vietnam's accession to the CMEA may have been initially welcomed by the USSR, but it was probably viewed with considerably less enthusiasm by the East European membership.

Whereas the Soviet Union gains important political benefits from Vietnam's membership in the CMEA (especially a powerful ally on China's southern border and a foothold in Southeast Asia), other CMEA members may see the SRV only as a further drain on their already overburdened resources. Accepting additional pressures on their own economies to subsidize Vietnamese development in return for long-term political and economic gains (which flow predominantly to the USSR) must be particularly unpalatable. Clearly Moscow may be using up valuable political capital among its European allies to extract support for the SRV in addition to the steadily growing burden of Cuba. How long the USSR will be willing to pay this political price is, of course, open to speculation and could present the Soviets some difficult choices in the next decade.

IV. Vietnamese Economic Dependence— Soviet Benefits

Thus far the discussion has concentrated on the evolution of Soviet-Vietnamese economic relations and resultant costs to the USSR. The Soviets are clearly committed to playing a dominant role in Vietnam's economic development. The decision could be an increasingly costly one, both economically and politically. A look at the benefits which the Soviets hope to derive may help place developments in a proper perspective.

Although Soviet economic aid and trade flows to Vietnam far exceed any current economic return to the USSR, there have been some economic benefits. The most obvious of them are trade related.

In return for its exports of equipment, petroleum, and agricultural products, the USSR imports from the SRV primarily consumer goods such as clothing, carpets, handicrafts, and foodstuffs. Since 1975 the Soviet Union has also imported Vietnamese rubber and rubber goods. (See Table 8 for Soviet imports from the SRV.)

Not only do Vietnamese exports help satisfy massive Soviet demand for consumer-oriented goods, but they also result in direct and indirect economic benefits to the Soviet Union. For example, Soviet imports of Vietnamese vodka have been increasing since 1960. It is possible that the USSR imports Vietnamese vodka for domestic consumption, freeing its own readily marketable vodka for export to hard currency markets.

An indirect economic benefit is hard currency earnings saved through Soviet access to Vietnam's rubber resources. Prior to 1975 the Soviet Union had no trade relations with the then government of South Vietnam. However, after 1975 Hanoi was able to tap the country's large rubber resources in the South, and in 1976 Soviet imports of Vietnamese rubber reached the equivalent of $6.4 million. (Data on Soviet rubber imports after 1976 are unavailable.) To the extent that Vietnam provides an alternative source of rubber (the USSR has traditionally imported much of its rubber from Malaysia—equivalent to over $640 million between 1970 and 1975), the Soviets realize a net hard currency savings.

Table 8

Major Soviet Imports from the SRV, 1974–77 (In Millions of Rubles)

Description	1974	1975	1976	1977
Tin	0.3	0.1	0.2	—
Rubber, resins, and resin-based goods	—	—	4.7	—
Parquet bordering	.1	.2	2.0	8.3
Tea	1.1	1.0	2.6	3.9
Pineapples	—	.1	.8	1.1
Bananas	.4	.6	1.0	1.1
Vodka	1.1	1.4	2.5	4.2
Liqueurs	1.7	2.1	2.3	3.0
Carpets	.5	.4	1.0	4.4
Overcoats and outer clothing	22.0	21.5	14.0	4.6
Knitted clothing	1.2	1.7	1.6	1.3
Rubber footwear	.2	.4	1.1	.9
Sport shoes	2.5	3.7	5.4	2.8
Cultural and household goods	4.1	5.1	9.7	2.5
Reed rugs and mats	5.1	6.0	6.3	9.1
Subtotal	40.2	44.2	55.8	9.4
Other	3.2	3.6	7.8	0.4
Total:				
Million rubles	43.4	47.8	63.6	129.8
Million dollars[1]	57.3	66.4	85.9	176.5

Source: *Vneshniaia torgovlia SSSR.*

[1]Ruble-dollar conversion factors used: 1974-0.758; 1975—0.719; 1976—0.741; and 1977—0.735.

However, by far the single most important economic benefit to the USSR hinges on development of Vietnam's potentially large, but as yet unproven, oil reserves, estimated by some industry experts to be capable of producing one million barrels per day (e.g., more than Malaysia and less than Indonesia). If these estimates prove accurate, in addition to freeing the two million barrels of Soviet supplied products for other uses, Vietnamese oil production of one million barrels annually holds out the prospect of large new sources of oil which might be available for Soviet use to meet its domestic and

CMEA supply requirements. However, even at the most optimistic pace of development, SRV oil production would not reach marketable quantities until the mid to late 1980s and would therefore ease the economic burden of supporting Vietnam only over the longer term.

Although political issues are beyond the immediate economic scope of this paper, Moscow's political gains from increasingly close ties with Hanoi should also be noted. Some observers have drawn close parallels between Cuba's direct military support of Soviet goals in Africa and Vietnamese activities in Southeast Asia, which also appear to fit well into Soviet objectives. As occurred in Cuba, a closer linkage to Soviet policies could develop as Vietnamese economic dependency grows.

In summary, during the long and not always smooth course of Soviet-Vietnamese economic relations, the USSR has been consistently willing to pay the economic price of at least a minimuim level of economic support for its Southeast Asian client. Thus far the bilateral relationship has developed much as the Soviet-Cuban relationship, with Soviet costs far exceeding any economic benefits. In both instances, therefore, political considerations loom large both as motivation for Soviet largesse and as potential sources of problems in future Soviet relations with the European CMEA. But the Cuban-Vietnam parallel may end there, for although Cuba, however reluctantly, has become locked into an economic-political alliance for which there appears to be virtually no viable alternative, Vietnam's future is still largely undecided. Because Vietnam's economy is more diversified, richer in natural resources (especially oil), and not yet as dependent on the Soviet Union, it is possible that the SRV can still maintain more economic and, hence, political independence than Cuba has. In the final analyisis oil will play the key role. Rapid development of this crucial resource could significantly influence the future course of SRV relations with both communist and noncommunist countries.

MONGOLIA

I. Introduction

Unlike Cuba and Vietnam, the economy of the Mongolian People's

Republic (referred to throughout this paper as the MPR or Mongolia) has been very closely linked with the Soviet Union almost since its establishment in 1924. It remains today as dependent on the USSR as it has ever been, and there is no evidence that its status will change.

For its part the Soviet Union continues to foot the bill for Mongolia's efforts to diversify its agriculture-based economy. In return for its investment, Moscow has gained some minor economic advantages and some major political benefits. Whereas the Soviet economic relationships with Cuba, and even more so Vietnam, are still evolving, Mongolia's path appears to be fixed.

II. A Brief History of Mongolian-Soviet Economic Relations

With the collapse of the Manchu Dynasty in 1911, China, Japan, and the Soviet Union struggled for dominance in Mongolia. The Soviets eventually prevailed, and in 1921 a procommunist government was established with Soviet help. In 1924 the Mongolian People's Republic was proclaimed and was immediately guided and protected by the USSR. Soviet troops prevented a Japanese takeover in 1938 and have since been called on periodically to put down insurrections.

The tenor of Soviet-Mongolian relations was set early on when in 1946 the two countries signed a Treaty of Friendship, Cooperation, and Mutual Assistance. Economic bonds between the two countries were cemented that same year with the signing of an Agreement of Economic and Cultural Cooperation. This agreement served as the basis for economic relations and provided for negotiation of protocols on trade and cultural exchanges, as well as the activities of Soviet engineers, technicians, and other specialists in the MPR.

After China recognized Mongolia in 1950, under pressure from the Soviet Union, the MPR received some Chinese economic assistance, largely in the form of labor for housing and road construction. However, with the Sino-Soviet split in 1960, the USSR once again became the principal source of economic assistance and the primary political forces. Since then Mongolia has consistently backed Soviet policies, and Moscow in return has provided generously for Mongolia's economic needs. In fact, without Soviet equipment, manpower, and capital, Mongolia would have remained an undeveloped agricultural nation.

Soviet aid to Mongolia prior to 1945 was largely military in nature. After 1945 and the signing of the Treaty of Friendship, Cooperation, and Mutual Assistance, Soviet aid took the form of credits and grants. Between 1945 and 1964 the USSR provided the MPR with the equivalent of $700 million in economic assistance. In addition to the grants and loans which were vital to Mongolian industrial development, the Soviet Union also provided equally valuable technical assistance on a variety of projects, including a petroleum refinery built in the 1950s. (In 1973, the last year for which information was available, production at the refinery was almost nil.)

Following the Sino-Soviet break, the pace of Soviet-Mongolian economic relations accelerated. In 1960 Mongolia joined the CMEA and in 1966 signed another Treaty of Friendship which replaced the 1946 Treaty and Agreement on Economic Cooperation. This twenty-year treaty provides for Soviet defense of Mongolia and permits construction of Soviet bases on Mongolian soil. During the 1961–65 period the Soviet Union assisted Mongolia in some 90 projects, including an open-pit coal mine, thermal electric power station, power transmission line, and a wide-gauge railroad.

Soviet aid increased after 1965, and the MPR was provided additional grants and loans equivalent to $550 million between 1966 and 1970. This figure was reportedly exceeded during the next five years, and it is likely that Soviet aid between 1975 and 1980 will also surpass the $500 million equivalent mark. In addition to grants the Soviet Union continued to provide enormous amounts of technical assistance. Mongolia's first power system went into operation in the late 1960s, and the large molybdenum-copper project at Erdenet was begun during the 1971–75 period.

Largely as a result of massive Soviet assistance, by 1978 over 1% of Mongolia's total 1,545,000 square kilometers was cultivated. In addition it is estimated that the industrial enterprises constructed with Soviet aid by 1978 were contributing more than 40% of Mongolia's total industrial output. For some industries the percentage was even greater; for example, electric power (90%) and coal mining (80%). During the current five-year plan period through 1980, Moscow has committed itself to assist the MPR on more than 240 projects, including a new fuel and power complex in central Mongolia and agricultural projects such as irrigation systems, land cultivation, and animal husbandry.

III. Mongolian Economic Dependence— Soviet Costs and Benefits

The costs to the USSR of developing and sustaining the Mongolian economy have been substantial. In addition to the costs of its technical assistance programs in Mongolia, the Soviet Union has incurred considerable economic costs in its trade with the MPR.

Since 1970 Mongolia has accumulated a trade deficit with the USSR of 1.7 billion rubles, equivalent to over $2 billion (see Table 9). Since Mongolia's sources of hard currency are exceedingly limited (only 4% of its trade is outside the soft currency CMEA network, and Western aid is estimated to have been $10 to $15 million between 1970 and 1976), the trade deficit was clearly financed by Soviet credits.

In addition to underwriting Mongolia's large and ever increasing trade deficit, another cost to the USSR derives from its petroleum and refined product exports to the MPR. Since 1965 the Soviet Union has supplied Mongolia with petroleum worth the equivalent of nearly $220 million (the bulk being refined products). While the terms of trade are unknown, it is likely that as with Cuba and Vietnam, these Soviet exports are provided at below market prices. And as indicated by the jump in value of 1976–77 exports, the cost to the Soviet Union of supplying petroleum products to Mongolia is likely to continue to increase over time. (See Table 10 for a list of Soviet exports to the MPR, 1974–77.)

The costs to the USSR in terms of technical manpower drain to Cuba and Vietnam have been noted before. However, Mongolia poses even greater problems since tens of thousands of Soviet technicians, advisers, and even laborers have already been committed to managing the MPR economy.

While the economic costs to the USSR of Mongolian economic

Table 9

Mongolian Trade with U.S.S.R., 1970–77 (In Equivalent U.S. Millions of Dollars)

	1970	1971	1972	1973	1974	1975	1976	1977
Mongolian imports	197.9	181.8	254.3	338.3	376.5	493.6	640.8	748.5
Mongolian exports	58.4	79.4	93.2	118.7	157.2	174.2	188.7	171.5
Balance	−139.5	−102.4	−161.1	−219.6	−219.3	−319.4	−452.1	−577.0

Table 10

Major Soviet Exports to Mongolia, 1974–77

	1974	1975	1976	1977
Machines, equipment and means of transport	167.7	221.6	315.6	375.9
Oil and oil products	12.5	13.1	25.7	35.0
Chemicals	1.4	1.3	1.4	1.8
Rubber	1.6	.4	—	—
Rubber goods	.2	.2	—	—
Construction materials	1.7	1.7	2.9	4.9
Lumber and paper products	2.0	2.5	3.4	4.2
Rope, hemp, nets	2.5	2.7	3.2	3.9
Tea	2.4	2.4	2.1	2.2
Meat and dairy products	2.6	3.0	4.4	1.8
Flour products	3.7	3.3	8.0	7.4
Sugar and vegetable oil	4.5	4.9	8.2	10.3
Cotton, woolen fabrics	14.4	15.0	14.7	15.9
Clothing	17.5	18.6	16.9	5.1
Shoes	4.3	5.1	5.1	3.1
Pharmaceuticals	3.3	3.9	3.7	3.7
Cultural and household goods	5.2	5.4	6.5	7.7
Wheat	—	1.4	—	4.6
Other	49.7	48.7	52.9	62.8
Total				
Million rubles	285.2	355.1	474.7	550.4
Million dollars[1]	376.5	493.6	640.8	748.5

Source: *Vneshniaia torgovlia SSSR.*

[1]Ruble-dollar conversion factors used: 1974—0.758; 1975—0.719; 1976—0.741; 1977—0.735.

Table 11

Soviet Imports from Mongolia (In Millions of Rubles)

	1974	1975	1976	1977
Fluorite	6.9	9.2	9.5	10.1
Wool	22.4	23.8	26.0	26.3
Beef cattle (for slaughter)	45.9	42.2	39.8	37.9
Meat and dairy products	26.8	28.2	37.8	26.1
Casein	.5	.5	.6	.7
Other	16.7	21.4	26.1	25.1
Total:				
Million rubles	119.1	125.3	139.8	126.1
Million dollars[1]	157.2	174.2	188.7	171.5

Source: *Vneshniaia torgovlia SSSR.*
[1]Ruble-dollar conversion factors used: 1974—0.758; 1975—0.719; 1976—0.741; 1977—0.735.

dependence are substantial, there are some economic returns. Mongolia is a major source of food for the Soviets. As indicated in Table 11, Soviet imports of Mongolian cattle, meat, and dairy products totaled 285 million rubles, equivalent to $385 million between 1974 and 1977. In addition, during that period the Soviet Union imported over 98 million rubles worth of wool and nearly 36 million rubles worth of fluorite for its steel industry. Mongolia has supplied an estimated 50% of USSR fluorite needs.

However, by far the most important returns to the USSR on its economic investment in Mongolia have been political. In 1944 the Soviets annexed Tannu Tuva, a large province in northern Mongolia. Of more importance to the USSR than the territory, however, is the installation of Soviet military bases in Mongolia and the stationing of Soviet troops along the Sino-Mongolian border. The Soviet presence in Mongolia is a painful thorn in China's side and possibly the single most important motivation for continued Soviet support of the Mongolian economy.

General Conclusions

The Soviets appear to follow a similar pattern in establishing economic ties with developing country client states. Cuba, Vietnam, and Mongolia can be viewed as three countries in different stages of evolution according to this pattern. The three are similar in that investments of Soviet resources yield a disproportionately small current economic return, but both the actual and potential political returns are large.

Although Moscow has willingly incurred the resource drain from its long-term support of Cuba and Mongolia, the addition of Vietnam as a client state could raise the costs substantially. Should the pattern be repeated with developing countries elsewhere, especially in Africa, the resource drain could become particularly costly for the already hard-pressed Soviet economy to handle.

Notes

1. Cuba's surplus with the USSR is partly offset by Soviet shipping charges since it generally imports from Cuba on an FOB basis.
2. Of which 3 million were at subsidized protocol prices and 800,000 at free market prices.
3. Inspite of the index mechanism, Cuba's sugar-for-oil terms of trade have deteriorated since 1974 as the apparent Soviet price paid for sugar increased 39% while the apparent cost (in terms of crude equivalent) of Soviet oil and products rose by 122%.
4. For more details on the economics of Cuban trade, see "Cuban Foreign Trade: A Current Assessment," unpublished staff research note, Office of East-West Policy and Planning, Industry and Trade Administration, Department of Commerce.
5. 1978 total Soviet exports of crude and products to Eastern Europe were estimated at 72 million tons.
6. Although a full member, Cuba apparently has not paid in its capital assessment (part in hard currency) to either bank.
7. Cuba withdrew from both in 1962 and has shown no interest in rejoining.
8. Cuba has frequently described its Soviet trade relations, in great detail, as an exemplary model for exchanges between developed and developing countries which should be followed by the capitalist world.

GEORGI MARINOV (BULGARIA)

Characteristics and Tendencies in the Economic Development of the Mongolian People's Republic, Cuba, and the People's Republic of Vietnam and Cooperation between Them and Bulgaria

The socioeconomic development of Cuba, Mongolia, and Vietnam shows once again the lasting relevance of the Marxist-Leninist theory of the social laws of the transition to socialism and the building of the new society. At the same time, it demonstrates its creative character and the ensuing possibilities of "every country that has moved along the socialist path, each in its own way to solve the problems of a socialist state system, the development of socialist industry, establishing cooperatives in the countryside, and the ideological reeducation of the popular masses."[1] As the concrete national conditions show, the experience of these three countries in building up the foundations of socialism may serve as an example and a reference point in tackling the complex economic and social problems in other countries that have chosen the socialist path of development. This applies first and foremost to the developing countries with a socialist orientation, whose problems cannot be regarded and

"Osobennosti i tendentsii v ikonomicheskoto razvitie na MNR, Kuba i SRV i s''trudnichesvoto na NRB s tiakh," *V''nshna t''rgoviia*, 1981, no. 11, pp. 8–13. Translated by Michel Vale.

resolved separately and in isolation from the general processes and phenomena that take place within the world socialist system or from the possibilities and prospects of development of their own economies on the basis of an international socialist division of labor, and at a certain stage, under the conditions of socialist integration as well.[2] For this reason it is of unquestionable practical and theoretical interest to examine the problems of the construction of the national economies of Mongolia, Cuba, and Vietnam, which not only participate in the international socialist division of labor, but as regular members of the CMEA have been actively drawn into the process of socialist integration.

As is known, the economic development of Mongolia, Cuba, and Vietnam is distinguished by a number of specific factors which give them a special place in the world socialist system and in the integrated community. These special factors are due primarily to their historical development, their natural and climatic conditions, the extent to which they are provided with mineral, material, financial, and labor resources, their geographical position, and their distance from the European members of the CMEA. All these things have an influence on their socioeconomic development in the first stage of socialist construction and on their participation in the international socialist division of labor and in socialist integration, and they give a specific countenance to economic relations and forms of cooperation.

An analysis of the initial economic positions from which these three countries began their progress toward socialism shows on the whole that their national economies, despite national differences, are characterized by a seminatural or single culture structure, a strongly pronounced agrarian character, an undeveloped or onesidedly developed industry, a limited internal division of labor, and a not particularly active participation in the international division of labor. Thus, for example, the economic base inherited by socialist Cuba had a highly distorted structure at all levels, a lack of stable internal sources of accumulation, inadequate and low professional training of skilled personnel for the national economy, a strong dependence on foreign trade, etc. For specific reasons (transition from feudalism, long years of war, the danger of intervention) the economic base on which the present development of Mongolia and Vietnam is taking place is similar. Despite successes achieved in building up the material and technological basis of socialism, the economic level of development of these three countries is still considerably behind the level of development of the other CMEA countries.[3] This is why external factors, the most important of which are the international socialist division of labor and socialist integration, at a certain stage are of no less decisive importance than internal factors for their social and economic development both in the first years of socialist construction as well as at the present.[4] This question is becoming more and more timely for all countries which have broken from the capitalist and neocolonialist system and have chosen the path of socialist transformation.

With their relatively similar initial economic bases and the similar external and internal conditions under which the economies of Mongolia, Cuba, and Vietnam are developing, there is a shared tendency to employ economic structures inherited from the past to restore the national economy, to develop the economy in the first stages of socialist construction, and to resolve both current as well as longer-term economic problems. This possibility exists because of the realities of the times: namely, the existence of the world socialist system, which is a crucial factor of historical development and possesses a tremendous industrial and scientific and technological potential, a relatively high level of development of the international socialist division of labor and socialist integration, and a qualitatively new type of economic relationship between socialist countries with different levels of economic development.

There are certain similar tendencies and elements in the way CMEA member countries at a lower economic level shape their economic strategies. The problems that must be dealt with in the first stages of constructing a material and technological base for socialism are similar in character. In concentrated form the most characteristic traits and features of a strategy for economic development of these countries can be discovered in the way they conduct their structural policy and implement socialist industrialization. The following is a general outline of a structural strategy: priority to development of the traditional sectors of the economy, which in principle belong to the agrarian and industrial and mining spheres.

Under conditions of active participation in the international socialist division of labor and the process of socialist integration, the traditional export products of Mongolia, Cuba, and Vietnam will find a promising market, advantageous prices, guaranteed foreign exchange incomes, and other external sources for financing economic development. Favorable external conditions will mainly help to deal with the increasing economic effect of such an important current economic task as the expansion and stabilization of existing sources of accumulation by raising the technical level and improving the productivity of labor in traditional branches and, above all, in those branches which provide the bulk of export resources. This in turn ensures a steady inflow of foreign exchange earnings and funds for production based on imports for the purposes of industrialization. Such a structural policy enables CMEA countries with a lower economic level to simultaneously improve the economic and social effectiveness of social production and to deal quickly with a consequent important political effect, with the most sensitive social problems such as unemployment, public health, education, social security, etc.

Second, Mongolia, Cuba, and Vietnam have the possibility at the very beginning of socialist construction to implement a selective structural policy that takes into account the effect of lasting and long-term internal and external factors that have limited their economic development for a rather long historical period. Similarly, economic structures are built with a high level of stability, without this causing any essential changes in long-term prospects. Two main directions for this construction and improvement may be noted. The first involves improving the structure of traditional branches by diversifying production. Thus, for example, in addition to sugar cane production and the nickel industry in Cuba, the introduction of new technology made possible the organization of dozens of new facilities in the chemical, paper-pulp, foodstuffs, and light industries, as well as nonferrous metallurgy. The same processes are evident in Mongolia, where in addition to livestock raising, the backbone of the Mongolian economy, a whole series of industrial sectors are in the process of formation: the leather industry, meat and meat products production, dairy products, etc. In Vietnam an intensive diversification of production is taking place in tropical agriculture, the paper-pulp, chemical, and light industries, and the foodstuffs industry. The second direction comprises the opening up of areas of production that are completely new for the economies of these countries, including in heavy industry. These are areas of production that are the principal vehicles of scientific and technological progress. It should be stressed that the development of both traditional sectors and areas of production, as well as new ones, is taking place under conditions of close cooperation and integration with the other CMEA countries and in accordance with the needs of the entire integrated community. In other words, the aim is to improve the degree of participation of these countries in the international socialist division of labor and socialist integration. A number of economic projects in Mongolia, Cuba, and Vietnam are being built for specialization within the international socialist division of labor and later of the integrated community. The integration profile of the economies of these countries is based on the traditional sectors and areas of production, which serve as the foundations for the present and subsequent stages of socialist construction.

In accordance with the chosen strategy for economic development, certain specific features may be discerned in the process of industrialization in Mongolia, Cuba, and Vietnam. Since these countries have no or an extremely limited base for the production of capital goods and, in particular, the tools of labor, the process of industrialization is taking place mainly on an industrial base that comes from abroad (mainly from the developed countries of the CMEA) and begins by raising the technical level of the traditional sectors and areas of production. Parallel with this these countries are also developing some of the most necessary aspects of heavy industry, which are aimed initially at serving the technical reorganization of the traditional sectors (farm machinery, fertilizer, etc.) or are important for the overall development of the economy (for example, electric power). The creation of a national base for the production of capital goods, at a level that is optimal for the country, is in principle planned for the next stage, when the necessary conditions have become ripe, and above all when the traditional sources

Development of Mutual Trade among Bulgaria and Mongolia, Cuba, and Vietnam (in millions of foreign exchange levs)

	1960	1970	1975	1980
Cuba	0.6	64.2	200.8	268.8
Mongolia	2.5	8.5	13.0	16.6
Vietnam	4.8	12.9	12.1	45.7
Total	7.9	85.6	235.9	331.1

Source: *V''nshna t''rgoviia na NRB, Statiticheski danni*, Sofia, 1980, 1981, pp. 30–33.

of accumulation are stabilized. Hence the decisive role of accumulation in the traditional sectors for the overall development of the economy and for industrialization, for which they provide the main bulk of export resources.

For specific reasons the principal characteristics of the social and economic development of Mongolia, Cuba, and Vietnam are preserved in the stage of participation in socialist integration as well. Consequently the specific aspects of economic cooperation with them are also retained. At the present stage the other countries of the CMEA still must provide considerable help and assistance. But unlike in the stage in which relations were predominantly bilateral, the role of multilateral relations in dealing with the social and economic problems and tasks of these countries increased sharply after they were brought into the CMEA. Similarly, the mutual effect from cooperation has been multiplied considerably, and the economic and scientific-technical development of these countries has been greatly accelerated. The fundamental postulates for this were set forth in the Comprehensive Program, in which a special section[5] is provided for promoting the adoption of special measures to accelerate the economic development of Mongolia. When Cuba and Vietnam were brought into the CMEA (in 1972 and 1978 respectively), these postulates retained their full force for these countries as well.

Bulgaria is cultivating active economic ties with CMEA countries of a lower level of economic development. Mutual trade is rising steadily, and 80% of Bulgaria's trade with these countries goes to Cuba. Among the CMEA countries Bulgaria is one of the most important economic partners of Cuba. Cooperation is both bilateral and multilateral within the CMEA.

The development of Bulgarian economic cooperation with the CMEA countries of a lower level of economic development comprises two basic stages. This distinction is dictated by the circumstance that for one very long period cooperation was limited mainly to dealing with specific and in most cases current economic problems of Mongolia, Cuba, and Vietnam. We moved on to a higher stage of cooperation after the necessary material, organizational, and economic conditions were created in the countries with a lower level of economic development; these conditions make it possible to employ higher forms of economic relations, such as specialization and cooperation in production in structure-determining branches, joint ventures and organizations, joint research, etc. At the beginning of the second stage of cooperation, economic relations between Bulgaria and Cuba, for example, began. In principle it is not impossible that in some cases even more mature forms of economic ties will be employed even in the first stage of cooperation.

Despite the fact that economic relations between Bulgaria and Mongolia, Cuba, and Vietnam as CMEA member countries cover different periods (the beginning is marked by the entry of the given country into the CMEA), it may be concluded that by the end of the '70s cooperation was still concentrated in those areas that were of priority importance for the development of the economies of these three countries in the given stages. For Mongolia this was mainly livestock raising, geological prospecting, the mining and processing of nonferrous metals, the production of construction materials, etc. For Cuba it was agriculture as a whole, the construction materials industry, the infrastructure, geological prospecting, the training of skilled personnel, etc. It should be noted that after 1975 economic relations between Bulgaria and Cuba also began to cover a number of structure-determining and progressive branches: machinery construction, electronics and electrical engineering, chemistry, and the paper-pulp industry. As with Cuba, economic cooperation between Bulgaria and Vietnam in the first years of Vietnam's membership in the CMEA was concentrated on tropical agriculture, geology, and the training of native cadres.

The principal aim of bilateral economic ties in the first stage is to help these countries strengthen the traditional sources of accumulation and increase national income in this period. Likewise, the necessary preconditions for passing on to the second stage of development of their economies, the stage of acceleration of the process of socialist industrialization, are gradually created. At the same time, the foundations are laid for a closely integrated interaction between the economies of Bulgaria, Mongolia, Cuba, and Vietnam over the long term.

So that the cooperation established in mutually chosen areas will yield the maximum economic effect in the shortest possible time (especially for Mongolia, Cuba, and Vietnam), there is a tendency for such forms of economic ties as will be conducive to the achievement of this goal, to be established on both a bilateral and a multilateral basis.

Mongolia and Vietnam, and to a lesser extent Cuba, have considerable natural riches which, however, are at a low level of development, exploitation, and assimilation. This is why, for example, in the area of geological prospecting, multilateral measures undertaken under the auspices of CMEA agencies will yield the best and most rapid results. General agreements for stepping up geological prospecting on the territories of Vietnam, Cuba, and Mongolia have been concluded with these three countries. Bulgaria is most actively involved in the organization of international geological expeditions. Encouragement should be given to the tendency for joint geological prospecting to be used as a foundation for setting up new economic areas of cooperation on a bilateral basis by including Bulgaria in the subsequent stages of development of a particular type of mineral resources, including the manufacture of the final product. This creates the preconditions for establishing lasting and long-term productive, scientific and technological, and commercial ties and for a rational division of labor and the satisfaction of mutual needs over a longer term. In the same way conditions are created for the utilization of more effective forms of cooperation and integration. Thus, for example, the enterprise "Mongol-Bulgarmetal" was created jointly with the Mongolian People's Republic. The purpose of this enterprise is to discover deposits and set up the production and technological conditions for the mining of nonferrous metals. Because most Mongolian mineral resources have not yet been exploited, there are considerable possibilities in this area to develop long-term production relations. Similar prospects are being explored with Vietnam. Bulgaria's cooperation with these countries in discovering their resources and their subsequent assimilation takes place in other forms and in other areas of the economy as well. In Cuba, for example, Bulgaria is helping to develop the nickel industry; in 1975 a multilateral agreement was concluded to establish in a joint effort new productive capacities for the mining of nickel and cobalt ore. Bulgaria and other CMEA countries are interested in developing rich deposits of bauxite in Vietnam. Because of the limited financial and material means of Mongolia, Cuba, and Vietnam, the CMEA countries should unite their efforts to more rapidly develop and exploit the agricultural and mineral resources of these countries; this will be a substantial contribution not only to building up modern economic complexes in these countries but also will help meet the important needs of the other CMEA countries as well. There can be no doubt that their opportunities for an even more active participation in the process of socialist integration will increase many times over.

It should be pointed out that so far, the cooperation of Bulgaria with Mongolia, Cuba, and Vietnam has been greatest and most fruitful in the agroindustrial sphere. The rich experience and traditions of our country in this area have given the agroindustrial sphere a certain priority in bilateral economic relations. This is also promoted by the circumstance that agriculture and the industrial sectors related to it are the most important at the present stage of economic development in Mongolia, Cuba, and Vietnam. In this area cooperation has long gone beyond mere exchange of commodities in international trade. The predominant forms of relations are in the construction of complete industrial projects and other projects, the providing of considerable scientific and technological assistance and highly skilled specialists, and the professional training of the domestic work forces of these countries in Bulgaria and on their own territories in special centers of learning created for that purpose. Complete plants are provided to these countries on the basis of credits at favorable terms. In Mongolia Bulgaria has helped build 14 relatively large industrial enterprises in the past ten years (a meat combine, a plant for leather goods, citrus fruit greenhouses, a hog yard, a canned goods plant, etc.). In Cuba dozens of industrial enterprises have commenced operations in the past fifteen years: ice plants, canned goods plants, cold-storage warehouses, machine-building factories for the production of agricultural and irrigation technology, etc. In Vietnam Bulgaria is building cold-storage warehouses, drying houses for tobacco, canned goods plants, a plant for the production of citronella oil, etc. It may be concluded that the construction of complete plants with Bulgarian assistance in these three countries has proven itself to be a very important form of industrial cooperation, since in this way an important contribution is made to the development of their industrial potential. Complete projects are also built in other sections of the economy in addition to the agroindustrial sphere: e.g., industry for the construction of building materials, the chemical industry, the pharmaceutical industry, machinery construction, etc. For example, in the last few years Cuba has been the leading receiver of Bulgarian exports of complete plants to CMEA countries. It should be noted that some of these facilities have an extremely great national importance, and in some cases the enterprises built become centers around which new industrial branches, subbranches, and production lines are formed. For example, the fur plant "G. Dimitrov" in Darkhan (Mongolia), the machinery construction complex for the production of agricultural machinery and equipment "The Heroes of 26th of July," and the factory for the production of irrigation technology "V. Levski" in Cuba are such examples. These large industrial objects are very important for the development of economic ties, especially industrial ties, in the future as well. Cooperation looks very promising with regard to specialization and cooperative ventures in production (with Cuba), the reconstruction and modernization, as well as the expansion of already existing capacities, the introduction of scientific and technological progress, etc. The construction of complete facilities also has another important consequence for mutual economic relations: the trained personnel necessary for these enterprises are educated, trained, and retrained completely with Bulgarian cooperation. For example, for the needs of the two above-mentioned factories in Cuba, Bulgaria will train about 450 Cuban citizens. Mongolian and Vietnam workers are also improving their skills in Bulgaria.

Cooperation in the agroindustrial sphere is gradually passing on to a higher stage of development, especially with Mongolia and Cuba. Ties in other regions as well are growing in connection with the development of modern agroindustrial complexes in these countries. At the Thirty-fifth Session of the CMEA, which took place in July 1981 in Sofia, two multilateral agreements were signed: for the comprehensive development of the production of sugar and for the production and industrial processing of citrus fruits in Cuba. Analogous bilateral agreements were signed between Bulgaria and Cuba as special cases. Thus cooperation between Bulgaria and Cuba in these two areas, which we know will be the mainstay of the Cuban agroindustrial complex, will acquire new dimensions and broader perspectives. At the same time, cooperation is also expanding in other areas of the agroindustrial sphere, especially in those aspects aimed at raising the technical level of agricultural production. Agroindustrial complexes are being built with Bulgarian aid in Mongolia. The first agroindustrial complex in the country specialized in the production of cereal foods, fruits, and vegetables, both fresh and canned, is being built near the city of Darkhan. The construction of irrigation systems is another important area of cooperation with Mongolia at the present stage. There are also good prospects for deepening cooperation in the agroindustrial sphere with Vietnam as well. Possibilities exist for establishing effective ties in the production of certain tropical crops: coffee, pineapples, rubber, etc. And progressive forms of cooperation, joint organizations, enterprises, etc., are being used. The rich mineral resources of Vietnam constitute another prospective development in cooperation in production and trade, namely, the oil industry.

Cooperation between Bulgaria and Mongolia, Cuba, and Vietnam in science and technology is in general taking place in the areas described. In practice every form of scientific and technological cooperation and integration known in the CMEA is being used. Cooperation in the area of technical assistance and the training of the domestic labor force is especially considerable. In Cuba the group of Bulgarian specialists is almost as large as the group from the USSR.

The number of Cuban citizens receiving an education and improving their skills in Bulgaria is growing. In the past five-year period about 500 Mongolian engineering and technical personnel improved their skills in Bulgaria. The training of specialists with various profiles for the needs of the Vietnam economy is on an even greater scale. There is a clear tendency emerging for scientific and technological cooperation to be closely linked with the basic directions of economic development in Mongolia, Cuba, and Vietnam. In addition it is concentrated in areas where active productive relations in machine-building technology can be expected to develop.

As mentioned, the conditions are gradually being created for moving on to a higher stage of cooperation and integration between Bulgaria and Mongolia, Cuba, and Vietnam. This is a stage of active structural adaptation, complementarity, and intertwining of the economic structures on a bilateral and multilateral basis. This process will open up new prospects for mutual economic relations under conditions of integration. We can expect cooperation to take place increasingly within the framework of multilateral agreements in accordance with the Comprehensive Program and the Coordinated Plan for Multilateral Integration Measures. The strategic problems of productive integration will be resolved on the basis of specialization and cooperation in production. The tendency for a gradual shift of economic and scientific and technological cooperation between Bulgaria and the CMEA countries still at a lower economic level from traditional branches to progressive and structure-determining branches, and from foreign trade to the production sphere, is an objective process which will leave its stamp on economic relationships henceforth. For example, there is already a shift to specialization and cooperation in jointly coordinated subbranches, of high priority for both countries, in machinery building, electronics, and electrical engineering. Similar additional opportunities are opening up for cooperation with Vietnam in a number of areas of machine building. Likewise, such possibilities exist with Mongolia as well. The development of these areas of production, which are fundamentally new for Cuba, Vietnam, and Mongolia, and the concentration of cooperation and integration in these areas mean that these countries will be needing considerable assistance in building up an adequate productive and material and technological basis. The complexity and duration of the process of creating such a base demands not only close coordination of economic plans but also a switch to agreements concerning long-term economic strategy on a bilateral and a multilateral basis within the CMEA. This is an objective tendency in the development of integrative processes in the CMEA at the present stage and is a legitimate pattern.

Notes

1. L. I. Brezhnev, *Mir sotsializma—torzhestvo velikikh idei*, Moscow, 1978, p. 589.

2. "The change in the social political structure of countries with a socialist orientation requires examination from the methodological positions of Marxist-Leninist theory for the transitional period from capitalism to socialism" (F. V. Stanis, *Vozniknovenie i stanovlenie ekonomiki sotsializma*, Moscow, 1980, p. 44).

3. For example, with regard to the index for electric power production per capita in 1980 (USSR = 100), these countries still lag behind considerably: Bulgaria - 80.6, UNR - 45.7, GDR - 121.1, Vietnam - 1.5, Cuba - 20.8, Mongolia - 17.2, Poland - 70.2, Romania - 60.3, Czechoslovakia - 97.3 (*Razvitie ekonomiki stran-chlenov SEV za 1971–1980 gg. Ekonomiko-statisticheskii obzor*, Moscow, 1980, p. 70). The relative share of machinery construction in total industrial output is low. Structurally speaking, the major economic links are still lacking. Foodstuffs and mineral raw materials with a low level of industrial processing, etc., predominate in the export structure of these countries.

4. "Under contemporary conditions external factors are beginning to show their beneficial impact, especially on the groundwork of domestic factors" (G. Aroio, *Sblizhavane i izravniavane na ravnishcheto na ekonomicheskoto razvitie na stranite-chlenki na SIV*, Varna, 1977, p. 55). These observations are especially true for CMEA countries at a lower level of economic development.

5. *Kompleksna programa*, Sofia, 1971, pp. 21–22. We have in mind the references to the construction of major economic facilities, the provision of credits on favorable terms, the employment of incentive and preferential prices, the accelerated training of a domestic workforce, etc.

P. NAVROZOV AND E. PLOTNIKOV (USSR)

Soviet-Vietnamese Friendship—a Factor of Peace and Construction

I

The relations between the Soviet Union and Vietnam are one of the clearest examples of the life-affirming force of the principles of socialist internationalism. Throughout the entire history of relations between these two states, these principles have demonstrated a creative revolutionary spirit, corresponding to the high ideals of freedom, peace, and socialism. The real charter of Soviet-Vietnamese brotherhood was the agreement on friendship and cooperation between the USSR and the People's Republic of Vietnam signed in Moscow more than five years ago, on November 3, 1978. As the logical consequence of multifaceted Soviet-Vietnamese relations that had survived the test of the radical turnings of history, this document established a legal foundation for a broad range of mutual relations. The agreement opened up a new page in the chronicle of indestructible friendship and fruitful cooperation between the USSR and the Republic of Vietnam and raised the relationships between our parties and states to a qualitatively higher level.

The agreement also served such extremely important goals as strengthening solidarity and comradely mutual assistance and mutual support and the securing of peaceful and constructive labor of the peoples of the two countries.

Russian text © 1984 by "Nauka" Publishers. "Sovetsko-v'etnamskaia druzhba—faktor mira i sozidaniia," *Mirovaia ekonomika i mezhdunarodnye otnosheniia*, 1984, no. 1, pp. 18–27. Translated by Michel Vale.

This historical document is an authoritative affirmation of the unshakable principles of Marxism-Leninism and socialist internationalism. Article 1 of the agreement stresses the endeavor of the Soviet Union and Vietnam to "unswervingly develop political relations and deepen comprehensive cooperation, to provide comprehensive support to one another on the basis of mutual respect of state sovereignty and independence, equal rights, and noninterference in one another's internal affairs."

The agreement clearly shows the broad range of its application: the political relations between the USSR and the Republic of Vietnam, economic and scientific and technical cooperation, relations between the agencies of state power and social organizations, contacts in science and culture, education, literature, and art, the press, radio and television, public health, environmental conservation, tourism, and athletics between the workers of both countries. An exchange of knowledge and experience accumulated in socialist and communist construction is provided for, along with long-term coordination of the economic plans of the Soviet Union and Vietnam, a coordination of long-term measures to develop the most important branches of the economy, science, and technology and a pooling of efforts to raise steadily the living standards of the peoples of both nations.

But the importance of the Soviet-Vietnamese agreement goes far beyond the framework of bilateral relations. The preamble and nine of the articles express the firm resolve of the Soviet Union and socialist Vietnam to contribute to the strengthening of peace in Asia and in the entire world, to struggle for the further consolidation of the unity of all the countries of the socialist community, for peace, national independence, democracy, and social progress, and to contribute to the development of good relations and mutually advantageous cooperation between states having different social systems.

The preamble of the agreement says that the Soviet Union and Vietnam see it as their international duty to "help one another strengthen and protect socialist achievements gained through the heroic efforts and self-sacrificing labor of their peoples." The statements of Article 5 of the Agreement, according to which both parties "will actively resist all the designs and intrigues of imperialism and the forces of reaction,'' were not to the liking of those who would whip up international tension and strike discord among the socialist countries. Article 6, in turn, says that ''if one of the parties should be the object of aggression or the threat of aggression, the supreme parties to the agreement will immediately enter into mutual consultations for the purposes of eliminating this threat and undertake the appropriate effective measures to ensure the peace and security of their countries.'' But the agreement ''does not affect the rights and duties of the parties as spelled out in existing bilateral and multilateral agreements concluded with their participation and is not aimed against any third country'' (Article 7).

The Soviet-Vietnamese agreement is a long-term document. It was concluded for an initial period of twenty-five years with automatic prolongation for ten years on each occasion if one of the parties does not declare its desire to terminate its validity. However, even within the past five years, it has already demonstrated its vital force. Its principles have become enriched by concrete historical experience and have been materialized in the weighty achievements of our countries.

As the leadership of the CPSU and the Republic of Vietnam have stressed more than once, the most important point in the agreement is that it was intended to serve, and indeed actually does serve, the interests of peaceful, constructive labor of our peoples. It is sufficient to recall the complexity of the circumstances surrounding Vietnam at the time the agreement was concluded and the difficulties the hostile policies of the forces of imperialism and hegemonism had created for socialist construction in the Republic of Vietnam.

While the Vietnamese people were still nursing the wounds inflicted on the country by the long years of aggression and intervention of American imperialism, the antipopular Pol Pot regime mounted an undeclared border war against Vietnam. This war, which continued until the end of 1978, ended with the collapse of the genocidal regime. Relying on the assistance of the Vietnamese People's Army, the Kampuchean patriots overthrew the criminal clique of Pol Pot, Yeng Sari, and Khieu Sampan and installed a genuinely popular order in the country. Peace and tranquillity set in on the southwestern borders of Vietnam.

But the peaceful respite proved to be short-lived. This time, the constructive labors of the Vietnamese people were interrupted by aggression from the north, from those who took it upon themselves to "teach a lesson" to a sovereign nation. This aggression, which was tacitly sanctioned by the American administration, was a total failure as a result of the heroism demonstrated by the Vietnamese border guards and militia and of the resolute and effective measures undertaken by the Soviet Union and other countries of the socialist community in support of the Vietnamese people.

Much has been done to develop the legal foundations of bilateral relations since the Soviet-Vietnamese agreement was signed. A number of accords and protocols, opening up fundamentally new areas of cooperation between our countries, have been signed. Some that are especially worthy of mention are the accord to create a Soviet-Vietnamese enterprise for geological survey and the extraction of oil and gas on the continental shelf in southern Vietnam, the acceptance of Vietnamese citizens for study and work in the USSR, and conditions for exchange journeys for the citizens of both countries and for legal assistance.

The Soviet-Vietnamese agreement of 1978 has become an important part of the system of official acts regulating relations between Vietnam and its fraternal socialist countries. Today the Republic of Vietnam has agreements on friendship and cooperation with Laos, the GDR, Bulgaria, the Mongolian People's Republic, Czechoslovakia, and the Republic of Cuba; it also has an agreement on friendship, peace, and cooperation with the Republic of Cambodia. The fundamental internationalist orientation in foreign policy of the countries of the socialist community is clearly embodied in all these documents. Thus Article 5 of the Vietnamese-Bulgarian agreement stipulates that Vietnam and Bulgaria will continue to apply their efforts to defend international peace and security, will actively combat all the designs and intrigues of imperialism and the forces of reaction, and will support the struggle for the ultimate liquidation of colonialism, neocolonialism, and racism in all their forms. They are for disarmament and the maintenance and deepening of the process of détente in international relations, for the final abolition of aggression and aggressive wars, for peace, national independence, democracy, and socialism. The Vietnamese-Mongolian agreement states that Vietnam and Mongolia, faithful to their international duty, will apply all efforts for the comprehensive consolidation of solidarity and unity among the countries of the socialist community on the principles of Marxism-Leninism and socialist internationalism and will strengthen the world system of socialism.

The signing of agreements with the countries of the socialist community was accompanied by the conclusion of new, increasingly broader accords on mutual activity in various areas of the economy, science, technology, etc. The most important result of this process has been to place cooperation between Vietnam and the fraternal states on a long-term basis, which has created favorable possibilities for clearer long-term planning and for taking into account current needs. In Vietnam's foreign trade relations with the socialist countries there is a gradual transition taking place from traditional channels of trade and commerce to industrial cooperation.

Today there is practically no area of the economy, science and technology, and culture in which the countries of the socialist community have not aided Vietnam. Since 1978 Vietnam has been a member of the CMEA. The highly effective and multifaceted aid of fraternal countries has made a major contribution to the development of industry, the intensification of agricultural production, and provision for the vital needs of the Vietnamese people. As the General Secretary of the Central Committee of the Communist Party of Vietnam, Le Duan, pointed out in an article dedicated to the fiftieth anniversary of the Communist Party of Vietnam, "The signing of agreements of friendship and cooperation between Vietnam and the Soviet Union and other fraternal states and Vietnam's entry into the Council of Mutual Economic Assistance have effectively helped to consolidate relations of solidarity and cooperation of our country with the world socialist community and have given the Vietnamese people a firm basis for the general development of the fatherland and the defense of its territorial integrity."[1]

II

The foundation of Soviet-Vietnamese relations is a concordance of views and actions of the vanguards of the peoples of the two countries—the Communist Parties of the Soviet Union and Vietnam. This political and ideological unity derives from their belief in immortal Marxist-Leninist theory and in proletarian socialistic internationalism. The foundations of relations of friendship, solidarity, and mutual assistance between Soviet and Vietnamese communists were laid in the 1920s. The great son of the Vietnamese people, Ho Chi Minh, deserves credit for this; as he wrote: "The more the working class and the people of Vietnam think about their hard, humiliating, and enslaved past and the various stages of their tormented and selfless struggle, at the same time replete with glorious victories, the more profound becomes their awareness of how much they owe to Lenin and the October Revolution."[2]

The revolutionary activity of communists of the two nations has been intimately intertwined throughout all stages of history. During the period of French colonial rule, Vietnamese revolutionaries bravely defended the first stage in the world revolution of workers and peasants and spread true information about the young country of soviets. For the Soviet people solidarity with Vietnam has been a command of the heart and reason both in the years of peaceful construction and during the struggle of the Vietnamese people against the French and American imperialists.

For the party of Vietnam communists, the union with the CPSU and with the land of the great October Revolution has become a firm historical tradition and is the cornerstone of the foreign policy of the party and the state. The basic line of the Republic of Vietnam, namely, the consolidation of fraternal friendship, militant solidarity, and general cooperation with the USSR, is set down in Vietnam's new constitution.

The principal lines of development of Soviet and Vietnamese relations and their basic content are laid down during top-level meetings. There have been seven such meetings since the signing of the Soviet-Vietnamese agreement. During the talks that took place in Moscow on July 29, 1983, Iu. V. Andropov and Le Duan exchanged information on major questions having to do with the party and state life of the two countries and examined current problems of the international situation of mutual interest to the two. Special attention was devoted to the problems of the struggle for peace and eliminating the threat of war. Le Duan expressed his full support to the peaceful initiatives of the Soviet Union and other fraternal socialist countries. Iu. V. Andropov declared that the USSR would continue to aid constructive efforts in Vietnam. The leaders of the two parties also analyzed some of the specific trends toward improving economic relations.

Interparty collaboration is evolving vigorously. The optimal paths for dealing with routine problems are determined on the basis of a comprehensive exchange of experience of the party leaderships in socialist construction.

A Soviet delegation of party and government officials, headed by G. A. Aliev, member of the Politburo of the Central Committee of the CPSU and First Vice-President of the Council of Ministers of the USSR, made an official visit of friendship to Vietnam on October 27–November 4, 1983. This visit was a new contribution to the further consolidation of friendship and improving cooperation between the two countries and parties. In the discussions, which reflected a thorough mutual understanding and unity of views of both parties, effective measures for further deepening Soviet-Vietnamese relations of friendship and cooperation were weighed, and current international problems were touched on. The long-term program of development of economic and scientific and technological cooperation between the USSR and Vietnam was signed.

The joint declaration on the results of the visit stresses that Soviet-Vietnamese relations are vigorously developing in full accord with the spirit and the letter of the Soviet-Vietnamese agreement, which "embodied the desire of the CPSU and the Communist Party of Vietnam and of the Soviet and Vietnamese peoples for a further strengthening of solidarity and the steady deepening and expansion of bilateral relations in all areas" and had become "a reliable instrument in the struggle for peace and stability in southeast Asia, for the security of nations, and against the belligerent forces of imperialism and international reaction, and finally, had a positive effect on the development of the situation on the Asiatic continent."[3]

On the international arena the USSR and the Republic of Vietnam uphold common positions on all the most important problems. Vietnam actively supports the efforts of the Soviet Union to strengthen peace and international security. Together with the CPSU and other fraternal parties, the Communist Party of Vietnam works actively to consolidate the socialist community and unity in the world communist movement against imperialism and all forms of reaction. Both states are for the adoption of concrete measures to curb the arms race, and for the conclusion of accords to abolish nuclear and chemical weapons and prohibit the creation of new forms of weapons of mass destruction.

Socialist Vietnam plays the role of a pillar of peace and socialism in southeast Asia. Given the continuing interference of reactionary forces, above all U.S. imperialism, in the affairs of this region, Vietnam, together with the Laotian People's Democratic Republic and the People's Republic of Cambodia, consistently upholds the causes of peace and good neighbor policy and pursues a line of constructive dialogue with the member nations of ASEAN.

This constructive line was specified in a four-point program put out by the government of the Republic of Vietnam in July 1976, which laid the foundations for the foreign policy of Vietnam in this region. The program provided for the development of fruitful political, economic, and other relations between the countries of this area on the basis of principles of peaceful coexistence, the abolition of foreign military bases, nonpermission of the use of the territory of the nations of this region for interference in the internal affairs of neighboring states, and the resolution of all disputed questions in a spirit of equality, mutual understanding, and mutual respect.

However, the struggle for a normalization of the situation in southeast Asia has encountered the active resistance of imperialism and hegemonism. The member nations of ASEAN are being pressured to reject the establishment of good neighbor relations with the Republic of Vietnam and the Laotian Democratic People's Republic and a recognition of the only lawful government of popular Kampuchea.

Yet the consultations and exchange of opinions between the Republic of Vietnam, the Laotian Democratic People's Republic, and the countries of ASEAN are nevertheless continuing. The proposals, full of a love of peace and goodwill, of the conferences of Foreign Ministers of Vietnam, Laos, and Kampuchea in 1980–83 provide for regulating the situation in southeast Asia by, for instance, the signing of bilateral or multilateral agreements between the two groups of states in the region, Indochina and ASEAN, on nonaggression and peaceful coexistence; regional conferences with their participation or consultations to discuss problems of mutual interest; the signing of agreements on peace and stability in southeast Asia followed by the convoking of an international conference to guarantee peace and stability; an international conference on southeast Asia with participation of the countries of the region, the five great powers who participated in preceding conferences on Indochina, as well as India and Burma; the adoption, on the basis of consultations, of ASEAN's proposal to create a zone of peace, freedom, and neutrality in the region, etc.

The summit conference of the three countries of Indochina in February 1983 in Vientiane was an important event. This meeting once again persuasively demonstrated that despite all attempts to disrupt dialogue in the region, the fraternal nations of Indochina are steadfastly endeavoring to continue their policy of peace, friendship, cooperation, and good neighborliness. The telegram of the Central Committee of the CPSU, the Presidium of the Supreme Soviet of the USSR, and the Council of Ministers of the USSR to the participants at the Vientiane conference expressed solidarity with this constructive course aimed at reducing tensions in the region and establishing the principles of peaceful coexistence between the countries of Indochina and the member nations of ASEAN.

The partial withdrawal of Vietnamese volunteer troops from Kampuchea, which has now taken place twice in 1982 and 1983, and the decision to withdraw some volunteer forces each year from this country depending on the further stabilization of the internal situation, was testimony to the goodwill of the peoples of Indochina.

In the joint Soviet-Vietnamese declaration adopted with regard to the results of the official visit of friendship of the Soviet party and government delegation to the Republic of Vietnam in October-November 1983, it is stated that "The Soviet Union fully supports the peace-loving foreign policy of the Republic of Vietnam, the constructive proposals of the Socialist Republic of Vietnam, the Laotian People's Democratic Republic, and the People's Republic of Kampuchea to improve the situation in southeast Asia and to transform it into a zone of peace, stability, and cooperation."[4]

Taking into account the fundamental interests of mankind, and guided by the resolutions of party congresses, the USSR and Vietnam are carrying on a consistent struggle to normalize relations with China.

Placing fundamental stress on the vital interest of all peoples, the struggle to ward off the threat of a new world war, and the regulation of regional conflicts, the Soviet Union and Vietnam attach major significance to the establishment of a just and stable peace in the Near East on the basis of a withdrawal of Israeli forces from all Arab territories occupied since 1967 and the securing of the legal rights of the Palestinian people, including its right to self-determination and the creation of its own independent state.

The peoples of the Soviet Union and Vietnam express fully solidarity with the Democratic Republic of Afghanistan and Cuba, sharply condemn the U.S. aggression in Grenada, support the just struggle of the patriots of Namibia headed by SWAPO, and support the total abolition of the iniquitous system of apartheid. They attach special significance to so important an international factor as the nonaligned movement, which is leading the struggle for peace, against imperialism, and for an equal and mutually advantageous international cooperation.

The USSR and the Socialist Republic of Vietnam are active supporters of the idea of transforming the Indian Ocean into a peace zone. They are for the banning of nuclear weapons in this area, the abolition of foreign military bases, and the reduction of the level of foreign military presence.

In 1983 demonstrations against the new turn in the arms race unleashed by U.S. imperialism, against the deployment of American middle-range missiles in Europe, and in support of the peaceful proposals of the Soviet Union acquired a broad scope in Vietnam. The Communist Party, the government, and the people of Vietnam fully supported the declaration of Iu. V. Andropov, General Secretary of the Central Committee of the CPSU and Chairman of the

Presidium of the Supreme Soviet of the USSR.

III

The dynamic vigor of Soviet-Vietnamese economic relations plays an important role in building a new society in the Republic of Vietnam, helping that country solve many economic problems, develop science and culture, and build a powerful legion of qualified scientific workers, engineers, and technicians. In the years that have passed since the agreement on friendship and cooperation was signed, dozens of projects, including the "Kaoshon" coal mine producing one million tons of coal per year (first shift), the "Mongzyung" mine (first shift, 450,000 tons coal per year), and five modern piers in the port of Haiphong have been put into operation in Vietnam. The Soviet Union constructed a surface space communications station like "Intersputnik" in Vietnam and has helped to restore normal traffic on the Hanoi–Ho Chi Minh City railroad.

In the current five-year period the USSR and the Republic of Vietnam are cooperating in the construction of about forty large economic projects. Special support is given to the development of sectors which will make it possible to utilize most effectively the riches of the country, both its natural and its labor resources.

Considerable attention is being devoted to the development of the fuel and energy sector. The Soviet Union provides technical aid to Vietnam in the construction of such major projects as the Horbin hydroelectric power plant on the Black River (2 million kilowatts) and the Falay thermoelectric power station (640,000 kilowatts). Joint efforts are being applied to prospecting for oil and gas deposits on the continental shelf in the south of the country. An agreement signed on July 18, 1981, resulted in the creation of the joint venture "Vetsovpetro," which is operating in Vungtau, a small city in southern Vietnam. A large on-shore industrial base has been constructed there to provide for offshore drilling for oil and gas. The first stationary drilling platform for future wells is almost ready to be towed out to sea.

This bilateral cooperation helps Vietnam deal with so complex a problem as transport as well. The construction of the Thanglong Bridge across the Red River, the largest bridge in southeast Asia and unique in its construction, is nearing completion in Hanoi. The Hanoi railroad depot is being modernized. Problems in the reconstruction of the Hanoi-Haiphong railroad are being dealt with.

Thousands of Soviet people are fulfilling their international duty in helping Vietnam construct new factories and plants and other projects. About 200 industrial enterprises built between 1955 and 1982 today provide 35% of all electric energy, 89% of the coal mined, 100% of superphosphate, and 76% of all milling machinery.

The Soviet Union is the largest trading partner of the Republic of Vietnam. Whereas in 1978 trade between the two countries amounted to 457.8 million rubles, in 1982 it exceeded 1 billion rubles and continues to grow. The USSR furnishes equipment for energy production, mines, and conveyance and transport, road-building and agricultural technology, trucks, ferrous metals, petroleum products, chemical fertilizers, food, and mass consumption goods. In addition to exports on commercial terms, nonremunerated supplies have been sent to fraternal Vietnam during these years.

Vietnamese exports to the USSR have also increased (by 50% in 1982 compared with 1980). Vietnam supplies the USSR with flooring, natural rubber, coffee, tea, essential oils, arts and crafts products, drugs, and carpets and mats. The inhabitants of the Soviet Far East receive Vietnamese fruits and vegetables in steadily increasing quantities.

New forms are being introduced into the trade and economic relations between the two countries. A number of industries in Vietnam (the textile and shoe industries, carpet manufacture, etc.) are operating partly on Soviet raw materials. Cooperation in compensation projects is being refined (for example, in the production of rubber and tin). In 1983 Vietnam began to supply articles from local industry some of which was processed from Soviet raw material.

A further increase in the effectiveness of cooperation is on the order of the day. An important aspect in the resolution of this task is coordination of economic plans; this first came into practice when the five-year plans for economic development of the two countries for the period 1981–85 were compiled.

The Soviet Union helps Vietnam train and retrain cadres. In the twenty-five years of cooperation in this area (1955–80), 70,000 specialists of higher and middle-level qualification have been trained. Today about 5,000 Vietnamese students are studying in 150 colleges and universities in 33 Soviet cities. Since 1981 the USSR has provided training and advanced training to Vietnamese managerial cadres in the party and state apparatus and familiarized them with the Soviet experience in building party, economy, and state.

There is one other new form of cooperation, namely, training Vietnamese workers in factories, plants, and building sites in the Soviet Union. The USSR has for many years been helping Vietnam perfect its system of vocational and technical training. After an agreement was signed between the two governments on April 2, 1981, young Vietnamese citizens began to be sent to Soviet enterprises to learn the areas of specialization necessary for the economy of the Republic of Vietnam.

IV

An agreement signed in April 1982 promotes the further development and deepening of cultural and scientific ties between the USSR and Vietnam. Soviet research institutes provide Vietnamese scientists with broad possibilities for working in their laboratories, at the same time helping to establish a scientific base on Vietnamese soil. Scientists of both countries are turning with increasing frequency to joint work on problems of mutual interest and are organizing scientific conferences and symposia. A clear indication of the level of scientific cooperation was the flight of the space ship Soyuz-37 in July 1980, whose crew consisted of Commander V. Gorbatko, Soviet cosmonaut, and the Vietnamese research cosmonaut Fam Tuan.

Exchange of exhibitions, performing groups, individual performers, films, television programs, and social and political and artistic literature is growing from year to year. For example, in the past five years the exchange of printed material between the USSR and the Republic of Vietnam has increased by more than threefold. Mutual journeys of writers, cinematographers, and representatives of artists' unions have become a regular phenomenon.

The USSR culture days in Vietnam, the first of which occurred in December 1982, have become a rather important event in the chronicle of cultural cooperation between the two countries. A large brigade of Soviet artists has performed in Vietnam, there have been numerous exhibitions, and Soviet films have been shown in more than 2,500 cinemas and clubs.

The publication of Lenin's *Complete Works* in 55 volumes in Vietnamese between 1971 and 1981 has a permanent value; it created the conditions for a broader and all-embracing study and creative utilization of Lenin's theoretical heritage in the Republic of Vietnam. This was the great service of a group of specialists and translators from the Soviet publishers "Progress" and the Vietnamese publishers "Shytkhat" ("Truth") and scholars from the Institute of Marxism-Leninism of the Central Committee of the CPSU and a number of scientific establishments of the Central Committee of the Communist Party of Vietnam. A telegram from the Central Committee of the Communist Party of Vietnam on the occasion of the completion of the publication of Lenin's *Complete Collected Works* stated that "The publication of Lenin's works in the Vietnamese language is a priceless gift of the CPSU, the government of the USSR, and the entire Soviet people to the Communist Party of Vietnam, the government of the Republic of Vietnam, and the Vietnamese people. Since the day it was formed, our party has always considered and continues to consider the dissemination of Lenin's works to be its prime ideological task."[5]

The past five years have seen a new development of traditional relations between social organizations of the two countries—professional trade unions, youth associations, etc.—and between certain work collectives of factories, plants, and educational institutions.

V

The multifaceted and fruitful relations with the Soviet Union and other fraternal countries has had a deep effect on the course of social and economic transformations in the country. The peaceful conditions in which the Republic of Vietnam lives, despite the intrigues of imperialism and other reactionary forces constantly provoking trouble on the Vietnamese borders, have been cemented by the agreement between the USSR and the Republic of Vietnam and by the tireless foreign political activity of the CPSU and the Communist Party of Vietnam and the active struggle for peace by the countries of the socialist community.

The Vietnamese people are today constructing socialism in a reunited country and are overcoming the postwar devastation and the acute social and economic differences between the different regions of the country. Thus at the time of unification, South Vietnam was in the first stages of the development of capitalism, while the northern part of the country had already moved on to the construction of the material and technical basis for socialism. In 1974 Le Duan said: "Our economy is called socialistic, but in reality it is still petty production and is basically of an agrarian character."[6] United Vietnam has begun to move along the path of socialism, with production per capita as follows: electrical energy—51 kilowatt hours; coal—109 kg; ferrous metals—2.8 kg; cement—11.3 kg; chemical fertilizers—9.4 kg; cotton fabric—3.1 meters; paper 0.9—kg; sugar—1 kg (1975). The national income per capita was $135.

By the beginning of the '80s a good portion of industrial and agricultural projects that had been destroyed by the American military clique had been restored. In South Vietnam the private property of the large bourgeoisie, the compradors, and traitors was abolished, and the attack was begun on the social cancers of neocolonialism: illiteracy, unemployment, prostitution, and drug addiction.

In the first years after the reunification of Vietnam, the party of communism carried on a relentless search for ways and means to resolve social and economic problems. Basing themselves on Marxist-Leninist theory and the experiences of the USSR and other fraternal countries, and taking into account the situation in Vietnam as it was in March 1982, the Fifth Congress of the Communist Party of Vietnam formulated four basic tasks for social and economic development in the 1980s:

• To satisfy the most essential and important needs, to gradually stabilize and then partly raise the material and cultural standards of the population, and above all, to find a reliable solution to the food problem.

• To continue the construction of the material and technical base of socialism, primarily with a view toward raising agricultural production, the production of consumer goods, and goods for exports and for preparing for an even more vigorous development of heavy industry in the next stages.

• To complete the socialist transformations in the provinces of the southern part of the country, continue the improvement of socialist production relations in the north and consolidate socialist production relations in the whole country.

• To satisfy the needs of the country's defense, to strengthen defensive capacity, and to maintain security and order.[7]

The Vietnamese communists believe that to resolve these problems, all the means of the Vietnamese economy must be put to use, local sources of raw materials and energy must be developed more fully, and a high return from all sectors of the economy—the state sector, cooperative sector, mixed sector, and private sectors—must be guaranteed. The congress called for the effective use of foreign aid, the improvement of planning and the system of economic management, and the resolute end to parasitical attitudes.

In the domain of capital goods construction, the party shifted emphasis to the reconstruction and expansion of existing enterprises and improving the effectiveness of their operations. To eliminate the squandering of means for capital construction, 42 projects of prime importance were defined for which funds will be allocated in the upcoming years (these projects are mainly projects of Soviet-Vietnamese economic cooperation), and work on those projects for which the conditions have not yet become ripe was stopped or postponed.

Since 1981 Vietnam has had good harvests of rice and other food crops, which has made it possible to sharply reduce the import of food products. Thus in 1982 the total yield of food crops was 16,590,000 tons, including 14,710,000 tons of rice. In 1982 state purchases of food crops reached the highest level ever at 2.9 million tons, almost 900,000 tons more than in 1981. In 1983, 3.9 million tons are scheduled to be purchased. The number of head of hogs, buffalo, and cows has increased in recent years.

Industrial production is also on the rise despite the shortages in electrical energy, raw material, spare parts, and petroleum products. Whereas in 1976–80 the average annual growth of industrial production was 0.6%, in 1981–82 it was already 10.9%, with the highest indices being recorded in local industry (15.2%) and the domestic industries (19.7%). The increase in value of industrial output for the first eight months of 1983 was 8.2%.

• • •

Assessing the importance of Soviet-Vietnamese cooperation, Le Duan stated in his report to the Fifth Congress of the Communist Party of Vietnam: "The Soviet Union is the most powerful and reliable ally of Vietnam, has resolutely stood on the side of our people, and has promptly and generously met the needs of strengthening the defensive capacity and protection of our country. The Soviet Union has provided our economy with the materials, technology, and goods most necessary for production and for the life of our people and has given us help in building quite a number of large projects that have laid the foundations for the material and technical basis of socialism in our country."[8]

The fruitful development of Soviet-Vietnamese relations, for which the agreement on friendship and cooperation between the USSR and the Socialist Republic of Vietnam was a powerful incentive, enables us to look confidently into the future of these relations. Fraternal friendship, ideological and political unity, and an comprehensive cooperation between the USSR and the Socialist Republic of Vietnam are not only an invaluable possession of the Soviet and Vietnamese peoples but also the source of inexhaustible possibilities for securing the peace and security of nations.

Notes

1. Le Duan, *Collected Articles and Speeches*, Moscow, 1981, p. 232.
2. Ho Chi Minh, *Works (1920–1969)*, Hanoi, 1971, p. 348.
3. *Pravda*, November 5, 1983.
4. *Pravda*, September 5, 1983.

5. *Pravda*, November 6, 1981.
6. Le Duan, *Selected Articles and Speeches, 1970–1975*, Moscow, 1975, p. 179.
7. See *Fifth Congress of the Communist Party of Vietnam*, Moscow, 1983, p. 32.
8. Ibid., p. 96.

DJAFAR AL KHADAT (YEMEN)

The Role of Foreign Financial Aid in the Financing of Capital Investments in the People's Republic of Yemen

The financing of capital investments derives from two principal sources—external and internal. The main source of capital investments is national income. Here we shall examine external sources of financing of capital investments and will distinguish two principal forms of financing—reimbursed and nonreimbursed.

The financing of capital investments on a reimbursed basis, in which funds made available by another country are used, requires that the credits obtained (in commodity and in value form) be returned within a specified period against the payment of a certain interest.

In nonreimbursed financial assistance the funds obtained are used to finance capital investments without their being returned to the creditor.

Given the economic structure established in the majority of developing countries, one of the most important factors in expanded reproduction is foreign trade, especially the sale of manufactured products in the form of exports. Furthermore the character and degree of dependence of the developing countries' economies on the world market are not identical. They are dependent on the product

"Roliata na v''nshnata finansova pomoshch za finansiraneto na kapitalnite vlozheniia v NDR Iemen," *Finansi i kredit*, 1983, no. 8, pp. 46–51. Translated by Michel Vale.

The author is a graduate student from the People's Republic of Yemen.

structure of exports, the extent of its concentration on specific types of production, the pattern of demand, prices, and a number of other factors. Also bear in mind that in the developed capitalist countries, about four-fifths of the value of exports is accounted for by finished products, while raw materials and food products account for one-tenth, whereas for the developing countries (especially economically backward ones), almost nine-tenths of the value of exports is represented by various raw materials (petroleum, coal, ore, agricultural products in unprocessed form) and foodstuffs. According to UN data, finished products did not represent even one-fifth of the exports of developing countries in 1980.[1]

In the light of the above we should point out that the intricacies of the foreign exchange and financial situation of the People's Republic of Yemen have to do with the inadequate level of development of the economy, the dependence on foreign financial assistance, the limited domestic financial resources, the considerable predominance of imports over exports, the subversive activity of the agents of imperialism and reaction, etc. Despite efforts of the government to cut back on imports, which resulted in a lowered rate of increase of imports in the period 1976–79, the People's Republic of Yemen covered roughly 80% of its needs with imports. Moreover, in the past few years, exports amounted to about 16 million dinars per year, while imports amounted to 30 million dinars.

The following factors have a considerable influence on ensuring the country's solvency: income from tourism, monetary remittances from citizens working abroad, loans, and nonreimbursed aid. However, it seems to us that in the 1980s the country will encounter serious difficulties in paying back its loans from abroad, since its balances of trade and payments are not in equilibrium.

At the beginning of the '70s agricultural production amounted to 40% of the value of exports of the countries of Asia, Africa, and Latin America. If, however, we exclude those countries that are mainly oil exporters we find that for the majority of developing countries, agricultural production accounts for over three-fourths of exports.[2] Given the substantial differences in the prices of finished industrial products and agricultural goods on the international markets in favor of the former, it is clear that most of the developing countries are unable to accumulate capital through the channels of foreign trade for the financing of capital investment. If expanded reproduction is to be achieved, they must inevitably resort to external financial assistance.

The developing countries use credits from both the developed capitalist countries and from the socialist countries, and lately credit relations between the developing countries themselves have intensified.[3] Here we shall be examining questions having to do with obtaining reimbursed and nonreimbursed financial aid in the form of credits from the developing countries in the above-indicated groups of countries.

The distribution of financial aid from socialist countries is based on a variety of factors (economic, political, and social) which constitute their foreign trade policy. The most important role is played by the mutual economic interests of the participating countries; these are satisfied through the establishment of a mutually advantageous international division of labor. The relations between the countries of the socialist community and the developing countries with a socialist orientation are the most stable. The latter are characteristically undergoing profound socioeconomic transformations and are playing an active role in the national liberation movement. As L. Brezhnev has written: "Respect of the sacred right of all peoples, and all countries, to choose their own path of development is an inviolable principle of a Leninist foreign policy. But we shall not conceal our views. In the developing countries, as everywhere, we see countries on the path of progress, democracy, and national independence, and we relate to them as friends and companions in battle."[4]

An important factor for an increase in financial assistance for these countries is the strengthening of their state sector and the compilation of national plans and programs for development. All this considerably facilitates mutual cooperation. In the mid-'70s over 40% of the financial assistance of the CMEA member countries in the form of credits was allocated to these countries.[5]

Immediately following the victory of the national democratic forces in the People's Republic of Yemen, the socialist member nations of the CMEA began to offer effective financial aid to the country, which for the most part was nonrepayable.

The USSR was the country that gave the greatest financial assistance to the People's Republic of Yemen. In the '70s the Soviet Union granted a series of credits for the procurement of various kinds of machinery (power, hydrotechnical, textile, agricultural, etc.), including spare parts, and a number of raw materials (sheet metal, cement, cotton, etc.), foodstuffs and provisions, etc.[6]

The financial help of the USSR in building up the fishing industry in the People's Republic of Yemen has been especially valuable.

Ships outfitted with all the necessary equipment for fishing have been provided without repayment. On the basis of an agreement between the People's Republic of Yemen and the USSR for the development of maritime fishing in the Gulf of Aden and the Indian Ocean (since 1969), the Soviet Union is financing a comprehensive program for the development of the fishing resources of the republic, including scientific research to determine fish reserves in coastal waters, the organization of industrial fishing, building up the fishing equipment in harbors in Aden and elsewhere, the construction of a fish cannery, etc., as well as the organization of expeditions to study and develop the ocean wealth of the country, the annual income of which in the '70s will reach $3 million.[7]

On the basis of an agreement between the two countries, the Soviet Union is financing the construction of a series of small artificial lakes and pools, the building of a radio station and a hospital, the repair of runways for take-offs and landing at the Aden airport, geological expeditions, etc.

In 1970 the GDR granted the People's Republic of Yemen a credit of $7 million which was to be used to finance the construction of a telephone station in Mukala (about 93,000 dinars), a mill costing 370,000 dinars, a candy factory costing 300,000 dinars, a factory for plastic goods for 41,000 dinars, the procurement of highway construction equipment for 200,000£, etc. The GDR also has furnished, without reimbursement, various types of equipment, farm items, etc., costing about 500,000 dinars.

Romania has given the People's Republic of Yemen two credits, one of which is for $5 million with a ten-year repayment condition at 2.5% annual interest for the construction of irrigation systems and the development of new lands, and the other for $8.5 million dollars to build a cement factory. Romania is also financing a geological expedition for heavy minerals.

The People's Republic of Cuba has provided, without reimbursement, equipment for a repair center for farm equipment, a soap and oil factory, and equipment for the outfitting of eight cooling plants, etc. In addition, 50 tractors, 20 bulldozers, 4,000 tons of wheat, 84,000 tons of sugar, and other goods have been provided on credit.

Poland has financed the procurement of equipment and materials for the development of electric power in the People's Republic of Yemen, for geological survey work, etc., and has provided credits for all. In addition in 1973 Poland granted Yemen nonrepayable aid up to an amount of $37 million.

Czechoslovakia has granted $6.3 million credit to the People's Republic of Yemen for a number of projects in the first five-year plan, including building a beer factory, a radio station, etc.

Yugoslavia has given Yemen a trade credit for a total sum of $10 million, as well as unrepayable aid in the form of supplies of sugar, medicine, medical equipment, etc.

Bulgaria has also granted considerable financial and trade credits to the People's Republic of Yemen.

These data show only some of the vast amount of aid given by the socialist countries to the People's Republic of Yemen over the past eight years. In the annual report of the Yemeni Communist Party to the Extraordinary Congress of 1980, it was pointed out that credit from the socialist countries amounted to 61% of all the capital investment funds for the years of the first and the beginning of the second five-year plan, while financial proceeds from internal sources during this period was 22%.[8] Comrade Ali N. Mohamed especially stressed the tremendous role played by Soviet aid for "developing new lands, building canals, artificial lakes, and artesian wells, the introduction of modern technology into agriculture, the creation of a national fishing fleet, the creation and development of an economic base for the fishing industry, assistance in construction and industry, in the service sector, in culture, geological surveying for oil and ore, and even scientific and technical training of thousands of cadres. During the last visit of a delegation from the

People's Republic of Yemen to the USSR (1980) a new agreement was signed according to which Yemen would receive a financial loan of $75.4 million for various vitally important projects."[9]

As we have already pointed out, one of the main types of financial assistance from the socialist countries to the People's Republic of Yemen is credits. The credits granted by socialist countries have many preferential conditions. Most of these are given for 10–12 years at an annual interest rate of 2.5–3%. The credits are to be paid back mainly with the export of traditional export goods: fish, coffee, leather, fruits, etc.[10]

The financial assistance from the developed capitalist countries to the People's Republic of Yemen is extremely limited, since after the victory of the revolution in 1968 they have mainly adopted a wait-and-see attitude. The turn of the country's development onto a path of socialist orientation and the strengthening of cooperation with the USSR and the countries of the socialist community, in addition to the consolidation of the state sector in the economy, has considerably reduced the interest of the capitalist countries in investing capital to reap large profits.

Without reimbursement France gave the People's Republic of Yemen equipment for X-ray labs costing 250,000 French francs, two small trucks, and five medical vehicles (first-aid vehicles).[11]

Japan has cooperated economically with the People's Republic of Yemen mainly in the fishing industry. The Nishepo Company has provided, without repayment, two ships (1,600 and 320 tons) with refrigeration and has concluded an agreement permitting trawling for sepia (a type of ocean fish) in the territorial waters of the country. This company is also building a 100-ton refrigeration unit.

The Danish firm Danida concluded an agreement for the construction of refrigeration units in four provinces of the country for the storage of fish.

Italy has promised to help the People's Republic of Yemen construct a tomato cannery and a cigar factory and to complete some agricultural projects; however, these pledges have not yet been made good on.

The Arab countries—Algeria, Kuwait, Iraq, Syria, etc.—play an important role in Yemen's economic and financial cooperation. In the '70s credit relations between the Arab countries expanded considerably, especially as a consequence of the accumulation of considerable foreign exchange reserves in the oil-exporting countries. Thus, for example, in the period 1973 to 1977 alone, the OPEC countries granted other less developed Arab countries credits for capital in the amount of $37.2 billion, including $21.1 billion on preferential conditions.[12]

Algeria granted Yemen a credit of $4 million dollars to prospect for oil deposits by the joint venture Siapko. In addition, aid without remuneration amounting to 67,000 dinars was given to Yemen for the procurement of various types of equipment.

Kuwait granted nonrepayable aid for the construction of a school (220,000 dinars) and a boarding school (167,000 dinars); for doing a study on the possibilities of irrigating 120,000 fedans of land in Abiyan and preparing a technical project (200,000 dinars); for prospecting for sources of drinking water, the procurement of sounding equipment ($65,000), etc. The two countries have also signed a protocol for the creation of a joint fishing venture with a capital of 1 million dinars for the purpose of freezing, processing, and exporting fish and other types of marine life.

Yemen received considerable financial aid from the Iraqi Republic. In the period 1971 to 1975 it received two credits (for 3 million pounds and 3 million dinars) for cleaning up and deepening the harbor in Aden with a view to increasing its ability to berth tankers of up to 120,000 tons displacement, for the construction of a canning factory, for procuring various machinery and equipment, etc.

Syria provided Yemen with 100 tractors and financial assistance for an education and general information program for the population; this also was without repayment.

Yemen has received financial aid for capital investments from various international organizations as well.

Yemen is a member of the Arab Organization for Agricultural Development, the purpose of which is to carry out integrated measures in agriculture aimed at increasing productivity and modernizing that sector, dealing with the problems of processing agricultural products in Arab countries in the Arab Federation for the food industry, etc., for which funds amounting to $3.9 billion are earmarked.[13] The Arab Reserve Fund for Economic and Social Development, created together with the above-mentioned organization, provides financial resources on privileged terms to the less developed countries at a 4% annual interest. OPEC gave this fund $80 million on a special account to grant noninterest-bearing loans to the People's Republic of Yemen, Sudan, the United Arab Republic, Morocco, and Mauritania.[14]

The direction of the development program of the UN also has given considerable financial aid to the People's Republic of Yemen amounting to about $7 million. This is intended for the construction of a highway, a telephone exchange, schools, factories, geological prospecting work, the development of desert lands, food supplies, etc.

The International Bank for Reconstruction and Development is financing a project for the development of fish breeding and the construction of a highway; the amount is $2 million.

From what we have said in the foregoing on the role of foreign financial assistance to the People's Republic of Yemen for implementing its investment policy for the 1970s, the following conclusions may be drawn:[15]

1. The USSR and the socialist countries have given the most financial aid to Yemen, some of which was even nonrepayable. The money was intended for the construction of various subsectors of industry, the modernization of agriculture and the fishing industry, the development of the infrastructure, etc.[16]

2. Financial aid obtained from the Arab countries and from various international organizations is mainly intended for the development of agriculture and the fishing industry, for squaring the country's balance of payments, for procuring foodstuffs, etc.

3. The developed capitalist countries have given very little financial aid to Yemen, a fact that has not had much importance for the acceleration of the country's economic development;

4. Very little of the foreign financial aid granted to Yemen has gone for the development of the country's industry (especially the machinery construction industry) but has been concentrated mainly on the development of energy and light industry. For these reasons the country is still very dependent on imports of capital goods

Table 1

Financing of Capital Investments in the People's Republic of Yemen for 1981–85 (in millions of Yemeni dinars)

Year	Internal sources	Foreign loans	Nonrepayable assistance	Total foreign sources
1981-1985	153.0	247.8	107.4	355.2
1981	44.2	51.0	18.7	69.7
1982	32.6	47.9	17.4	65.3
1983	28.1	48.7	21.8	70.5
1984	24.5	49.7	24.0	73.7
1985	23.5	50.1	25.2	75.3

Source: *Second Five-Year Plan for the Socioeconomic Development of the People's Republic of Yemen*, vol. 1, p. 114, Aden, Ministry of Planning, 1981.

(machinery, equipment, spare parts, etc.), and at the present time its export sector (mainly in fishing) is unable to provide the necessary foreign exchange.

The data in Table 1 show that foreign financial assistance to Yemen during the period 1981–85 will play an important role in the country's investment policy. It will grow to 355.2 million dinars and will increase from year to year in the period in question: from 69.7 million dinars in 1980 to 75.3 million dinars in 1985. The main reason is that funds for capital investment are still to a great degree spent mainly on the development of light industry, and the returns from these investments are relatively low. Under these conditions domestic sources for the financing of capital investments are insufficient (40% smaller than external sources) and will tend to decrease during the period in question, in 1985 amounting to only 23.5 million dinars.

Regarding the development of domestic sources for the financing of capital investment, it may be predicted that considerable funds, in the form of state subsidies, will still be set aside for maintaining price stability on a number of food items of primary necessity (about 16.5 million dinars in 1980). At present, because of continuing inadequate savings on fuel, administrative costs, the inflation of administrative payrolls, etc., the state budget deficit is increasing, and according to the 1982 plan will have to rise by about 60 million dinars, and will probably be about 20 million dollars more.

Despite the considerable size of nonrepayable financial aid (107.4 million dinars), which has grown over the years in this period, the country still has a number of important unresolved problems bearing on investment policy. The most important of these have to do with allocating more funds for the development of those branches of industry creating new capacities and modernizing existing capacity. Thus the export basis of the country will be strengthened and the possibility for accumulation will increase. The role of the subjective factor in planning capital investments with a view toward improving their economic and social effectiveness is also important.

Notes

1. *UN World Economic Survey, 1969–1970. The developing countries in 1960. The problem of appraising progress*, New York, 1971, p. 224.
2. Ibid.
3. We shall not dwell in detail on international credit relations and the mechanism of their functioning since that will be an object of a separate study.
4. L. Brezhnev, *Leninskim kursom*, 10 volumes, p. 86.
5. See *Sotrudnichestvo sotsialisticheskikh i razvivaiushchichsia stran novyi typ mezhdunarodnykh ekonomicheskikh otnoshenii*, Moscow, 1980, p. 72.
6. In 1979 and 1980 alone, exports from the USSR to Yemen were in the form of credits totalling about 149 million rubles according to the data from the *Statistical Manual* of the Ministry of Foreign Trade of the USSR; see *Vneshniaia torgovlia*, 1980.
7. These and all other data in the following are from *Ekonomika narodnodemokraticheskoi respubliki Iemen*, P. Alkhimov and V. Gusakov, Moscow, 1976, pp. 158–75.
8. See Ali N. Mokhamed.
9. Ibid.
10. Experts from the International Bank for Reconstruction and Development came to the conclusion on the basis of calculations that the degree of privilege in credits given from the socialist countries to the developing countries was 46 points, thereby exceeding the score for the developed capitalist countries (14–32 points), data from *World Bank DA Annual Report*, 1977, Washington, 1977, p. 48.
11. Data from P. Alkhimov and V. Gusarov.
12. Data from UNCTAD, TD/V (p. 3), 158, p. 76.
13. *Euromoney*, August 1978, Supplement, p. 69.
14. See "Valiutnye problemy razvivaiushkikhsia stran," *MĖ i MO*, 1977, p. 76.

15. The data on foreign financial assistance are not complete because of the absence of data for a number of financial and credit agreements between Yemen and other countries.

16. V. Filimoshin points out that "so far about 50 major projects have been or are being constructed or are scheduled for construction with the assistance of CMEA member nations. Of these 30 are in operation. See *Ekonom. sotrudnichestvo stran-SEV*, 1981, vol. 1, p. 93.

N. BOGATYI AND A. O. OL'SHANYI (USSR)

Economic and Trade Cooperation between the CMEA Countries and India

Each year on January 26 the Indian people celebrate their national holiday, Republic Day. On this day in 1950 India ceased to be a British dominion and ended its colonial dependence. Thirty-four years is a short time for a country whose history goes back thousands of years, but in these years some considerable positive changes have taken place in the country. India has made some major achievements in the political, economic, social, cultural, and other spheres.

The total national product of the country increased by more than tenfold, the production of electric power twentyfold, oil extraction sevenfold, and coal fourfold.

The country, which in the early '50s was still a semicolonial appendage of the West, today is one of the industrially developed countries. Modern machinery, vessels, airplanes, tractors, combines, and radio technology are produced in Indian firms not only for the domestic market but are also eagerly bought abroad.

Multifaceted relations with the Soviet Union and the other

Russian text © 1984 by "Nauka" Publishers. "Torgovo-ekonomicheskoe sotrudnichestvo stran-chlenov SEV i Indii," *Vneshniaia torgovlia*, 1984, no.2, pp. 7–12. Translated by Michel Vale.

Table 1

Foreign trade volume of the CMEA countries with India (in millions of rubles)

	1960	1970	1980	1981	1982
Volume	198.6	641.4	2,283.2	3,145.7	3,289.4
Export	94.7	264.4	1,179.4	1,517.4	1,420.5
Import	103.9	377.0	1,103.8	1,628.3	1,868.9

Sources: Calculated from the handbooks of the CMEA countries.

CMEA member nations have played an important role in the development of the leading sectors of India's economy and in the consolidation of its economic independence. Cooperation with these countries is based on the principles of respect for national sovereignty, equality, mutual advantage, and noninterference in each others' internal affairs.

Cooperation between the CMEA countries and India in the economy, in trade, and in science and technology takes place on a planned basis and is of a mutually advantageous and long-term character.

Foreign trade. The volume of foreign trade between the CMEA countries and India is the most comprehensive indicator of mutual economic relations since it includes all the shipments of goods made in various forms of cooperation. The increase in the economic potential of the countries of the socialist community as their economic integration proceeds and specialization and cooperation in production deepens has created the necessary material conditions for the development of economic and trade relations not only within the CMEA but also with liberated countries, including India. On the other hand, India's accomplishments in developing its economy, and above all in industrialization, have served to alter its import needs and export possibilities, and this includes its trade with the CMEA countries.

During the period from 1970 to 1982 alone, the volume of foreign trade of the CMEA countries with India increased by a factor of five, reaching 3.3 billion rubles in 1982.

Table 2

Volume of trade of individual CMEA countries with India (in millions of rubles)

	1960	1970	1980	1981	1982
Bulgaria	1.1	26.6	39.9	130.8	105.3
Hungary	11.6	37.6	59.8	98.0	88.0
GDR	27.1	59.3	94.9	127.3	106.6
Cuba	—	0.3	4.8	12.7	10.0
Poland	13.0	58.0	97.5	122.2	161.1
Romania	13.5	28.1	147.6	143.3	184.5
USSR	104.0	364.9	1,739.8	2,397.9	2,514.0
Czechoslovakia	28.3	66.6	98.9	113.5	119.8

come one of the major trading partners of the countries of the socialist community.

Whereas in the early '50s the share of the CMEA countries in India's foreign trade was less than 1%, in 1982, according to data in the Indian periodical *Financial Express*, these countries accounted for 25% of India's total exports and 13% of India's total imports.

The volume of trade of the CMEA countries with India is developing at a rapid pace. This is unequivocal evidence of the stability of the economic relations between them. India's most important trading partner among the countries of the socialist community is the Soviet Union, which accounted for more than three-fourths of India's trade volume with these countries in 1982.

Trade between the CMEA countries and India is growing on the basis of long-term, mainly five-year trade agreements between the governments. These agreements, the first of which was concluded between the USSR and India on December 2, 1953, defined the contractual basis and the basic principles of trade relations between the countries of the socialist community and India; it contained indicative lists or quotas of goods for mutual trade, which were subsequently concretized and specified by corresponding protocols on trade volume.

Some changes in the structure of reciprocal trade have taken place in the last decades. In the '60s new industrial sectors were created in

India, and key sectors of industry were expanded, so that the country needed machinery and equipment. In some years the share of machinery and equipment in the exports of CMEA countries to India was as high as 69% (for Soviet shipments even as high as 75%). The export of machinery, equipment, and means of transportation from the USSR to India was 2.2 billion rubles alone in the period from 1961 to 1982.

In the '70s the relative proportion of machinery, equipment, and means of transportation in the exports of the CMEA countries to India began to decrease, owing to the development of India's own national production in these goods, but shipments of oil and petroleum products, fertilizers, and other chemical products increased markedly.

The Soviet Union provides the Indian market with machinery and equipment for deep pit and open mining of minerals, equipment for drilling and exploitation of oil wells, and machinery and equipment for power production and the metallurgical, machinery construction, electrotechnical, petroleum-processing, chemical, and textile industries, underground transport and highway construction equipment, oil and petroleum products, ballbearings, chemical products, newsprint, etc.

Over 60% of Czechoslovak exports to India consist of machinery, equipment, and means of transportation, including equipment for electric power plants, the metallurgical, machinery construction, textile and leather industries, farm machinery, high-grade and sheet steel, pipes, and fittings.

Poland exports mining, foundry, and energy equipment, metal-cutting machinery and hoisting cranes, as well as fertilizer and other chemical goods.

The exports of the GDR include equipment for enterprises in the chemical, textile, foodstuffs, and metal-processing industries, farm machinery, ships, and other goods. Recently the delivery of fertilizers from the GDR (mainly potassium fertilizers) has increased sharply.

Hungary provides India with equipment for the coal industry, power stations, nonferrous metallurgy, the chemical, foodstuffs, textiles, and leather and shoe industries, as well as ferrous metals and chemical goods.

Romania's exports to India have increased mainly because of an increase in the delivery of fertilizers, oil-drilling equipment, equipment for petroleum processing, power stations, and the production of building materials (factories for concrete fabrication and brick factories).

Bulgaria's exports are made up mainly of fertilizer and other products of the chemical industry, as well as rolled steel. Recently deliveries of Bulgarian radio and electronic equipment and equipment for the foodstuffs and tobacco industries have begun.

Traditional agricultural and industrial raw materials (tea, coffee, tobacco, spices, jute, and leather goods) occupy an important place in the product structure of India's exports to the CMEA countries. However, recently a considerable diversification of Indian exports has taken place: shipments of the products of developing national industries have increased to the countries of the socialist community. In the early '80s the share of finished and semifinished products in Soviet and Czechoslovak imports from India was 55% and 40%, respectively, whereas in India's total exports the share of these goods did not exceed 30%.

The Soviet Union heads the list of India's trading partners with regard to imports from a number of industrial sectors. This applies especially to products such as cables, garage equipment, cotton fabric, embroidered and knitted goods, detergents, cosmetics, etc. The large orders from the USSR and other CMEA countries help the development of old Indian industries and the creation of new ones. For example, the production of knitted goods in India is concentrated in the city of Ludhiana. More than 90% of the goods produced there are delivered to the USSR, securing jobs for 500,000 people or half the population of the city.

Each year the CMEA countries increase their purchases of nontraditional goods, i.e., machinery and equipment, from India. The USSR alone has expanded its imports of products of this group from 2.1 million rubles in 1970 to 154 million rubles in 1982. Soviet organizations are expanding their purchases of garage and electrotechnical equipment, repair and maintenance instruments, and other goods from India.

"Trade with the Soviet Union and other CMEA countries is extremely advantageous for India," observed the general manager of India's Institute of Foreign Trade, D. N. Saksen. "In contrast to the Western nations, which dictate extortionary terms and demand political concessions, the socialist countries erect no protectionist obstacles to Indian exports, nor do they seek political advantages. Indian-Soviet trade is graphic demonstration of what impressive achievements can be attained by countries with different socioeconomic systems in the area of economic cooperation if their relations are based on planning, equal rights, and mutual advantage."[1]

In economic and trade relations bilateral clearing, with the Indian rupee used as the unit of accounting, is employed in accounts between most of the CMEA countries (USSR, Czechoslovakia, Romania, Poland, GDR) and India. This system of accounting is extended to all trade and nontrade payments between organizations and firms of the partner countries. The Western press has repeatedly attempted to sow the seeds of doubt about the advantages of such a system of accounting for India. However, as the Indian newspaper *The Economic Times* wrote, economic and trade relations (with an accounting system in rupees) with most of the countries of the socialist community are very important for India. At present European socialist countries are the only region where India has a positive trade balance, whereas the overall foreign trade deficit of India, which has reached unprecedented heights, continues to grow. The Indian government, says the *Times*, intends to maintain the existing system of payments in trade with the socialist countries of Europe.

This newspaper, referring to government circles, observes that the system of accounting in rupees has had the following advantages for India:

- it has made it possible to considerably expand the market for many Indian goods (India was almost totally dependent on the Western countries and Japan until it began actively to trade with the European CMEA countries in the '50s);
- India has been able to sharply increase its exports of nontraditional goods (their share in total Indian exports at present is more than 50%, whereas in the '70s it was only 20%);
- it has enabled India to begin to export machinery and chemical products to the European socialist countries, which are playing a "pioneer role" in the imports of many Indian goods in these sectors;

• finally, in the process of industrialization this system of payments has enabled India to acquire the necessary machinery and equipment, raw materials, and materials from European members of the CMEA without having to spend freely convertible currency (for example, in 1980–81 these countries provided India with 14% of its total imports of oil, 39% of its imported petroleum products, 26% of imported fertilizers, 25% of nonferrous metals, and more than 20% of imported machinery and equipment).

The trade agreements for 1981–85 signed between the CMEA countries and India opened up new prospects for increasing the volume of trade and diversifying its structure.

Economic and technical cooperation. The trade between the CMEA countries and India is becoming more and more a part of the entire system of economic relations comprising technical cooperation, industrial cooperation, and other forms.

Economic and technical assistance from the CMEA countries to India today bears a number of distinctive features:

• it promotes the development of the state sector on a planned basis;

• it has an industrial orientation and helps to create administrative and industrial complexes;

• it is based for the most part on long-term agreements between the governments.

Thanks to technical assistance from the CMEA countries, over 400 industrial enterprises and other ventures, mainly in the sphere of material production, have been built or are being built, mainly in India's state sector. All these projects were created in conformity with five-year plans for the development of India's economy.

One distinctive feature of cooperation between the CMEA countries and India is its industrial orientation: over 70% of the total volume of economic and technical assistance is in the area of industry and energy.

The figures themselves bespeak the economic importance of enterprises built in India with the assistance of the CMEA countries. In the last few years projects built under Soviet-Indian cooperation smelted about 38% of all the steel, extracted over 35% and processed 41% of the oil, generated about 10% of the electric power, and produced a considerable portion of heavy metallurgical, mining, and energy equipment.

Industrial enterprises built with the cooperation of CMEA countries provide a foundation for the further industrialization of India. Thus, whereas in the construction of the first-generation metals plant at Bhilai, India's share in the deliveries of equipment and metal constructions was 13% and 22% respectively, this share had increased to 60% and 92% respectively in equipping a factory at Bokaro.

The construction of large plants has fundamentally changed the life of all areas, has promoted the rapid development of productive forces and the creation of local skilled personnel, and has raised the living standard of the population. Large numbers of small enterprises producing goods necessary for construction and operation of large industrial complexes have grown up around the latter. On the estimates of Indian economists, just nine large plants built under Soviet and Indian cooperation have spawned more than 800 different small firms.

An important area of cooperation between CMEA countries and India is metallurgy. The metals plants at Bhilai and Bokaro were constructed and are being expanded with the assistance of Soviet organizations alone (to 4 million tons of steel per year in each). Effort is being applied across a broad front to build a metals plant in Vizakhapatman, which will have a capacity of 3 million tons of steel per year.

Firms built with the help of CMEA countries usually function more reliably and consistently and reach their planned capacities more quickly than projects built by Western firms.

In the '50s, in addition to the Bhilai factory, metals plants were built in Durgapur and Rurkel (with the aid of England and West Germany). According to the estimates of Indian specialists, the plant at Bkhilai was the most effective of these three metals plant in all economic and technical indicators. According to the data from the end of the '70s and beginning of the '80s, the level of utilization of productive capacity in steel smelting reached in this plant was 1.3 times higher than the average for all of India's metallurgical industry.

The countries of the socialist community have made a major

contribution to the development of India's nonferrous metallurgy. The construction of an aluminum plant with a capacity of 200,000 tons (with Hungary's assistance) and one with a capacity of 100,000 tons per year (with the assistance of the Soviet Union) has been completed in Korba.

Soviet organizations have developed for India a technical plan for a mine and a concentrating plant and a mining and concentrating complex having a capacity of 3 million tons of copper ore per year, have provided the technological and economic documentation for the construction of an aluminum plant with a capacity of 600–800,000 tons of aluminum per year in the state of Agra-Pradesh, and a small plant for the production of gallium as a by-product in the production of aluminum at plant in Korba.

A plant with a capacity of 600,000 square meters of copper foil and 490,000 square meters of sheet metal with copper plating per year is being built in Djaipur with the assistance of the GDR. Once this plant begins operation, India will no longer be dependent on importing these products.

Cooperation with the CMEA countries is of major importance for India in dealing with problems having to do with the assertion of their sovereign rights to prospect for and exploit their national natural resources, including the development of their fuel and energy resources.

The USSR and Romania are giving India technical assistance in surveying and developing oil and gas deposits and in constructing petroleum-processing plants. As a result of the combined efforts of India and Soviet specialists, large oil deposits have been drilled in the states of Gujarat and Assam and in the western part of the Indian shelf near Bombay. A total of fifty oil and gas deposits have been drilled in India with the assistance of the USSR. The Indian State Commission on Petroleum and Natural Gas, created in 1956, extracted more than 75 million tons of oil and over 9 billion cubic meters of gas during the period of its cooperation with Soviet organizations.[2]

Three oil-processing plants, including those in Koiyali and Barauni with a capacity of 3 million tons of oil each (later the Indians expanded this to 7.3 and 3.3 million tons respectively) and in Matur, with a capacity of 6 million tons of oil per year, were built as a cooperative venture between the Soviet Union and India. Romania helped to build a plant for processing 1.25 million tons of oil per year in Gauhati.

Once these plants began operation, India was able to cover a good deal of its needs in petroleum products and to reduce its imports of them.

The CMEA countries have helped India build several modern plants for producing heating and coking coal. Soviet organizations have helped to design, build, and remodel plants for coal production having a total capacity of about 45 million tons as well as other concentrating plants with a capacity of 20 million tons per year. Coal mines with a capacity of 4 million tons per year and a coal-washing factory with a capacity of 2.8 million tons per year have been built with the cooperation of Romania. Hungary has also helped to build coal mines. Specialists from the GDR helped to develop Indian lignite deposits.

CMEA countries have also helped considerably to develop India's electric power production. Power stations with a total capacity of 3.5 thousand MV have been built with the USSR's assistance. A contract has been signed for the construction of the first section of the thermoelectric power plant "Vindyachal," with a capacity of 1,260 MV. Hungary, Poland, and Czechoslovakia have helped to build power plants with a total capacity of about 1,000 MV.

Measures to create an independent national economy have required the rapid development of a modern machinery construction industry. The core of Indian heavy machinery construction is large factories built with the help of the Soviet Union and Czechoslovakia. The heavy machinery factory in Ranchi produces various equipment for the metallurgical, petroleum, cement, and other industries.

A factory constructed with the Soviet Union's assistance in Durgapur is the main producer of mining equipment in India. It produces coal combines, crushing machines, various concentrating equipment, conveyors, ventilators, and pumps. Many of India's mines are outfitted with equipment from this factory.

Up to 60% of heavy energy equipment is manufactured in the factory in Hardvar, built with the help of the Soviet Union, and the largest one of its kind in southern and southeastern Asia. The plant produces equipment for hydroelectric and thermal electric power plants. Turbines with a capacity of 200 MV, which have been installed in various power plants throughout the country, are now being produced for the first time in India.

Czechoslovakia has made an important contribution to the development of India's machinery industry. It helped to build a factory for heavy electrical equipment in Haiderabad to produce turbines and generators of a total power of 900 MV per year, a factory for power plant boilers in Tiruchchirappalli, and a factory for chemical equipment in Vizakhapatnam. Czechoslovakia has also helped to build four machine tool plants, the largest of which is the heavy tooling plant in Ranchi.

The training of local personnel is given major attention in cooperation between the CMEA countries and India. During the period of cooperation, the countries of the socialist community helped to train over 150,000 Indian specialists; they were trained directly on the work site or in plants already in operation, in schools and centers built in the country with the cooperation of the countries of the socialist community, and in colleges and universities and factories in the CMEA countries themselves.

The Soviet Union helped to create four faculties at Indian universities and six technical schools, to equip the Bombay Technological Institute, which is designed to train more than 2,000 specialists per year, and to build several large centers of learning. Czechoslovakia helped to set up the Institute for Machine Tools in Bangalore. Other CMEA nations helped equip various educational institutions and centers of learning.

Cooperation between CMEA countries and India in other sectors of industry, in agriculture, and in science and technology is successfully developing.

Industrial cooperation and other forms of economic relations. The development of new forms of cooperation alongside the traditional forms are furthering the expansion and deepening of economic relations between the CMEA countries and India. Industrial cooperation, which has some auspicious prospects for development in the future, is growing in importance among these new forms.

There are various forms of cooperation relations, e.g., forms of cooperation in which one partner provides the other one parts, units, and whole assemblies over a long period of time as components for some final product which the manufacturing partner itself sells. For example, on a contractual basis Soviet organizations transfer production technology on a cooperative basis to their Indian partners and supply complementary items and units for more complicated equipment produced in machinery plants in Ranchi, Durgapur, and Hardvar, all built with the help of the USSR.

The production of Zetor tractors at a factory in Barod and Yava motorcycles in a factory in Mysore has been organized on the basis of shipments provided on a cooperative basis from the USSR. First the tractors were delivered in a disassembled form, but later individual units and parts began to be delivered in a volume which decreased steadily as their production in India began to function smoothly. The production of metal-working tools on the basis of components obtained from Czechoslovakia has been set up in factories in Ranchi and Adjmir. The factory in Ranchi alone produces fifteen types of machine tools on the basis of Czechoslovak units and subassemblies.

Hungary supplied the necessary equipment and helped build a lightbulb factory, and Hungarian know-how was used to begin to manufacture components and lightbulb units and neon tubes in India.

Hungary is supplying equipment for a microwave system extending 4,000 kilometers and has transferred to India the technical know-how necessary for manufacturing similar equipment. Indian specialists are being trained in Hungary to produce and operate microwave equipment.

Economic and technological cooperation on a compensation basis is also growing. Soviet organizations are expanding their purchases of heavy machine constructed at plants in India as a result of compensation offered for assistance in construction. A list of equipment from factories in Ranchi and Durgapur to be delivered to the USSR in 1981–85 has been agreed on. Currently these factories are fulfilling Soviet orders for the manufacture of about 30,000 tons of equipment.

Poland's expenditures on the export of equipment for small wool-spinning factories in India are being compensated by counter-deliveries of cloth.

In the '70s India began to produce and export a broad list of complex types of machinery and equipment. This created the preconditions for the development of fruitful cooperation between Indian firms and organizations in the CMEA countries on markets of third countries. For example, Indian enterprises cooperated with factories in the USSR and Czechoslovakia to produce oil-drilling equipment and excavators for third countries.

Factories in Ranchi and Durgapur provided some of the deliveries of complex technological and other equipment to build metals plants in Turkey, Egypt, Sri Lanka, an aluminium plant in Yugoslavia, and various projects in Hungary, Bulgaria, and Cuba on the basis of orders from Soviet organizations.

In accordance with an agreement on cooperation in the oil-processing industry signed between Romania and India, specialists from both countries are doing geological prospecting for oil (using Romanian drilling equipment) not only in India but also in third countries (for example, in Libya).

In recent years cooperation in the form of mixed companies has been growing steadily in industry and other sectors. This form of cooperation differs from all those above in that it provides for joint capital investment, management, and allocation of earnings and expenditures. Joint ventures with the participation of CMEA organizations are formed in the developing countries, usually as mixed companies.

Czechoslovak organizations are providing India with technical assistance in the construction of electric power plants and cement, chemical, and oil-processing plants through the mixed company Shkoda India Private, Ltd (62% of the capital belongs to the Indian firm and 38% to Shkoda Eksport of the USSR).

The company K Diesels Pragoinvesta (84% of the founding capital belongs to the Indian firm and 16% to Transakt of the USSR) installed a technological assembly line for the production of components for diesel motors built on Czechoslovak license in an Akhmadabad plant. Czechoslovakia purchases a portion of the output of this plant.

The mixed enterprise Temis (75% of the shareholders' capital belongs to an Indian firm and 25% to a Hungarian firm) set up the production of Vitamin B_{12} and other medicinal preparations. In addition this firm packages and sells a number of pharmaceutical products delivered from Hungary.

The organization of large-scale and long-term cooperation, including industrial cooperation between the CMEA countries and India, requires mutual coordination of measures of an industrial, financial, and contractual law nature. Long-term programs of cooperation signed at the governmental level between the partner countries play an important role in this system. Commissions set up between the two governments supervise the implementation of these programs. One such long-term program of economic, trade, and scientific and technical cooperation extending over ten to fifteen years was signed between the USSR and India on March 14, 1979.

Economic and trade relations between India and Bulgaria, Hungary, GDR, Romania, and Czechoslovakia are also developing on a long-term basis.

Such a system of long-term programs and agreements is especially important for India because they have a regulating effect on progressive processes of reorganization of the economic structure taking place in the country, promote the development of planning in the economy, and create the possibility of optimal utilization of both internal and external sources. But these long-term programs and agreements also enable the partners to plan together and coordinate all the principal directions of mutual economic, trade, and scientific and technological relations and to provide the necessary material and financial resources for this.

The full utilization of the advantages that lie in the various forms of economic and trade cooperation is in the fundamental interests of both the CMEA countries and India. Economic and trade relations between the CMEA countries and India, which are growing and becoming stronger, are an important contribution to the cause of peace and international cooperation on a democratic basis.

Notes

1. Quote in M. I. Stasov, *Indiia i sotsialisticheskie strani*, Moscow, 1980, p. 76.
2. *Built with the economic and technological assistance of the Soviet Union*, Moscow, 1982, p. 186.

V. KORNYSHEV (USSR)

Commercial and Economic Relations between the USSR and Argentina Are in Full Swing*

This year marks the tenth anniversary of the signing of a number of intergovernmental agreements between the USSR and Argentina; these agreements have served as a basis for the dynamic development of commercial and economic relations between the two countries in the following years. Among them are the Agreement on the Development of Commercial and Economic and Scientific-Technical Cooperation, the Agreement on the Delivery of Machinery and Equipment by the USSR to Argentina, the Agreement on Scientific-Technical Cooperation (all three signed on February 13, 1974), and the Agreement on Merchant Shipping August 24, 1974.

The signing of these agreements testifies to the desire of both countries to develop mutually advantageous cooperation in the most important sectors of their economies, science, and technology. The agreements not only defined the possible areas but also the forms of cooperation, with particular emphasis on mutual trade. In the same year, 1974, the mixed Soviet-Argentine Committee on Commercial and Economic and Scientific-Technical cooperation was created. Its functions include examining questions of cooperation between the two countries in the indicated areas, supervision of the fulfillment of corresponding Soviet-Argentine agreements, and the development of recommendations for the further development of cooperation.

The agreements signed in 1974, together with the trade agreement signed earlier in 1971, created a stable contractual and legal

 "SSSR–Argentina: torgovo-ekonomicheskie sviazi razvivaiutsia," *Vneshniaia torgovlia*, 1984, no. 3, pp. 30–3. Translated by Michel Vale.

basis for cooperation between the two countries, which has had an auspicious effect on the development of bilateral relations, mainly in the area of trade. Thus in 1975 the trade volume between the USSR and Argentina grew by almost fourfold compared with 1973, amounting to 304.4 million rubles.

The trade between the two countries continued to develop in the succeeding years, and in 1983 its volume was about 1.2 billion rubles (estimate).

Argentina is one of the oldest trading partners of the USSR in Latin America. It currently occupies first place in terms of trade volume with the Soviet Union among the countries of this region and third place among the developing countries. The signing of the agreement to deliver Soviet machinery and equipment was of prime importance for the development of mutual trade; this agreement provides on the one hand for installment payments of up to ten years on advantageous conditions for the sale of Soviet technology to Argentina, and on the other hand, the use of the proceeds from these deliveries to purchase Argentine merchandise. At the same time as this and other agreements were concluded, negotiations were going on with organizations in Argentina's state sector concerning the delivery of Soviet machinery and equipment for the petroleum and coal industry, electric power, and metallurgy under commercial credit conditions, and contracts were concluded that specified these deliveries over the course of several years.

In 1974, again as a result of the successful participation of the foreign trade organization "Energomasheksport" in trade, a contract was concluded for the delivery of turbines and generators for the Argentine-Uruguayan hydroelectric power plant "Salto Grande," with a capacity of 1.9 million kilowatts, one of the largest power plants in Latin America. The delivery of Soviet equipment for this plant was the first major act of cooperation between the two countries in the area of electric power.

At present two more electric power plants are being constructed in Argentina; the equipment for them is being supplied by Soviet organizations; these are the power plants "Costa Nera" (310 megawatts) and "Bahia Blanca" (620 megawatts). The equipment for Costa Nera has already been delivered, and its assembly is being completed; the delivery of the equipment for the second power plant is scheduled for 1984.

The organizations of the two countries are concluding negotiations for deliveries of Soviet equipment for the hydroelectric power plant "Piedra del Aguila," 2.1 million kilowatts. A qualitatively new aspect of the work in constructing this project is that the main equipment for the plant will be manufactured in cooperation with Argentine industry. This will enable the largest Argentine machinery construction companies not only to more completely utilize their production capacities but also, with the aid of Soviet specialists, to acquire experience in manufacturing large hydroturbines and generators which until now have not been produced in Argentina.

Considering the experience accumulated and the positive results of the joint work of Soviet and Argentine organizations in developing electric power in Argentina, one can assume that this sector will remain one of the most promising in commercial and economic cooperation between the two countries. Argentina's program for developing this sector provides, for example, for the construction of the "Parana Medio" hydroelectric complex, one of the largest future projects of this type in Latin America.

Soviet organizations have provided engineering services to Argentine specialists in developing the first draft of the complex and have expressed their willingness to participate broadly in the construction of the project.

In the ten years that have passed since the conclusion of the agreement on the delivery of machinery and equipment, Soviet foreign trade organizations have exported equipment to Argentina valued at about 160 million rubles, including, in addition to power equipment, petroleum storage tanks, automatic and pneumatic cranes, trucks, pumps for the petroleum industry, mining equipment, special types of rolling mills, etc. The vast majority of these deliveries were to state companies, which continued to be the principal buyers of Soviet technology.

Machinery and equipment are the basis of Soviet exports to Argentina. Among other exports the largest and most constant item is sodium bichromate, which is the initial material for the production of chemicals necessary for Argentina's leather industry.

Argentina's exports to the USSR consist almost wholly of agricultural products and articles resulting from their processing. Argentina is one of the largest exporters of farm products in the world and traditionally supplies the USSR with wool, uncured and semifinished leather, cereals, vegetable oils, and quebracho, a tanning extract.

In 1980 Argentina did not take part in the boycott declared by the United States against the Soviet Union on the delivery of cereal grains and did not cut back commercial and economic relations with the USSR, the development of which is in the interests of both countries. On Argentine initiative an agreement to deliver fodder grain (maize and sorghum) and soybeans to the Soviet Union was concluded, and in 1981 an agreement on meat deliveries was signed. Both agreements are working well. With the signing of these agreements the Soviet Union assumed first place among Argentina's trading partners, and its share in Argentine exports is over 20%. In addition to the grains other major items in Soviet imports from Argentina are meat, vegetable oils (linseed, sunflower, tung), and in some years wine and sugar have been purchased. Soviet imports from Argentina also include certain kinds of industrial goods, for example, compressor pump pipes.

Because of the considerable volume of purchases of Argentine farm products, trade between the two countries shows a considerable positive balance in favor of Argentina, and this to some extent has held back the further development of mutual trade. Understanding this, the Argentine government has shown interest in substantially expanding its imports from the USSR, and in particular to purchase machinery, equipment, and other Soviet export goods to a total value of about $500 million; and it has made concrete initiatives for the further development of economic and scientific-technical cooperation on the basis of existing intergovernmental agreements.

These questions in particular were discussed at the latest (seventh) session of the mixed Soviet-Argentine Committee in July 1983 in Moscow. The results of this meeting once again confirmed that the countries are reliable business partners, and that the winds blowing in the foreign policy arena have not affected relations between them. The exchange of opinion on a broad range of questions at this meeting confirmed the interests of both sides in continuing and developing mutually advantageous relations. The course of fulfillment of earlier agreed upon purchases of equipment by Argentine state companies and prospects of their further development were examined. The state of negotiations on cooperation in projects scheduled to be constructed and modernized in Argentina in the upcoming years was also discussed. In particular the parties agreed to continue exploring questions of cooperation in the building of fishing ports (Puerto Madrin, Ujuaia), the reconstruction of the seaport Bahia Blanca, and the modernization and electrification of the Buenos Aires-Rosario railroad. The possibilities of cooperation in other areas, e.g., geology, mining, the gas industry, and other sectors of industry were also discussed. Considering that Argentina has not thus far exploited very intensely its fish resources in its territorial waters, cooperation in maritime fishing, both in the form of joint research in the fishing industry and by creating joint fishing companies, seems to be promising.

As regards scientific-technical cooperation, only the first steps have been taken. To stimulate cooperation in this area, the parties decided to develop a program of joint measures for the period 1984–85. The program will be agreed on in the near future at the first meeting of the mixed Soviet-Argentine Committee on Scientific-Technical Cooperation, formed in May 1983.

However, despite the considerable growth of Soviet-Argentine trade relations, it must be said that the size of bilateral cooperation reached in the past decade does not measure up to its full potential.

The objective reasons for this are primarily inadequate knowledge about opportunities in each of the countries and the traditional orientation of Argentine business circles toward to the development of relations with Western partners. Considering this, the two countries devoted considerable attention to questions of developing and consolidating business contacts between organizations and firms in the two countries, ranging from a broader mutual exchange of information to determine possibilities for mutually advantageous cooperation, to questions concerning organizing exhibitions, to advertizing measures, etc.

One of the major measures designed to promote the export of Soviet goods to Argentina will be a permanent exhibition hall for Soviet machinery and equipment and other items in Buenos Aires, which should be opened in this year. An agreement to set up this exhibition hall to allow Argentinian business circles to become better acquainted with samples of Soviet technology and other export goods was also concluded at the meetings of the joint commission.

The activity of the House of Argentine-Soviet Trade, set up about ten years ago on the initiative of a group of private Argentine firms which were regular partners of Soviet foreign trade organizations, is actively assisting to expand and consolidate multifaceted business contacts and activity. The House attracts interested Argentine companies to Soviet-Argentine trade and helps them establish ties with Soviet organizations. It should be noted that Argentina is the first and so far the only country in Latin America where such a house exists as an instrument of national companies interested in developing commercial and economic relations with the USSR.

A regular commercial Aeroflot flight from Moscow to Buenos Aires was started in March 1983.

The new constitutional civilian government which recently came to power in Argentina expressed the intention of following the principle of rejecting "ideological barriers" to the development of foreign economic relations consonant with national interests and, in particular, of continuing to expand commercial and economic relations with the USSR. The goodwill of both sides, as well as the accumulated positive experience in Soviet-Argentine mutually advantageous and egalitarian cooperation, permits us to hope that commercial and economic relations between the two countries will continue to grow stronger and to expand.

ISTVÁN DOBOZI (HUNGARY)

Factors Affecting Hungary's Economic Relations with the Third World up to 2000*

Introduction

The aim of this article is to define the main elements of those external economic conditions which affect, directly or indirectly, the long-term cooperation between Hungary and the developing countries and to spell out the direction and intensity of their effects.[1] In our opinion this long-term evolution is affected by three basic "environmental elements": (1) the quantitative, dynamic, equilibrium, structural, and organizational-institutional features of the present economic relations of Hungary and the developing countries; (2) the international economic environment and, within it, intra-CMEA cooperation, the expected evolution of world trade and of the developing countries' economies and of progress toward a new international economic order, which together constitute the system of objective external conditions of the relations of Hungary and the developing countries; (3) the internal evolution of the Hungarian economy.

I. The Present Features of the Economic Relations between Hungary and the Developing Countries

After World War II Hungary's economic relations with the developing countries were slow and sluggish to develop. In 1950 the share of

*Paper presented at the Roundtable on Yugoslav and Hungarian Experiences in Economic Cooperation with Developing Countries, October 6–7, 1983, Budapest.

Table 1

Share of Developing Countries in Total Hungarian Foreign Trade (on the basis of provenance/destination data; in %)

	1970	1972	1973	1974	1975	1976	1977	1978	1979	1980	1981	1982
Exports	4.9	5.2	4.8	6.3	6.0	8.0	8.6	8.7	9.1	9.8	11.7	12.9
Imports	3.9	6.0	6.5	7.6	6.9	9.5	9.9	8.7	8.2	9.2	8.3	10.2

Source: Various volumes of *Külkereskedelmi Statisztikai Évkönyv*, Budapest, Központi Statisztikai Hivatal; for 1982, data provided by the Minstry of Foreign Trade, Budapest.

the developing countries in Hungarian foreign trade was smaller than it had been before the war. The following two and a half decades were characterized by excessive turnover fluctuation, but no permanent increase ensued. Share indices in 1973 approximately equaled those of the fifties but still fell short of several of the pre-World War II years.[2]

This situation did not change significantly until the seventies. As shown in Table 1, both the imports and exports shares of developing countries in Hungarian trade increased 2.6-fold between 1970 and 1982.

Table 2 shows that with the exception of 1979, Hungary's actual trade turnover with the developing countries regularly chalked up a deficit in the seventies. Thus, instead of improving it, trade with developing countries actually worsened the general balance of the Hungarian external economy. This is especially true for the period 1974–78, when the deficit amounted to some 30–33% of all Hungarian exports to developing countries. It was not until 1979 that the balance deficit had been eliminated, with a relatively significant surplus attained in 1981 and 1982, due primarily to an annual 27% increase in Hungarian exports to the Third World (meanwhile, total exports increased by only 6.5% annually, and exports to the developed capitalist countries even decreased by 8.5% during 1981–82).

Hungary's trade with the developing countries is characterized by a marked asymmetry of *commodity patterns* (see Table 3). Manufactures (SITC 5–8) constitute four-fifths of the total of Hungarian

Table 2

Evolution of Trade Turnover between Hungary and the Developing Countries (in million forints)

	Exports	Imports	Balance
1970	8,069.4	10,487.6	−2,418.2
1971	8,190.5	9,375.9	−1,185.4
1972	9,214.3	10,219.7	−1,005.4
1973	10,080.4	12,233.0	−2,152.5
1974	14,939.1	19,560.6	−4,621.5
1975	15,671.2	21,516.6	−5,845.4
1976	16,293.5	21,796.3	−5,482.2
1977	20,520.3	26,526.1	−5,988.0
1978	20,907.8	26,101.7	−5,183.3
1979	25,739.2	25,318.7	+ 423.4
1980	27,513.3	27,521.4	− 3.6
1981	34,972.8	26,005.8	+8,967.0
1982	41,732.0	33,239.3	+8,492.7

Source: Various volumes of *Külkereskedelmi Statiszitkai Évkönyv*; for 1982, data provided by the Ministry of Foreign Trade, Budapest.

exports to developing countries, but only 14% of the imports originating in the same. The discrepancy is greatest between the exports and imports shares (35 and 9%, respectively) of machinery and transport equipment (SITC 7) and is even more conspicuous if compared to the structure of total Hungarian trade turnover, in which manufactures represent 67% of both exports and imports. It is clear from the above that the pattern of the developing countries' exports to Hungary is less *developed*, whereas that of Hungary to the developing countries is *more developed* than their respective overall exports.[3] In the course of the seventies, Hungary failed to increase the share of machinery in its exports to developing countries; its share even decreased somewhat. This, no doubt, is partly related to the fact that Hungary could not penetrate the machinery markets of the newly industrializing countries, which have for some time been among the major and most dynamically expanding machine-absorbing markets of the Third World. As regards the exploitation of machine export opportunities, Hungary lags behind not only the

Table 3

The Commodity Pattern of Trade between Hungary and the Developing Countries (as % of total Hungarian exports to and imports from developing countries)

		1970	1974	1975	1976	1977	1978	1979	1980
Exports to developing countries									
SITC	0+1	10.8	16.6	14.6	14.7	20.0	25.3	19.4	15.8
	2+4	0.2	0.6	0.6	1.0	1.0	0.6	1.3	0.9
	3	0.0	0.1	0.0	0.1	0.2	0.8	0.7	1.3
	5	6.1	8.7	6.9	7.4	7.2	8.6	11.7	11.5
	7	37.0	33.2	47.5	44.5	39.7	32.4	33.7	35.0
	6+8	45.7	40.8	30.4	32.3	32.7	32.3	32.8	34.5
	5−8	88.8	82.7	84.8	84.2	79.6	73.3	72.2	81.0
Exports, total									
SITC	0+1	22.3	23.3	21.7	22.1	21.9	20.3	19.5	21.0
	2+4	4.7	5.0	4.3	5.2	5.2	5.7	5.2	5.8
	3	1.1	1.1	2.0	3.0	3.1	3.5	4.2	4.8
	5	6.8	7.5	7.0	8.3	8.8	8.9	9.4	9.5
	7	34.2	33.3	37.0	33.5	33.5	34.5	34.0	32.1
	6+8	30.9	29.7	28.7	27.9	27.6	27.2	26.7	25.7
	5−8	61.9	70.5	72.7	69.7	69.9	70.6	70.1	67.4
Imports from developing countries									
SITC	0+1	57.2	34.9	36.3	42.8	59.7	51.1	46.8	44.5
	2+4	29.2	26.8	21.4	24.2	15.8	16.8	16.0	17.6
	3	0.0	15.5	28.3	18.3	12.2	19.9	23.1	23.2
	5	2.9	7.8	2.1	1.5	1.1	0.9	1.0	0.8
	7	0.8	0.3	0.6	0.7	1.0	1.1	2.7	0.9
	6+8	10.0	14.6	11.2	12.5	10.2	10.2	10.4	13.0
	5−8	13.7	22.7	13.9	14.7	12.3	12.1	14.1	14.7
Imports, total									
SITC	0+1	9.9	10.6	8.2	9.9	10.8	8.5	7.8	8.1
	2+4	13.5	11.2	10.6	9.7	9.0	9.0	9.0	9.4
	3	9.1	8.5	13.5	12.4	12.3	13.6	16.0	16.4
	5	9.1	15.0	11.6	13.3	12.9	12.9	12.4	13.6
	7	32.1	29.9	31.7	31.0	31.3	32.8	32.4	29.2
	6+8	26.2	24.7	24.5	23.6	23.5	18.6	22.1	22.5
	5−8	67.4	69.6	67.8	67.9	67.7	65.3	66.9	67.3

Source: Various volumes of *Külkereskedelmi Statiszitikai Évkönyv*.

Note: SITC 0 Food and live animals; 1 Beverages and tobacco; 2 Crude materials, inedible, except fuels; 3 Mineral fuels, lubricants, and related materials; 4 Animal and vegetable oils and fats; 5 Chemicals; 6 Manufactured goods classified chiefly by material; 7 Machinery and transport equipment; 8 Miscellaneous manufactured goods

Table 4

Evolution of Hungarian Imports from Developing Countries, 1970–81

	Value index						Price index						Volume index					
	Developing countries (preceding year = 100)	Total imports (preceding year = 100)	Developing countries 1970 = 100	Developing countries 1975 = 100	Total imports 1970 = 100	Total imports 1975 = 100	Developing countries (preceding year = 100)	Total imports (preceding year = 100)	Developing countries 1970 = 100	Developing countries 1975 = 100	Total imports 1970 = 100	Total imports 1975 = 100	Developing countries (preceding year = 100)	Total imports (preceding year = 100)	Developing countries 1970 = 100	Developing countries 1975 = 100	Total imports 1970 = 100	Total imports 1975 = 100
1970	100.0	100.0	100.0		100.0		100.0	100.0	100.0		100.0		100.0	100.0	100.0		100.0	
1971	89.4	119.3	89.4		119.3		99.9	101.7	99.9		101.7		89.5	117.3	89.5		117.3	
1972	109.0	97.1	97.4		115.9		100.5	102.4	106.0		104.1		108.5	94.8	97.0		111.3	
1973	119.7	109.4	116.6		126.8		138.2	106.3	138.7		110.7		86.6	102.9	84.1		114.5	
1974	159.9	136.8	136.6		173.4		141.4	116.4	196.2		128.9		113.1	117.5	95.1		134.5	
1975	110.0	120.6	205.1	100.0	209.9	100.0	95.2	114.2	186.7	100.0	147.2	100.0	115.5	105.6	109.9	100.0	142.1	100.0
1976	101.3	96.9	207.8	101.3	202.7	96.9	109.5	93.3	204.4	109.5	137.3	93.3	92.5	103.8	101.7	92.5	147.6	103.9
1977	121.7	116.2	252.9	123.3	235.5	112.6	130.0	107.0	265.8	142.4	147.0	99.9	93.6	108.6	95.1	86.6	160.2	112.7
1978	98.4	112.6	248.9	121.3	265.2	126.8	93.1	100.0	247.5	132.6	147.1	99.9	105.7	112.6	100.6	91.5	180.3	126.9
1979	97.0	102.6	241.4	117.7	272.1	130.1	101.4	106.1	250.9	134.4	156.0	106.0	95.7	96.7	96.2	87.6	174.4	122.7
1980	108.7	97.1	262.4	128.0	264.2	126.4	99.2	98.3	248.9	133.3	153.3	104.2	109.6	98.8	105.4	96.0	172.3	121.3
1981	94.5	104.8	247.9	120.9	276.8	132.4	98.8	104.6	245.9	133.7	160.3	108.9	95.6	100.2	100.7	91.7	172.6	121.5

Source: Various volumes of *Külkereskedelmi Statisztikai Évkönyv*.

Table 5

Evolution of Hungarian Exports from Developing Countries, 1970–81

	Value index						Price index						Volume index					
	(preceding year = 100)		Developing countries		Total imports		(preceding year = 100)		Developing countries		Total imports		(preceding year = 100)		Developing countries		Total imports	
	Developing countries	Total imports	1970 = 100	1975 = 100	1970 = 100	1975 = 100	Developing countries	Total imports	1970 = 100	1975 = 100	1970 = 100	1975 = 100	Developing countries	Total imports	1970 = 100	1975 = 100	1970 = 100	1975 = 100
1970	100.0	100.0	100.0		100.0		100.0	100.0	100.0		100.0		100.0	100.0	100.0		100.0	
1971	101.5	107.9	101.5		107.9		98.3	100.3	98.3		100.3		103.2	107.6	103.2		107.6	
1972	112.5	121.2	114.2		130.8		99.9	101.6	98.2		101.9		112.6	119.3	116.3		128.4	
1973	109.4	118.1	124.9		154.6		105.2	105.0	103.3		107.0		104.0	112.5	120.9		144.5	
1974	148.2	111.6	185.1		172.5		121.2	107.7	125.2		115.3		122.3	103.6	147.8		149.6	
1975	104.9	111.2	194.2	100.0	191.8	100.0	94.8	106.1	118.7	100.0	122.3	100.0	110.6	104.8	163.6	100.0	156.8	100.0
1976	104.0	103.1	202.0	104.0	197.7	103.1	98.5	95.4	116.9	98.5	116.6	95.4	105.6	108.1	172.8	105.6	109.6	108.1
1977	125.9	116.5	254.3	131.0	230.3	120.1	103.0	103.4	120.4	101.5	120.6	98.7	122.2	112.7	211.2	129.1	191.0	121.7
1978	101.9	100.9	259.1	133.5	232.4	121.2	95.8	99.4	115.4	97.2	119.9	98.1	106.4	101.5	224.5	137.3	193.8	123.5
1979	123.1	117.2	319.0	164.3	272.4	142.0	105.8	104.2	122.0	102.8	124.9	102.2	116.4	112.5	261.5	159.8	218.1	138.9
1980	106.9	99.6	341.0	175.7	271.3	141.5	101.7	98.7	124.1	104.5	123.3	100.8	105.1	100.9	274.8	168.1	220.1	140.4
1981	127.1	106.5	433.4	223.3	288.9	150.6	104.3	103.8	129.4	108.9	127.9	104.6	121.9	102.6	334.9	204.9	225.8	144.0

Source: Various volumes of *Külkereskedelmi Statisztikai Évkönyv*.

developed capitalist countries but some of the CMEA countries as well. The share of manufactures imports within the total imports from the Third World decreased significantly in the second half of the seventies, a trend diametrically opposed to the more or less universal tendency manifesting itself in the imports structure of the developed countries. Besides the above-mentioned shortcomings of adaptation, and Hungary's staying away from one of the mainstreams of the international industrial division of labor, the decrease is also related to the fact that hard currency problems have rendered Hungarian manufactures imports more difficult since the mid-seventies.

Owing to the specific structural features of Hungary's commodity turnover with the developing countries, the *deterioration of the terms of trade* was especially marked. Between 1970 and 1981 the terms of trade with the developing countries deteriorated by 53%, that is, faster by a factor of 2.5 than in the case of total turnover. Since 1978 the terms-of-trade index has improved. It should be mentioned, however, that the significant increase in the relative share of developing countries within overall Hungarian trade in the seventies is closely related to the marked deterioration of the terms of trade. The increase in the imports share is due almost exclusively to the outstanding price increase, whereas the *volume* of the imports stagnated between 1970 and 1981 (see Table 4). Owing to the extraordinary deterioration of the terms of trade, a dynamic increase in export volumes has become a must for reasons of equilibrium. In the same period, while the volume of imports remained level, that of exports increased by a factor of 3.3, that is, much faster than the volume of total exports (see Table 5).

Marked geographical concentration of both exports and imports is a characteristic feature of the *geographical distribution pattern* of Hungary's trade with the developing countries (see Table 6). This geographical concentration is *excessive*; the interests of the long-term development of relations and the security of the turnover demand a much more diversified and balanced geographical distribution pattern.

Table 6

Geographic Concentration of Trade between Hungary and the Developing Countries

Exports	Percentage share in exports and imports of the: first partners	first three partners	first five partners	first ten partners	first twenty partners	Imports	Percentage share in exports and imports of the: first partners	first three partners	first five partners	first ten partners	first twenty partners
1950	45.3	80.9	91.1	97.9	99.8	1950	76.2	99.4	99.7	—	—
1960	16.1	41.7	60.5	78.0	92.7	1960	34.1	69.7	87.0	95.6	99.9
1970	20.3	40.8	54.1	78.0	91.5	1970	16.6	41.2	58.0	77.0	94.2
1973	13.1	32.0	48.6	75.4	89.0	1973	14.6	36.9	44.0	54.2	76.2
1974	20.3	37.9	52.3	73.6	89.2	1974	16.9	43.6	57.1	77.0	95.9
1975	23.7	42.7	55.7	72.9	86.2	1975	15.3	38.2	53.6	74.1	95.7
1976	22.1	44.3	59.4	72.8	84.4	1976	28.1	55.3	66.9	82.4	93.5
1977	15.0	35.0	52.5	76.1	89.8	1977	32.1	50.3	61.7	79.0	91.1
1978	17.5	38.1	53.8	75.7	86.3	1978	24.4	48.4	57.1	73.5	91.4
1979	20.1	37.2	48.8	68.8	83.6	1979	28.9	54.4	63.5	78.6	91.3
1980	15.9	36.7	48.7	71.8	87.3	1980	25.0	50.6	61.3	78.8	92.6

Source: Various volumes of *Külkereskedelmi Statisztikai Évkönyv*.

Table 7

Trade between Hungary and the NICs*
(in million forints)

	Imports	Exports	Balance
1970	2,571.3	629.1	−1,942.2
1971	1,987.0	328.1	−1,658.9
1972	2,343.3	453.8	−1,889.5
1973	3,179.4	1,095.8	−2,083.6
1974	4,143.3	1,039.2	−3,004.1
1975	4,768.8	771.8	−3,997.0
1976	6,901.4	717.3	−6,184.1
1977	10,385.0	733.5	−9,651.5
1978	8,811.4	881.5	−7,929.9
1979	9,229.4	1,726.8	−7,502.6
1980	9,143.4	1,221.7	−7,921.7
1981	10,813.5	2,073.5	−8,740.0

Source: Various volumes of *Külkereskedelmi Statisztikai Évkönyv*.
*Newly industrializing countries: Hong Kong, Singapore, South Korea, Taiwan, the Philippines, Malaysia, Thailand, Brazil, Argentina, Mexico.

In the seventies the evolution of the geographical distribution pattern of Hungarian exports was characterized primarily by the fact that exports were directed first and foremost to the *nearest countries of the Middle East and North Africa with an increased purchasing power and dynamically expanding economy*. Out of the ten most significant importing partners, nine belong to this region; in 1980, 66.5% of all Hungarian exports went to these countries. During the last decade trade with this group of countries brought regular surplus to Hungary.

On the other hand, Hungary failed to develop widespread, stable, and dynamic trade relations with the other rapidly growing group of countries of the Third World, i.e., the *newly industrializing countries* (NICs). This means that Hungary could not integrate itself into the division of labor of those countries of the Third World which are industrializing most vigorously and have quickly expanding and diversified imports markets. This is *one of the most serious*

Table 8

Share of the NICs in Hungarian Foreign Trade (in million forints)

	In Hungarian imports from		In Hungarian exports to	
	the developing countries	the world	the developing countries	the world
1970	23.5	1.8	7.7	0.4
1971	20.9	1.1	4.0	0.2
1972	22.6	1.3	4.8	0.2
1973	25.6	1.7	10.7	0.6
1974	20.8	1.6	7.5	0.5
1975	21.9	1.5	4.8	0.3
1976	21.7	3.0	4.4	0.3
1977	39.2	3.8	3.6	0.3
1978	33.7	2.9	4.2	0.4
1979	36.5	2.9	4.9	0.5
1980	33.2	3.1	4.4	0.4
1981	41.6	3.5	6.0	0.6

Source: Various volumes of *Külkereskedelmi Statiszitikai Évkönyv*.

Table 9

Trade between Hungary and the NICs of Latin America* (in million forints)

	Imports	Exports	Balance
1970	2,037.7	596.9	−1,440.8
1971	1,472.9	272.4	−1,200.5
1972	1,783.2	383.8	−1,399.4
1973	2,607.0	981.3	−1,625.7
1974	3,184.0	997.1	−2,186.9
1975	3,900.0	705.3	−3,194.7
1976	5,944.2	457.5	−5,486.7
1977	9,187.6	576.6	−8,611.0
1978	7,577.7	706.8	−6,870.9
1979	7,867.3	1,213.7	−6,653.6
1980	7,184.5	905.8	−6,278.7
1981	9,025.5	1,635.2	−7,390.3

Source: Various volumes of *Külkereskedelmi Statisztikai Évkönyv*.
*The Latin American NICs are: Mexico, Brazil, Argentina.

Table 10

Trade between Hungary and the NICs of Asia*
(in million forints)

	Imports	Exports	Balance
1970	533.6	32.2	− 501.4
1971	514.1	55.7	− 458.4
1972	560.1	70.0	− 490.1
1973	572.4	114.5	− 457.9
1974	959.3	142.1	− 817.2
1975	868.8	66.5	− 802.3
1976	957.2	259.8	− 697.4
1977	1,197.4	156.9	−1,040.5
1978	1,233.7	174.7	−1,059.0
1979	1,362.1	513.1	− 849.0
1980	1,958.9	315.9	−1,643.0
1981	1,788.0	438.3	−1,349.7

Source: Various volumes of *Külkereskedelmi Statisztikai Évkönyv*.
*The Asian NICs are: the Philippines, Hong Kong, Malaysia, Singapore, Thailand, South Korea, Taiwan.

shortcomings of Hungarian trade policy with respect to the Third World.

Tables 7 and 8 present the evolution of the trade turnover of Hungary and ten of the NICs (Hong Kong, Singapore, South Korea, Taiwan, the Philippines, Malaysia, Thailand, Brazil, Argentina, and Mexico) in the period 1970–81. As can be seen, Hungary chalked up a chronic and significant deficit in trade with this group. Tables 9 and 10 show that deficit persists not only with the NICs of Latin America (with regular and significant deficits, especially in the case of Brazil) but also with the NICs of Asia. It is interesting to note that most developed countries in the West have trade surpluses with the developing countries in question.

While the share of the NICs in total Hungarian imports from the Third World increased from 23.5% in 1970 to 41.6% in 1981 (mainly as a result of the vigorous increase in agricultural imports from Brazil), their rather small share in Hungarian exports tended to decrease—with some fluctuation—until 1980. It cannot be discerned as yet with sufficient clarity whether the share increase of 1981 was just another phase of fluctuation, or whether it marks the beginning of a new trend. In 1981 almost four-fifths of the Hungarian exports directed to the NICs went to three Latin American states (Brazil, Argentina, and Mexico).

It is evident from the above that *solely as an importer Hungary took a minor share of the economic dynamism* of the NICs, and as an exporter it failed to establish organic links with them.

The past decade brought significant progress in the *payments and settlement system* of cooperation with the developing countries. Bilateral clearing was replaced in most cass by hard currency settlement, and that often exerted a positive influence on trade turnover.

In the Fifth Five-Year Plan period (1976–80), the *credit-intensity of Hungarian machine exports* to the developing countries *declined*, contrary to the credit granting of the Western countries, which was characterized in that period by a dynamic expansion of credit offer and an extraordinarily vigorous credit competition. The intensifying credit competition manifested itself in the growing proportion of state-granted interest-rate subsidies, the extension of credit repayment periods, the spreading of so-called combined credits (that is, export credits and foreign aid), and the more significant export credit guarantees offered by the state. The competitiveness of the "financial package" of a business deal has become as important a transaction condition as price or technical level.[4] The inadequacy of the volume of Hungarian export credits and of their competitiveness was most probably instrumental in the sluggish expansion of Hungarian machinery exports to the developing countries.

At the beginning of 1982 there were only 16 *joint ventures* with Hungarian holdings located in 12 developing countries. For various reasons five joint ventures ceased functioning in 1980 and 1981. The Hungarian exports generated by the joint companies operating in the developing countries represented only 4% of all Hungarian exports to the developing countries in the past decade. By the end of the seventies even this small share had declined to 2%.[5] This is explained by the fact that some of these joint enterprises, although formally in existence, are virtually nonoperative. Recently, however, Hungarian enterprises have become more interested in joint ventures with the developing countries, owing to the difficulties encountered in other markets; but because of the existing constraints, no serious breakthrough is to be expected in the near future in this form of cooperation.

Production cooperations with the developing countries also have a negligible effect on trade, although their number surpasses that of joint enterprises. Cooperation between Hungarian and developing-country enterprises has progressed slowly; neither did that already established prove successful enough. The existing Hungarian system of enterprise regulation, motivation, and financing and the economic environment in general do not provide enough of a stimulus to founding joint enterprises and production cooperations. Most Hungarian firms are reluctant to participate in joint ventures or production cooperations involving a much greater risk and uncertainty than routine undertakings. This attitude is partly generated by insufficient information and the lack of experience. Further problems occur in connection with the financing of the Hungarian part of the cooperation and, in case of failure, the rehabilitation of finances.

II. The Anticipated Evolution of the International Economic Environment as It Affects the Long-term Economic Relations of Hungary and the Developing Countries

1. Economic Cooperation with the European CMEA

The problems in intra-CMEA cooperation in several fields, and especially the fact that there is little hope for a quick solution, will accelerate the expansion, both in breadth and depth, of economic cooperation with the non-CMEA countries and the Third World countries among them.

The long-term cooperation of Hungary with the developing countries will be affected most by the following CMEA problems: (1) the expected long-term increase in raw material and fuel imports originating in the CMEA; (2) the evolution of CMEA cooperation in the field of manufacturing; (3) the mechanisms of intra-CMEA cooperation.

Our forecasts, covering the most fundamental fuels and raw materials, indicate further difficulties in raw material and energy imports from CMEA sources until 2000.[6] The general CMEA-level shortage of these commodities will further increase, and they will become even "harder" commodities. The quantitative limits to imports from CMEA sources will make themselves felt more vigorously than before; the cost advantages of these imports relative to nonsocialist imports and to the development of domestic mining will, in general, substantially diminish, and in certain cases even cease. The increasing difficulties of CMEA imports are basically connected with the specific development problems of Soviet mineral mining and with the inadequacies of CMEA cooperation.

The growth rate of several branches of the Soviet extractive industry will likely diminish during the period until 2000, which in turn will in most cases also constrain the expansion rate of exports. The fall in the growth rate of Soviet raw material and energy exports to CMEA countries is due to the following major factors:

1. The shift to trans-Ural regions of the centers of production of the basic sectors of Soviet extractive industry will speed up in the period under review, with a steep rise in marginal production costs. This will create so immense a need for development capital that the country, relying on own resources at a time of relatively moderate increase in national income, can hardly be expected to meet it. Reliance on foreign loans may be substantial in relation to several developed market-economy countries but, in relation to the other CMEA countries, especially in a situation when the intra-CMEA terms of trade have changed in the past decade in favor of the Soviet Union and, consequently, a substantial need for consolidation credits has arisen in the net resource importing countries, may hardly mitigate to any appreciable extent the accumulation burdens of the Soviet Union. As a result, the export-oriented expansion of Soviet mineral mining is likely to encounter the constraint of limited development capital in the period under review.

2. In certain cases (e.g., oil) the expansion of exports is also limited by reserve availability problems.

3. The technological problems of mineral mining confronting more and more difficult geological and climatic circumstances.

4. Increasing bottlenecks in transporting raw materials and energy owing to the shift toward the East of the geographical center of extraction.

5. The Soviet Union is likely to maintain in its resource exports the proportions established in the 1970s between the East European CMEA countries and the developed market-economy countries and over the long term will probably not expand its exports to CMEA countries to the detriment of its nonsocialist exports. Parallel with the shift toward Eastern regions of the extractive and partly of the manufacturing industry, an upswing is expected in the "Eastern" trade of the Soviet Union, that is, a dynamic expansion of its raw material and energy exports to Japan, Southeast Asia, and possibly North America. This may influence the country's export capabilities vis-à-vis the European countries.

6. In view of the falling growth rate of raw material and energy production, the trade-off between preferring exports and satisfying relatively dynamically expanding domestic needs will probably be even more pronounced. In an economy with high specific raw material and energy consumption, the artificial reduction of (or the costly substitution for) domestic use in the interest of exports may involve serious growth-impeding effects. Hence the USSR can in the years ahead probably give priority to exports only at the expense of domestic economic sacrifices greater than those experienced in the past. Therefore export priority is likely to subside in areas where the above problems appear to be most pronounced.

7. A deepening of integration in the extractive industry is unlikely to take place within the CMEA in the period under review to such an extent that it could make intra-CMEA resource flows significantly more dynamic. The long-term raw material and energy target program was drawn up in a one-sided demand approach, and it seems as if the financial resources for joint cooperation projects envisaged in the program are insufficient in the CMEA. A massive reliance on non-CMEA financial resources would result in an inadmissibly large increase in indebtedness, and therefore this alternative may be excluded. In addition, the energy target program is heavily reliant on nuclear power and did not envisage cooperation in the satisfaction of the demand for oil and natural gas.

From what has been discussed above one can draw the conclusion that the more rapid the increase in the supply costs of raw materials and energy imported from CMEA sources, *ceteris paribus*, the higher the relative profitability of imports from alternative sources. As a recent Soviet assessment has put it,

> . . . the improvement of the existing forms of cooperation (between the CMEA countries and the developing countries) and the introduction of novel forms of relations could very well lead to a situation where, even under the changed price patterns of the world market, imports of fuels and minerals from the developing countries may prove no less efficient than imports from the Soviet Union.[7]

In view of the inadequacy of domestic fuels and raw materials bases, the excessively costly nature of the development of the domestic extractive industry, the expected growth rate of fuels and raw materials demand, and the problems discussed above of import procurement from a socialist source, *the gradual outward reorientation* of the raw materials and fuel supply of the smaller CMEA countries, Hungary among them, seems inevitable.

The qualitative problems of intra-CMEA cooperation are most manifest in the *manufacturing industry*.[8] The 1980s will probably bring a further exacerbation of the problems of intra-CMEA manufacturing exports because export growth in every European socialist country will have to be stimulated by the qualitative improvement of manufacturing. "Soft goods" imports from the partners, however, will not provide a sufficient base for that.

The crucial condition for the significant qualitative improvement of intra-CMEA manufacturing cooperation is the widespread evolution of direct interfirm cooperation. That, however, requires autonomous enterprises, which in turn means that the future of the whole system of manufacturing cooperation is a function of the economic reform of the CMEA countries. However, in most of the member countries the implementation of a reform that is not just symbolic cannot be predicted with sufficient certainty. The currently prevailing national mechanisms and the mechanism of CMEA-level cooperation reinforce one another and run counter to the widespread development of manufacturing integration. The established system of cooperation fails to stimulate the creation of export capacities producing competitive goods for the world market. In such a situation the more intensive expansion of the division of labor with the non-CMEA countries is a natural outcome.

2. The Impact of the Expected Structural Changes in World Trade

The future evolution of East-West economic relations, as part of the world economic environment affecting the shaping of economic relations between Hungary and the developing countries, will play an important role in the future. While in the seventies the measure of East-West trade expansion was determined by the import demands of the CMEA countries, in the eighties their export capacity will be the determining factor. East-West trade will lose impetus as compared as to the seventies. In the resulting situation the significance of developing countries as *alternative* export and import markets will most probably increase.

The expected evolution of *trade between the developed capitalist countries and the developing ones* in the next two decades will exert a considerable, although indirect, influence on the external conditions of economic cooperation with the developing countries and the criteria of partner choice in the Third World.

The dynamic expansion of the exports of capital-intensive goods, beside the traditional labor-intensive goods, from the developing countries to the developed ones is a characteristic feature of the 1970s. In this period the newly industrializing developing countries diversified the pattern of their exports very rapidly, partly as an answer to the protectionist measures of the developed countries. *Product diversification* has become especially pronounced in the second half of the decade. The share of the developing countries in the developed capitalist markets grew exceptionally fast in the case of such nontraditional commodities as paper and printing, metal components, motor vehicles, photographic equipment, electrical appliances and optical goods, furniture, man-made fibers, tires, handtools, and various types of machinery. The NICs were exceptionally successful in maintaining dynamic exports by diversifying their pattern and complementing and partly replacing with new goods those traditional products whose exportation is facing serious obstacles (especially textiles and clothes). Most of the less developed Third World countries managed to counterbalance the protectionist measures of the developed capitalist countries only partly by the diversification and upgrading of their exports (and by gaining access to new markets).

In the period up to 2000 the manufactures exports of the developing countries are expected to maintain the dynamic growth established in the past decade despite the slow growth of the world economy and protectionist measures. The developing countries' traditional goods markets may also expand, although under the combined effect of the declining growth of demand and protectionist measures, market penetration will be slow.[9] The United States, the EEC, and Japan intend to cut or even abolish their preferences granted to the more advanced developing countries. The above factors will encourage a further diversification and product up-grading in the sphere of manufactures exports on the part of the developing countries. In the case of such labor-intensive goods as china and glassware and furniture, where the developing countries are represented by a relatively small market share, export to the developed countries will grow dynamically. A rapid export expansion is expected for products characterized by a high income elasticity, such as sporting goods. The export of semifinished goods and parts also provides great opportunities. The share of capital-intensive products (petrochemicals, man-made fibers, steel, aluminum, automotive parts) will grow at the expense of labor-intensive products.

In view of the above, the share of the developed capitalist countries in the overall trade relations of the developing countries will remain decisive up to the turn of the century.

Those developing countries that are most seriously affected by the limiting measures imposed by the developed capitalist countries and are less competitive than other Third World exporters might tend to enhance their economic relations with the CMEA in order to diminish their dependence on the markets of the developed capitalist countries and to intensify their exports by market diversification. An eventual *redirection of relations* in favor of the socialist coun-

Table 11

Share of the Developed Capitalist Countries, the European CMEA Countries and Hungary in the Developing Countries' Trade (percentage of total exports and imports)

Exports by developing countries to:	1970	1975	1976	1977	1978	1979	1980
Developed capitalist countries	74.0	70.2	71.2	70.7	70.6	71.1	69.1
European CMEA countries	6.3	4.7	4.2	4.2	4.3	3.7	3.8
Hungary	0.30	0.26	0.22	0.21	0.25	0.18	0.17
Imports by developing countries from:	**1970**	**1975**	**1976**	**1977**	**1978**	**1979**	**1980**
Developed capitalist countries	73.2	68.9	67.0	66.5	68.3	65.2	63.5
European CMEA countries	9.8	6.6	6.6	7.1	7.5	7.4	6.8
Hungary	0.25	0.21	0.21	0.19	0.20	0.22	0.20

Source: *Monthly Bulletin of Statistics*, June 1978; June 1979; July 1980; July 1981.

tries greatly depends on the degree to which the CMEA countries, Hungary among them, open their markets to the products of the developing countries and succeed in eliminating, by developing more advanced and stable forms of cooperation, their own relative disadvantage in the choice of partners by the developing countries.

Within the set of long-term conditions of cooperation with the developing countries, the intensification of *intra-Third World* division of labor is gaining more importance and, if approached passively, might contribute to Hungary's relative loss of ground in the Third World. A farsighted and aggressive marketing policy may temper the possible disadvantageous consequences of the process in question and may even open up new opportunities for cooperation for the Hungarian economy.

The strenghtening of intra-developing-country links has thus far manifested itself first and foremost in the dynamic increase of their trade with one another. In the long run the rate of growth of intra-developing-country trade will remain higher than that of world trade and that of the Third World's trade with the other groups of countries. Consequently, an increasing proportion of their exports will go to other developing countries, that is, *a growing share of the imports demands of the developing countries will be met by exports from the other developing countries.*[10]

The intensification of South-South economic cooperation has already had a significant impact on the *economic relations of the socialist countries and the developing countries*. As shown in Table 11, the European CMEA has lost more ground in the exports and imports markets of the developing countries than the developed capitalist states, although the socialist countries' share in these markets is very small. In the seventies Hungary's exports to and imports from the developing countries could not even keep pace with the average growth of the developing countries' total trade, and consequently its share in both diminished considerably. Moreover, in the second half of the seventies the greatest loss in Hungarian exports to the developing countries occurred in that very group (machinery and transport equipment) which underwent the most dynamic increase in intra-developing-country trade. Thus the main losers of the expansion of intra-developing-country trade have become the least competitive marginal partners. The promotion of integration into South-South cooperation is a very significant task for the Hungarian economy. Otherwise cooperation among developing countries will inevitably exert a permanent negative influence on Hungary's marketing ability in the Third World, with special regard to the manufactures (especially machines and transport equipment), a sphere where intra-Third World trade is expected to grow very fast.

3. *Anticipated Evolution of the Third World's Economic Growth*

In the seventies the developing countries adapted to the moderate growth of world trade and world output and higher energy prices in various ways. Although the growth rate of their GDP fell from 5.9% in the sixties to 5.1%, it was still much higher than that of the developed capitalist countries (3.3%) or the socialist countries (4.8%).[11]

The economic performance of the developing countries in the

1980s and 1990s will be shaped by several factors,

> . . . including their ability to increase the inflow of external capital and to raise the rate of domestic saving in order to finance investment aimed at restructuring their economies. Also of critical importance will be their success in increasing export growth and reducing dependence on imported oil, capital goods, and raw materials.[12]

Table 12, based on calculations by the World Bank, presents an optimistic (high case) and a pessimistic (low case) variant of the past and projected evolution of the main macroeconomic performance indicators in the oil-importing developing countries. As shown in the table, the net fuel imports expressed as a percentage of GDP (at constant 1978 prices) decreased from 3.3% in 1970 to 2.7% in 1980, and the projection suggests a further decline to about 2.1–2.3% by 1990. But even that requires considerable efforts of conservation and substitution of domestic for imported energy.

The oil-importing countries have reacted to the oil-price increases of 1979–80 by raising their foreign borrowing. As a result, their current account deficit increased from 2.3% of GDP in 1978 to 4.4% in 1980. However, in view of the burdens of debt service of the developing countries on the one hand and the limited availability of concessional capital on the other, reliance on foreign loans will certainly decrease in the long run. In the optimistic (high case) variant the greater domestic saving and the greater share of exports in GDP will replace, at least partially, foreign capital. The above, combined with the savings on fuel imports, will make it possible for the oil-importing countries to adapt to the higher oil prices and to reduce their dependence on foreign capital inflows.

According to the pessimistic (low case) variant, the above processes will work out less favorably in the developing countries. The proportion of domestic saving in GDP will remain approximately at the 1980 level. Weaker domestic economic performance will diminish the creditworthiness and thus limit the supply of foreign capital, and that in turn will necessitate cutting imports in order to reduce current account deficits. As a result of the above factors, economic growth must inevitably slow down.

In the optimistic variant the growth performance of the develop-

Table 12

Performance Indicators, Oil-Importing Developing Countries, 1970–79 (percentage of GGDP)

Item	1970	1975	1978	1980	High Case 1985	High Case 1990	Low Case 1985	Low Case 1990
Constant (1978 prices)								
Fuel imports, net	3.3	2.6	2.8	2.7	2.5	2.3	2.6	2.1
Nonfuel imports	21.8	21.0	19.9	20.2	20.4	23.8	17.9	18.4
Exports	19.2	19.7	21.1	21.6	23.5	28.0	21.7	22.1
Savings	19.9	19.2	20.8	21.5	21.7	21.9	20.7	21.1
Current prices								
Current account deficit	2.4	5.1	2.3	4.4	3.2	3.0	2.9	2.4
Fuel imports, net	1.0	2.9	2.8	5.2	5.8	6.1	5.9	5.6

Source: *World Development Report 1981*, Washington, The World Bank, 1981, p. 14.

ing countries may even improve as compared to the average annual rate of growth in the seventies. The high case projects about 5.7% a year for the eighties, but even the pessimistic one allows for 4.5% (see Table 13). In both cases the *projected growth of the developing countries will exceed by far* that of the other two groups of countries (advanced market and socialist economies) of the world economy. Developing country imports will increase at a faster rate (7% in real terms) than those of the other two country groups. The *shift of the dynamics of growth and imports demand toward the developing countries* will enhance their importance for the choice of foreign trade partners.

As shown in Table 13, in the eighties the growth performance of the developing countries will be almost as *diverse* as it was in the seventies. Oil-exporting developing countries are expected to expand reasonably rapidly. On the other hand, even the high case projects marginal improvements only for the sub-Saharan African countries. In the low case the latters' GDP is likely to grow less rapidly than their population, and below what was achieved in the seventies.

The middle-income oil-importing countries will be capable of a much better economic performance than the low-income ones thanks to their better resource endowments and more open trade policies. The overall growth rate of the group as a whole will be between 5 and 6% a year, but that of the East Asians might even reach 8% in the high case. The increasing disparity in terms of growth dynamism and level of economic and technologic development within the Third World requires the *formulation of a more differentiated foreign economic policy vis-à-vis these countries*, taking into account the various specificities of the subgroups.

The combined impact of the above processes in the world economy affecting the long-term economic relations between Hungary and the developing countries makes it possible and even imperative that the Third World's share in overall Hungarian trade be increased significantly. The *"push"* and *"pull" forces* discussed above, acting in the foreign economic environment of the Hungarian economy, suggest that in the coming two decades, *the greatest room for maneuver* will open up for the Hungarian external economy in the markets of the Third World. Although it would be misleading to draw far-reaching conclusions from short-term trends, the experiences of the early eighties seem to support the above statement, since Hungary's exports to the developing countries increased by 53% in 1981 and 1982 together, while exports to the developed capitalist countries declined by 1.4%, and exports to the socialist countries increased at a substantially slower rate than before (at 19.6%).[13]

Up to 1990 the share of the developing countries in overall Hungarian foreign trade may increase to 18–20% and might reach as much as 25% by 2000.[14] The intensification of Hungary's relations with the developing countries and the exploitation of the inherent cooperation opportunities require the performance of several *foreign economic tasks*, the most important of which seem to be the following:

1. Long-term economic strategy and, as part of it, structural policy and foreign economic policy should have clear and definitive ideas relating to the developing countries. *The Third World should be integrated into Hungarian structural policy.* Treating the Third World as a residual (that is, shortage-eliminating and surplus-discharging) sphere is untenable in the long run.

2. Instead of, and beside, the prevailing ad hoc relations, it

Table 13

Growth of Third World GDP, by Region, 1960–90 (average annual percentage)

			High Case			Low Case		
Region	1960-1970	1970-1980	1980-1985	1985-1990	1980-1990	1980-1985	1985-1990	1980-1990
Oil importers	5.7	5.1	5.0	5.8	5.4	3.8	4.4	4.1
Low-income oil importers	4.2	3.0	4.0	4.3	4.1	2.8	3.2	3.0
Sub-Saharan Africa	4.0	2.4	3.0	3.0	3.0	1.8	2.0	1.9
Asia	4.3	3.2	4.2	4.6	4.4	3.0	3.5	3.2
Middle-income oil importers	6.2	5.6	5.2	6.1	5.6	4.0	4.7	4.3
Sub-Saharan Africa[a]	4.1	3.5	3.0	3.3	3.1	2.7	3.0	2.8
East Asia and Pacific	7.9	8.2	7.8	8.5	8.1	6.3	6.5	6.4
Latin America/ Caribbean	5.3	6.0	5.1	6.0	5.6	4.4	4.8	4.6
Middle East, North Africa	4.1	4.9	4.1	4.1	4.1	3.0	3.3	3.2
Southern Europe	7.0	4.6	4.3	5.0	4.6	2.5	3.5	3.0
Oil exporters	6.5	5.2	6.2	6.8	6.5	4.9	5.9	5.4
All developing countries	5.9	5.1	5.3	6.1	5.7	4.1	4.9	4.5

Source: *World Development Report 1981*, Washington, The World Bank, 1981, p. 15.
[a]Excludes South Africa.

would be useful to establish *a long-term and stable division of labor* corresponding to the aims of Hungary's long-term structural policy endeavors, to the fundamental economic interests of the developing countries, and to the basic trends of the international division of labor.

3. The *excessive fluctuation* of trade with the developing countries is to be checked by a careful choice of partners and the establishment of more profound division of labor relations.

4. In this context the *geographical radius* of Hungarian trade and cooperation relations *is to be increased*, especially in the direction of the steadily and rapidly expanding solvent markets.

5. The present commodity pattern of the Hungarian exports and

imports is unsuitable for the dynamic development of mutual economic relations. The share of up-to_date machinery, equipment, and highly processed foodstuffs should be increased in exports. Hungarian *export policy* should put more emphasis on the so-called systems approach, i.e., the export of complete plants and vertically integrated production and service systems in those fields where previous experience promises the realization of a significant comparative advantage. This, however, requires an appropriate domestic enterprise regulation system and also adequate internal motivation and financing. In exports a deliberate structural policy is required to reduce the share of those products for which the developing countries present a growing challenge both in the Western and the Third World markets. The relatively high proportion of certain raw material and energy-intensive goods and semifinished products in Hungarian exports contradicts both the endowments of the Hungarian economy and the basic trends of industrialization in the developing countries.

6. Within *Hungarian imports* from the developing countries, the share of *nontraditional* goods, especially semifinished goods and certain manufactured products (machinery and consumer manufactures among others), should be increased.

7. The *organizational forms and mechanisms* of cooperation require substantial modernization and the widespread implementation of more flexible, complex, and permanent forms of cooperation. Past experience demonstrates that the intensity of cooperation depends, to a great extent, on the chosen institutional form. As opposed to the actual practice, Hungary should strive to create not only export- but also *import-oriented* cooperation deals. It would be useful in this respect to *redeploy*, partly or totally, those domestic productive activities which have lost their competitiveness at home to certain developing countries.

Notes

1. The present study relies to a great extent on the concluding chapter (written by the author) of a study prepared at the Institute for the World Economy of the Hungarian Academy of Sciences: "Követendö gazdaságpolitikánk, teendöink és feladataink a harmadik világ relćiójában a 2000-ig terjedö idöszakban" [Hungar-

ian Economic Policy and Required Actions vis-à-vis the Third World up to 2000], Bálint Balkay, Tibor Csighy, Kálmán Dezséri, Péter Farkas, Mariann Farkas, Judit Gergely, Róbert Hardi, Judit Kiss, László Láng, Imre Lévai, István Magas, János Nyerges, Margit Rácz, Zsolt Rostoványi, and István Szívós participated in the research project. Kálmán Dezséri gave valuable help with the calculations.

2. For more information about the pre-World War II evolution of economic relations between Hungary and the developing countries, see István Dobozi, "Hungary's Approach to the Third World in Historical Perspective," paper presented at the EADI General Conference "Emerging Development Patterns: European Contributions," November 11–14, 1981, Budapest; Rozália Bogó, *Hungary and the Developing Countries. A Historical Analysis of Hungary's Foreign Trade with the Developing Countries*, Studies on Developing Countries, No. 100, Budapest, Institute for World Economics of the Hungarian Academy of Sciences, 1979.

3. Judit Gergely, "A magyar ipar strukturális átalakulása és a fejlödö országokból származó késztermékbeszerzési lehetöségek" [Structural Transformation of the Hungarian Industry and the Possibilities of Manufactured Goods Imports from the Third World], Budapest, Institute for the World Economy, November 1981 (mimeo).

4. Dorottya Somogyi, "Új megállapodás a tökés exporthitelnyújtás rendezéséröl" [A New Agreement about the Settling of Capitalist Export Credit Granting], *Világgazdaság*, Budapest, November 12, 1981, p. 5.

5. For more details, see Kálmán Dezséri, "Magyarország és a fejlödö országok közötti kereskedelem intézményes keretei" [The Institutional Framework of Trade between Hungary and the Developing Countries], Budapest, Institute for the World Economy, 1981, p. 29 (mimeo).

6. István Dobozi, *Projected Trends of World Raw Material and Energy Markets until 2000*, Studies on Developing Countries, No. 110, Budapest, Institute for World Economics of the Hungarian Academy of Sciences, 1982.

7. "Sotrudnichestvo s razvivaiushchimisia stranami v reshenii toplivnosirevoi problemy stran SEV," *Toplivno-sirevaia problema v usloviiakh sotsialisticheskoi ekonomicheskoi integratsii*, edited by A. I. Zubkov, Moscow, Nauka, 1979, p. 126.

8. This section relies on Margit Rácz's paper discussing the topic in detail: "Az európai KGST-országok gazdasági együttmüködésének hatása a fejlödö országokkal fenntartott gazdasági kapcsolataikra" [The Impact of Intra-CMEA Cooperation and the European CMEA Countries' Economic Relations with the Developing Countries], Budapest, Institute for the World Economy, 1981 (mimeo).

9. Helen Hughes and Jean Waelbroeck, "Can Developing Country Exports Keep Growing in the 1980s?" *The World Economy*, June 1981, p. 144.

10. Judit Kiss, "A fejlöd'országok egymás közötti együttmködése" [Cooperation among Developing Countries], Institute for the World Economy, Budapest, 1981 (mimeo).

11. *World Development Report 1981*, Washington, World Bank, 1981, p. 14.

12. Ibid.

13. *Külkereskedelmi Statisztikai Évkönyv 1981*; for 1982, data provided by the Ministry of Foreign Trade, Budapest.

14. Let us remark that the developing countries are represented by greater,

sometimes significantly greater, export and/or import shares in the trade of several East and West European small countries than in the case of Hungary. In 1981 the share of the developing countries was 26.4 and 17.4% of total Romanian exports and imports, respectively; 17.4% of Bulgarian exports; 15.2% of the exports of the Soviet Union. The Third World's share was 19.8% in the exports of Switzerland and 13.6% in those of Austria. In 1981, 22.3% of the imports of the Netherlands and 16% of those of Belgium originated in the Third World. The share of the developing countries was 19% in the exports and 16% in the imports of Yugoslavia. (On the basis of the *Yearbook of International Trade Statistics 1980*; *Statistics of Foreign Trade 1982*; *Statisticheskii ezhegodnik stran-chlenov Soveta Ekonomicheskoi Vzaimopomoshchi 1981*.)

For Product Safety Concerns and Information please contact our EU representative GPSR@taylorandfrancis.com
Taylor & Francis Verlag GmbH, Kaufingerstraße 24, 80331 München, Germany

www.ingramcontent.com/pod-product-compliance
Ingram Content Group UK Ltd.
Pitfield, Milton Keynes, MK11 3LW, UK
UKHW022002180926
475701UK00003B/153
* 9 7 8 0 8 7 3 3 2 3 6 4 2 *